W9-DIL-562

Java Generics and Collections

Other Java™ resources from O'Reilly

Related titles

Enterprise JavaBeans 3.0	Java Cookbook™
Head First EJB	Java Enterprise in a Nutshell
Head First Java	Java I/O
Head First Servlets and JSP	Java in a Nutshell
Java 5.0 Tiger: A Developer's Notebook™	Learning Java

Java Books Resource Center

java.oreilly.com is a complete catalog of O'Reilly's books on Java and related technologies, including sample chapters and code examples.

OnJava.com is a one-stop resource for enterprise Java developers, featuring news, code recipes, interviews, weblogs, and more.

Conferences

O'Reilly brings diverse innovators together to nurture the ideas that spark revolutionary industries. We specialize in documenting the latest tools and systems, translating the innovator's knowledge into useful skills for those in the trenches. Visit *conferences.oreilly.com* for our upcoming events.

Safari Bookshelf (*safari.oreilly.com*) is the premier online reference library for programmers and IT professionals. Conduct searches across more than 1,000 books. Subscribers can zero in on answers to time-critical questions in a matter of seconds. Read the books on your Bookshelf from cover to cover or simply flip to the page you need. Try it today for free.

Java Generics and Collections

Maurice Naftalin and Philip Wadler

O'REILLY®

Beijing · Cambridge · Farnham · Köln · Paris · Sebastopol · Taipei · Tokyo

Java Generics and Collections
by Maurice Naftalin and Philip Wadler

Copyright © 2007 O'Reilly Media, Inc. All rights reserved.
Printed in the United States of America.

Published by O'Reilly Media, Inc., 1005 Gravenstein Highway North, Sebastopol, CA 95472.

O'Reilly books may be purchased for educational, business, or sales promotional use. Online editions are also available for most titles (*safari.oreilly.com*). For more information, contact our corporate/institutional sales department: (800) 998-9938 or *corporate@oreilly.com*.

Editor: Mike Loukides
Production Services: Windfall Software

Indexers: Maurice Naftalin and Philip Wadler
Cover Designer: Karen Montgomery

Printing History:

October 2006:   First Edition.

Nutshell Handbook, the Nutshell Handbook logo, and the O'Reilly logo are registered trademarks of O'Reilly Media, Inc. *Java Generics and Collections*, the image of an alligator, and related trade dress are trademarks of O'Reilly Media, Inc.

Many of the designations used by manufacturers and sellers to distinguish their products are claimed as trademarks. Where those designations appear in this book, and O'Reilly Media, Inc. was aware of a trademark claim, the designations have been printed in caps or initial caps.

While every precaution has been taken in the preparation of this book, the publisher and authors assume no responsibility for errors or omissions, or for damages resulting from the use of the information contained herein.

 This book uses RepKover™, a durable and flexible lay-flat binding.

ISBN-10: 0-596-52775-6
ISBN-13: 978-0-596-52775-4
[M]

We dedicate this book to
Joyce Naftalin, Lionel Naftalin, Adam Wadler,
and Leora Wadler

—Maurice Naftalin and Philip Wadler

Contents

Part I Generics

Part II   Collections

Preface

Java now supports *generics*, the most significant change to the language since the addition of inner classes in Java 1.2—some would say the most significant change to the language ever.

Say you wish to process lists. Some may be lists of integers, others lists of strings, and yet others lists of lists of strings. In Java before generics this is simple. You can represent all three by the same class, called `List`, which has elements of class `Object`:

list of integers	List
list of strings	List
list of lists of strings	List

In order to keep the language simple, you are forced to do some of the work yourself: you must keep track of the fact that you have a list of integers (or strings or lists of strings), and when you extract an element from the list you must cast it from `Object` back to `Integer` (or `String` or `List`). For instance, the Collections Framework before generics made extensive use of this idiom.

Einstein is reputed to have said, "Everything should be as simple as possible but no simpler". And some might say the approach above is too simple. In Java with generics you may distinguish different types of lists:

list of integers	List<Integer>
list of strings	List<String>
list of lists of strings	List<List<String>>

Now the compiler keeps track of whether you have a list of integers (or strings or lists of strings), and no explicit cast back to `Integer` (or `String` or `List<String>`) is required. In some ways, this is similar to *generics* in Ada or *templates* in C++, but the actual inspiration is *parametric polymorphism* as found in functional languages such as ML and Haskell.

Part I of this book provides a thorough introduction to generics. We discuss the interactions between generics and subtyping, and how to use wildcards and bounds; we describe techniques for evolving your code; we explain subtleties connected with casts and arrays; we treat advanced topics such as the interaction between generics and security, and how to maintain binary compatibility; and we update common design patterns to exploit generics.

Much has been written on generics, and their introduction into Java has sparked some controversy. Certainly, the design of generics involves swings and roundabouts: making it easy to evolve code requires that objects not *reify* run-time information describing generic type parameters, but the absence of this information introduces corner cases into operations such as casting and array creation. We present a balanced treatment of generics, explaining how to exploit their strengths and work around their weaknesses.

Part II provides a comprehensive introduction to the Collections Framework. Newton is reputed to have said, "If I have seen farther than others, it is because I stand on the shoulders of giants". The best programmers live by this motto, building on existing frameworks and reusable code wherever appropriate. The Java Collections Framework provides reusable interfaces and implementations for a number of common collection types, including lists, sets, queues, and maps. There is also a framework for comparing values, which is useful in sorting or building ordered trees. (Of course, not all programmers exploit reuse. As Hamming said of computer scientists, "Instead of standing on each other's shoulders, we stand on each other's toes.")

Thanks to generics, code using collections is easier to read and the compiler will catch more type errors. Further, collections provide excellent illustrations of the use of generics. One might say that generics and collections were made for each other, and, indeed, ease of use of collections was one of the main reasons for introducing generics in the first place.

Java 5 and 6 not only update the Collections Framework to exploit generics, but also enhance the framework in other ways, introducing interfaces and classes to support concurrency and the new enum types. We believe that these developments mark the beginning of a shift in programming style, with heavier use of the Collections Framework and, in particular, increased use of collections in favor of arrays. In Part II, we describe the entire framework from first principles in order to help you use collections more effectively, flagging the new features of Java 5 and 6 as we present them.

Following common terminology, we refer to the successive versions of Java as 1.0 up to 1.4 and then 5 and 6. We say 'Java before generics' to refer to Java 1.0 through 1.4, and 'Java with generics' to refer to Java 5 and 6.

The design of generics for Java is influenced by a number of previous proposals—notably, GJ, by Bracha, Odersky, Stoutamire, and Wadler; the addition of wildcards to GJ, proposed by Igarashi and Viroli; and further development of wildcards, by Torgersen, Hansen, Ernst, von der Ahé, Bracha, and Gafter. Design of generics was carried out under the Java Community Process by a team led by Bracha, and including Odersky, Thorup, and Wadler (as parts of JSR 14 and JSR 201). Odersky's GJ compiler is the basis of Sun's current javac compiler.

Obtaining the Example Programs

Some of the example programs in this book are available online at:

ftp://ftp.oreilly.com/published/oreilly/javagenerics

If you can't get the examples directly over the Internet but can send and receive email, you can use *ftpmail* to get them. For help using *ftpmail*, send an email to

   ftpmail@online.oreilly.com

with no subject and the single word "help" in the body of the message.

How to Contact Us

You can address comments and questions about this book to the publisher:

   O'Reilly Media, Inc.
   1005 Gravenstein Highway North
   Sebastopol, CA 95472
   (800) 998-9938 (in the United States or Canada)
   (707) 829-0515 (international/local)
   (707) 829-0104 (fax)

O'Reilly has a web page for this book, which lists errata and any additional information. You can access this page at:

   http://www.oreilly.com/catalog/javagenerics

To comment or ask technical questions about this book, send email to:

   bookquestions@oreilly.com

For more information about books, conferences, software, Resource Centers, and the O'Reilly Network, see the O'Reilly web site at:

   http://www.oreilly.com

Conventions Used in This Book

We use the following font and format conventions:

- Code is shown in a fixed-width font, with boldface used for emphasis:

```
class Client {
  public static void main(String[] args) {
    Stack<Integer> stack = new ArrayStack<Integer>();
    for (int i = 0; i<4; i++) stack.push(i);
    assert stack.toString().equals("stack[0, 1, 2, 3]");
  }
}
```

- We often include code that corresponds to the body of an appropriate `main` method:

```
Stack<Integer> stack = new ArrayStack<Integer>();
for (int i = 0; i<4; i++) stack.push(i);
assert stack.toString().equals("stack[0, 1, 2, 3]");
```

- Code fragments are printed in fixed-width font when they appear within a paragraph (as when we referred to a `main` method in the preceding item).

- We often omit standard imports. Code that uses the Java Collection Framework or other utility classes should be preceded by the line:

```
import java.util.*;
```

- Sample interactive sessions, showing command-line input and corresponding output, are shown in constant-width font, with user-supplied input preceded by a percent sign:

```
% javac g/Stack.java g/ArrayStack.java g/Stacks.java l/Client.java
Note: Client.java uses unchecked or unsafe operations.
Note: Recompile with -Xlint:unchecked for details.
```

- When user-supplied input is two lines long, the first line is ended with a backslash:

```
% javac -Xlint:unchecked g/Stack.java g/ArrayStack.java \
%     g/Stacks.java l/Client.java
l/Client.java:4: warning: [unchecked] unchecked call
to push(E) as a member of the raw type Stack
        for (int i = 0; i<4; i++) stack.push(new Integer(i));
```

Using Code Examples

This book is here to help you get your job done. In general, you may use the code in this book in your programs and documentation. You do not need to contact us for permission unless you're reproducing a significant portion of the code. For example, writing a program that uses several chunks of code from this book does not require permission. Selling or distributing a CD-ROM of examples from O'Reilly books does require permission. Answering a question by citing this book and quoting example code does not require permission. Incorporating a significant amount of example code from this book into your product's documentation does require permission.

We appreciate, but do not require, attribution. An attribution usually includes the title, author, publisher, and ISBN. For example: "*Java Generics and Collections*, by Maurice Naftalin and Philip Wadler. Copyright 2006 O'Reilly Media, Inc., 0-596-52775-6."

If you feel your use of code examples falls outside fair use or the permission given above, feel free to contact us at *permissions@oreilly.com*.

Safari® Enabled

When you see a Safari® Enabled icon on the cover of your favorite technology book, that means the book is available online through the O'Reilly Network Safari Bookshelf.

Safari offers a solution that's better than e-books. It's a virtual library that lets you easily search thousands of top tech books, cut and paste code samples, download chapters, and find quick answers when you need the most accurate, current information. Try it for free at *http://safari.oreilly.com*.

Acknowledgments

The folks at Sun (past and present) were fantastically good about answering our questions. They were always happy to explain a tricky point or mull over a design tradeoff. Thanks to Joshua Bloch, Gilad Bracha, Martin Buchholz, Joseph D. Darcy, Neal M. Gafter, Mark Reinhold, David Stoutamire, Scott Violet, and Peter von der Ahé.

It has been a pleasure to work with the following researchers, who contributed to the design of generics for Java: Erik Ernst, Christian Plesner Hansen, Atsushi Igarashi, Martin Odersky, Mads Torgersen, and Mirko Viroli.

We received comments and help from a number of people. Thanks to Brian Goetz, David Holmes, Heinz M. Kabutz, Deepti Kalra, Angelika Langer, Stefan Liebeg, Doug Lea, Tim Munro, Steve Murphy, and C K Shibin.

We enjoyed reading Heinz M. Kabutz's *The Java Specialists' Newsletter* and Angelika Langer's *Java Generics FAQ*, both available online.

Our editor, Michael Loukides, was always ready with good advice. Paul C. Anagnostopoulos of Windfall Software turned our LaTeX into camera-ready copy, and Jeremy Yallop produced the index.

Our families kept us sane (and insane). Love to Adam, Ben, Catherine, Daniel, Isaac, Joe, Leora, Lionel, and Ruth.

PART I

Generics

Generics are a powerful, and sometimes controversial, new feature of the Java programming language. This part of the book describes generics, using the Collections Framework as a source of examples. A comprehensive introduction to the Collections Framework appears in the second part of the book.

The first five chapters focus on the fundamentals of generics. Chapter 1 gives an overview of generics and other new features in Java 5, including boxing, *foreach* loops, and functions with a variable number of arguments. Chapter 2 reviews how subtyping works and explains how wildcards let you use subtyping in connection with generics. Chapter 3 describes how generics work with the Comparable interface, which requires a notion of *bounds* on type variables. Chapter 4 looks at how generics work with various declarations, including constructors, static members, and nested classes. Chapter 5 explains how to evolve legacy code to exploit generics, and how ease of evolution is a key advantage of the design of generics in Java. Once you have these five chapters under your belt, you will be able to use generics effectively in most basic situations.

The next four chapters treat advanced topics. Chapter 6 explains how the same design that leads to ease of evolution also necessarily leads to a few rough edges in the treatment of casts, exceptions, and arrays. The fit between generics and arrays is the worst rough corner of the language, and we formulate two principles to help you work around the problems. Chapter 7 explains new features that relate generics and reflection, including the newly generified type Class<T> and additions to the Java library that support reflection of generic types. Chapter 8 contains advice on how to use generics effectively in practical coding. We consider checked collections, security issues, specialized classes, and binary compatibility. Chapter 9 presents five extended examples, looking at how generics affect five well-known design patterns: Visitor, Interpreter, Function, Strategy, and Subject-Observer.

CHAPTER 1

Introduction

Generics and collections work well with a number of other new features introduced in the latest versions of Java, including boxing and unboxing, a new form of loop, and functions that accept a variable number of arguments. We begin with an example that illustrates all of these. As we shall see, combining them is *synergistic*: the whole is greater than the sum of its parts.

Taking that as our motto, let's do something simple with sums: put three numbers into a list and add them together. Here is how to do it in Java with generics:

```
List<Integer> ints = Arrays.asList(1,2,3);
int s = 0;
for (int n : ints) { s += n; }
assert s == 6;
```

You can probably read this code without much explanation, but let's touch on the key features. The interface List and the class Arrays are part of the Collections Framework (both are found in the package java.util). The type List is now *generic*; you write List<E> to indicate a list with elements of type E. Here we write List<Integer> to indicate that the elements of the list belong to the class Integer, the wrapper class that corresponds to the primitive type int. Boxing and unboxing operations, used to convert from the primitive type to the wrapper class, are automatically inserted. The static method asList takes any number of arguments, places them into an array, and returns a new list backed by the array. The new loop form, *foreach*, is used to bind a variable successively to each element of the list, and the loop body adds these into the sum. The assertion statement (introduced in Java 1.4), is used to check that the sum is correct; when assertions are enabled, it throws an error if the condition does not evaluate to true.

Here is how the same code looks in Java before generics:

```
List ints = Arrays.asList( new Integer[] {
  new Integer(1), new Integer(2), new Integer(3)
} );
int s = 0;
```

```
for (Iterator it = ints.iterator(); it.hasNext(); ) {
  int n = ((Integer)it.next()).intValue();
  s += n;
}
assert s == 6;
```

Reading this code is not quite so easy. Without generics, there is no way to indicate in the type declaration what kind of elements you intend to store in the list, so instead of writing List<Integer>, you write List. Now it is the coder rather than the compiler who is responsible for remembering the type of the list elements, so you must write the cast to (Integer) when extracting elements from the list. Without boxing and unboxing, you must explicitly allocate each object belonging to the wrapper class Integer and use the intValue method to extract the corresponding primitive int. Without functions that accept a variable number of arguments, you must explicitly allocate an array to pass to the asList method. Without the new form of loop, you must explicitly declare an iterator and advance it through the list.

By the way, here is how to do the same thing with an array in Java before generics:

```
int[] ints = new int[] { 1,2,3 };
int s = 0;
for (int i = 0; i < ints.size; i++) { s += ints[i]; }    → length
assert s == 6;
```

This is slightly longer than the corresponding code that uses generics and collections, is arguably a bit less readable, and is certainly less flexible. Collections let you easily grow or shrink the size of the collection, or switch to a different representation when appropriate, such as a linked list or hash table or ordered tree. The introduction of generics, boxing and unboxing, *foreach* loops, and *varargs* in Java marks the first time that using collections is just as simple, perhaps even simpler, than using arrays.

Now let's look at each of these features in a little more detail.

1.1 Generics

An interface or class may be declared to take one or more type parameters, which are written in angle brackets and should be supplied when you declare a variable belonging to the interface or class or when you create a new instance of a class.

We saw one example in the previous section. Here is another:

```
List<String> words = new ArrayList<String>();
words.add("Hello ");
words.add("world!");
String s = words.get(0)+words.get(1);
assert s.equals("Hello world!");
```

In the Collections Framework, class `ArrayList<E>` implements interface `List<E>`. This trivial code fragment declares the variable `words` to contain a list of strings, creates an instance of an `ArrayList`, adds two strings to the list, and gets them out again.

In Java before generics, the same code would be written as follows:

```
List words = new ArrayList();
words.add("Hello ");
words.add("world!");
String s = ((String)words.get(0))+((String)words.get(1))
assert s.equals("Hello world!");
```

Without generics, the type parameters are omitted, but you must explicitly cast whenever an element is extracted from the list.

In fact, the bytecode compiled from the two sources above will be identical. We say that generics are implemented by *erasure* because the types `List<Integer>`, `List<String>`, and `List<List<String>>` are all represented at run-time by the same type, `List`. We also use *erasure* to describe the process that converts the first program to the second. The term *erasure* is a slight misnomer, since the process erases type parameters but adds casts.

Generics implicitly perform the same cast that is explicitly performed without generics. If such casts could fail, it might be hard to debug code written with generics. This is why it is reassuring that generics come with the following guarantee:

Cast-iron guarantee: the implicit casts added by the compilation of generics never fail.

There is also some fine print on this guaranteee: it applies only when no *unchecked warnings* have been issued by the compiler. Later, we will discuss at some length what causes unchecked warnings to be issued and how to minimize their effect.

Implementing generics by erasure has a number of important effects. It keeps things simple, in that generics do not add anything fundamentally new. It keeps things small, in that there is exactly one implementation of `List`, not one version for each type. And it eases evolution, since the same library can be accessed in both nongeneric and generic forms.

This last point is worth some elaboration. It means that you don't get nasty problems due to maintaining two versions of the libraries: a nongeneric *legacy* version that works with Java 1.4 or earlier, and a *generic* version that works with Java 5 and 6. At the bytecode level, code that doesn't use generics looks just like code that does. There is no need to switch to generics all at once—you can evolve your code by updating just one package, class, or method at a time to start using generics. We even explain how you may declare generic types for legacy code. (Of course, the cast-iron guarantee mentioned above holds only if you add generic types that match the legacy code.)

Another consequence of implementing generics by erasure is that array types differ in key ways from parameterized types. Executing

```
new String[size]
```

allocates an array, and stores in that array an indication that its components are of type
`String`. In contrast, executing:

```
new ArrayList<String>()
```

allocates a list, but does not store in the list any indication of the type of its elements. In the
jargon, we say that Java *reifies* array component types but does not reify list element types
(or other generic types). Later, we will see how this design eases evolution (see Chapter 5)
but complicates casts, instance tests, and array creation (see Chapter 6).

Generics Versus Templates   Generics in Java resemble templates in C++. There are just
two important things to bear in mind about the relationship between Java generics and C++
templates: syntax and semantics. The syntax is deliberately similar and the semantics are
deliberately different.

Syntactically, angle brackets were chosen because they are familiar to C++ users, and
because square brackets would be hard to parse. However, there is one difference in syntax.
In C++, nested parameters require extra spaces, so you see things like this:

```
List< List<String> >
```

In Java, no spaces are required, and it's fine to write this:

```
List<List<String>>
```

You may use extra spaces if you prefer, but they're not required. (In C++, a problem arises
because >> without the space denotes the right-shift operator. Java fixes the problem by a
trick in the grammar.)

Semantically, Java generics are defined by *erasure*, whereas C++ templates are defined
by *expansion*. In C++ templates, each instance of a template at a new type is compiled
separately. If you use a list of integers, a list of strings, and a list of lists of string, there
will be three versions of the code. If you use lists of a hundred different types, there will be
a hundred versions of the code—a problem known as *code bloat*. In Java, no matter how
many types of lists you use, there is always one version of the code, so bloat does not occur.

Expansion may lead to more efficient implementation than erasure, since it offers more
opportunities for optimization, particularly for primitive types such as `int`. For code that
is manipulating large amounts of data—for instance, large arrays in scientific computing—
this difference may be significant. However, in practice, for most purposes the difference
in efficiency is not important, whereas the problems caused by code bloat can be crucial.

In C++, you also may instantiate a template with a constant value rather than a type, making
it possible to use templates as a sort of "macroprocessor on steroids" that can perform
arbitrarily complex computations at compile time. Java generics are deliberately restricted
to types, to keep them simple and easy to understand.

1.2 Boxing and Unboxing

Recall that every type in Java is either a *reference* type or a *primitive* type. A reference type is any class, instance, or array type. All reference types are subtypes of class Object, and any variable of reference type may be set to the value null. As shown in the following table, there are eight primitive types, and each of these has a corresponding library class of reference type. The library classes are located in the package java.lang.

Primitive	Reference
byte	Byte
short	Short
int	Integer
long	Long
float	Float
double	Double
bool	Boolean
char	Character

Conversion of a primitive type to the corresponding reference type is called *boxing* and conversion of the reference type to the corresponding primitive type is called *unboxing*.

Java with generics automatically inserts boxing and unboxing coercions where appropriate. If an expression e of type int appears where a value of type Integer is expected, boxing converts it to new Integer(e) (however, it may cache frequently occurring values). If an expression e of type Integer appears where a value of type int is expected, unboxing converts it to the expression e.intValue(). For example, the sequence:

```
List<Integer> ints = new ArrayList<Integer>();
ints.add(1);
int n = ints.get(0);
```

is equivalent to the sequence:

```
List<Integer> ints = new ArrayList<Integer>();
ints.add(new Integer(1));
int n = ints.get(0).intValue();
```

In practice, the compiler will arrange for the value of new Integer(1) to be cached, as we explain shortly.

Here, again, is the code to find the sum of a list of integers, conveniently packaged as a static method:

```
public static int sum (List<Integer> ints) {
  int s = 0;
  for (int n : ints) { s += n; }
  return s;
}
```

Why does the argument have type List<Integer> and not List<int>? Because type parameters must always be bound to reference types, not primitive types. Why does the result have type int and not Integer? Because result types may be either primitive or reference types, and it is more efficient to use the former than the latter. Unboxing occurs when each Integer in the list ints is bound to the variable n of type int.

We could rewrite the method, replacing each occurrence of int with Integer:

```java
public static Integer sumInteger(List<Integer> ints) {
  Integer s = 0;
  for (Integer n : ints) { s += n; }
  return s;
}
```

This code compiles but performs a lot of needless work. Each iteration of the loop unboxes the values in s and n, performs the addition, and boxes up the result again. With Sun's current compiler, measurements show that this version is about 60 percent slower than the original.

Look Out for This!   One subtlety of boxing and unboxing is that == is defined differently on primitive and on reference types. On type int, it is defined by equality of values, and on type Integer, it is defined by object identity. So both of the following assertions succeed using Sun's JVM:

```java
List<Integer> bigs = Arrays.asList(100,200,300);
assert sumInteger(bigs) == sum(bigs);
assert sumInteger(bigs) != sumInteger(bigs);  // not recommended
```

In the first assertion, unboxing causes values to be compared, so the results are equal. In the second assertion, there is no unboxing, and the two method calls return distinct Integer objects, so the results are unequal even though both Integer objects represent the same value, 600. We recommend that you never use == to compare values of type Integer. Either unbox first, so == compares values of type int, or else use equals to compare values of type Integer.

A further subtlety is that boxed values may be cached. Caching is required when boxing an int or short value between -128 and 127, a char value between '\u0000' and '\u007f', a byte, or a boolean; and caching is permitted when boxing other values. Hence, in contrast to our earlier example, we have the following:

```java
List<Integer> smalls = Arrays.asList(1,2,3);
assert sumInteger(smalls) == sum(smalls);
assert sumInteger(smalls) == sumInteger(smalls);  // not recommended
```

This is because 6 is smaller than 128, so boxing the value 6 always returns exactly the same object. In general, it is not specified whether boxing the same value twice should return identical or distinct objects, so the inequality assertion shown earlier may either fail or succeed depending on the implementation. Even for small values, for which == will compare values of type Integer correctly, we recommend against its use. It is clearer and cleaner to use equals rather than == to compare values of reference type, such as Integer or String.

1.3 Foreach

Here, again, is our code that computes the sum of a list of integers.

```
List<Integer> ints = Arrays.asList(1,2,3);
int s = 0;
for (int n : ints) { s += n; }
assert s == 6;
```

The loop in the third line is called a *foreach* loop even though it is written with the keyword for. It is equivalent to the following:

```
for (Iterator<Integer> it = ints.iterator(); it.hasNext(); ) {
  int n = it.next();
  s += n;
}
```

The emphasized code corresponds to what was written by the user, and the unemphasized code is added in a systematic way by the compiler. It introduces the variable it of type Iterator<Integer> to iterate over the list ints of type List<Integer>. In general, the compiler invents a new name that is guaranteed not to clash with any name already in the code. Note that unboxing occurs when the expression it.next() of type Integer is assigned to the variable n of type int.

The *foreach* loop can be applied to any object that implements the interface Iterable<E> (in package java.lang), which in turn refers to the interface Iterator<E> (in package java.util). These define the methods iterator, hasNext, and next, which are used by the translation of the *foreach* loop (iterators also have a method remove, which is not used by the translation):

```
interface Iterable<E> {
  public Iterator<E> iterator();
}
interface Iterator<E> {
  public boolean hasNext();
  public E next();
  public void remove();
}
```

All collections, sets, and lists in the Collections Framework implement the Iterable<E> interface; and classes defined by other vendors or users may implement it as well.

The *foreach* loop may also be applied to an array:

```
public static int sumArray(int[] a) {
  int s = 0;
  for (int n : a) { s += n; }
  return s;
}
```

The *foreach* loop was deliberately kept simple and catches only the most common case. You need to explicitly introduce an iterator if you wish to use the remove method or to iterate over more than one list in parallel. Here is a method that removes negative elements from a list of doubles:

do not test it w/ Arrays.asList...

```
public static void removeNegative(List<Double> v) {
  for (Iterator<Double> it = v.iterator(); it.hasNext();) {
    if (it.next() < 0) it.remove();
  }
}
```

Here is a method to compute the dot product of two vectors, represented as lists of doubles, both of the same length. Given two vectors, $u_1, \ldots, u_n$ and $v_1, \ldots, v_n$, it computes $u_1 * v_1 + \cdots + u_n * v_n$:

```
public static double dot(List<Double> u, List<Double> v) {
  if (u.size() != v.size())
    throw new IllegalArgumentException("different sizes");
  double d = 0;
  Iterator<Double> uIt = u.iterator();
  Iterator<Double> vIt = v.iterator();
  while (uIt.hasNext()) {
    assert uIt.hasNext() && vIt.hasNext();
    d += uIt.next() * vIt.next();
  }
  assert !uIt.hasNext() && !vIt.hasNext();
  return d;
}
```

Two iterators, uIt and vIt, advance across the lists u and v in lock step. The loop condition checks only the first iterator, but the assertions confirm that we could have used the second iterator instead, since we previously tested both lists to confirm that they have the same length.

1.4 Generic Methods and Varargs

Here is a method that accepts an array of any type and converts it to a list:

```
class Lists {
  public static <T> List<T> toList(T[] arr) {
    List<T> list = new ArrayList<T>();
```

```
    for (T elt : arr) list.add(elt);
    return list;
  }
}
```

The static method toList accepts an array of type T[] and returns a list of type List<T>, and does so for *any* type T. This is indicated by writing <T> at the beginning of the method signature, which declares T as a new type variable. A method which declares a type variable in this way is called a *generic method*. The scope of the type variable T is local to the method itself; it may appear in the method signature and the method body, but not outside the method.

The method may be invoked as follows:

```
List<Integer> ints = Lists.toList(new Integer[] { 1, 2, 3 });
List<String> words = Lists.toList(new String[] { "hello", "world" });
```

In the first line, boxing converts 1, 2, 3 from int to Integer.

Packing the arguments into an array is cumbersome. The *vararg* feature permits a special, more convenient syntax for the case in which the last argument of a method is an array. To use this feature, we replace T[] with T... in the method declaration:

```
class Lists {
  public static <T> List<T> toList(T... arr) {
    List<T> list = new ArrayList<T>();
    for (T elt : arr) list.add(elt);
    return list;
  }
}
```

Now the method may be invoked as follows:

```
List<Integer> ints = Lists.toList(1, 2, 3);
List<String> words = Lists.toList("hello", "world");
```

This is just shorthand for what we wrote above. At run time, the arguments are packed into an array which is passed to the method, just as previously.

Any number of arguments may precede a last *vararg* argument. Here is a method that accepts a list and adds all the additional arguments to the end of the list:

```
public static <T> void addAll(List<T> list, T... arr) {
  for (T elt : arr) list.add(elt);
}
```

Whenever a *vararg* is declared, one may either pass a list of arguments to be implicitly packed into an array, or explicitly pass the array directly. Thus, the preceding method may be invoked as follows:

```
List<Integer> ints = new ArrayList<Integer>();
Lists.addAll(ints, 1, 2);
Lists.addAll(ints, new Integer[] { 3, 4 });
assert ints.toString().equals("[1, 2, 3, 4]"));
```

We will see later that when we attempt to create an array containing a generic type, we will always receive an *unchecked* warning. Since *varargs* always create an array, they should be used only when the argument does not have a generic type (see Section 6.8).

In the preceding examples, the type parameter to the generic method is inferred, but it may also be given explicitly, as in the following examples:

```
List<Integer> ints = Lists.<Integer>toList();
List<Object> objs = Lists.<Object>toList(1, "two");
```

Explicit parameters are usually not required, but they are helpful in the examples given here. In the first example, without the type parameter there is too little information for the type inference algorithm to infer the correct type. It infers that the argument to toList is an empty array of an arbitrary generic type rather than an empty array of integers, and this triggers the unchecked warning described earlier. In the second example, without the type parameter there is too much information for the type inference algorithm to infer the correct type. You might think that Object is the only type that an integer and a string have in common, but in fact they also both implement the interfaces Serializable and Comparable. The type inference algorithm cannot choose which of these three is the correct type.

In general, the following rule of thumb suffices: in a call to a generic method, if there are one or more arguments that correspond to a type parameter and they all have the same type then the type parameter may be inferred; if there are no arguments that correspond to the type parameter or the arguments belong to different subtypes of the intended type then the type parameter must be given explicitly.

When a type parameter is passed to a generic method invocation, it appears in angle brackets to the left, just as in the method declaration. The Java grammar requires that type parameters may appear only in method invocations that use a dotted form. Even if the method toList is defined in the same class that invokes the code, we cannot shorten it as follows:

```
List<Integer> ints = <Integer>toList();  // compile-time error
```

This is illegal because it will confuse the parser.

Methods Arrays.asList and Collections.addAll in the Collections Framework are similar to toList and addAll shown earlier. (Both classes are in package java.util.) The Collections Framework version of asList does not return an ArrayList, but instead returns a specialized list class that is backed by a given array. Also, its version of addAll acts on general collections, not just lists.

1.5 Assertions

We clarify our code by liberal use of the `assert` statement. Each occurrence of `assert` is followed by a boolean expression that is expected to evaluate to `true`. If assertions are enabled and the expression evaluates to `false`, an `AssertionError` is thrown, including an indication of where the error occurred. Assertions are enabled by invoking the JVM with the `-ea` or `-enableassertions` flag.

We only write assertions that we expect to evaluate to `true`. Since assertions may not be enabled, an assertion should never have side effects upon which any nonassertion code depends. When checking for a condition that might not hold (such as confirming that the arguments to a method call are valid), we use a conditional and throw an exception explicitly.

To sum up, we have seen how generics, boxing and unboxing, *foreach* loops, and *varargs* work together to make Java code easier to write, having illustrated this through the use of the Collections Framework.

CHAPTER 2

Subtyping and Wildcards

Now that we've covered the basics, we can start to cover more-advanced features of generics, such as subtyping and wildcards. In this section, we'll review how subtyping works and we'll see how wildcards let you use subtyping in connection with generics. We'll illustrate our points with examples from the Collections Framework.

2.1 Subtyping and the Substitution Principle

Subtyping is a key feature of object-oriented languages such as Java. In Java, one type is a *subtype* of another if they are related by an `extends` or `implements` clause. Here are some examples:

`Integer`	is a subtype of	`Number`
`Double`	is a subtype of	`Number`
`ArrayList<E>`	is a subtype of	`List<E>`
`List<E>`	is a subtype of	`Collection<E>`
`Collection<E>`	is a subtype of	`Iterable<E>`

Subtyping is transitive, meaning that if one type is a subtype of a second, and the second is a subtype of a third, then the first is a subtype of the third. So, from the last two lines in the preceding list, it follows that `List<E>` is a subtype of `Iterable<E>`. If one type is a subtype of another, we also say that the second is a *supertype* of the first. Every reference type is a subtype of `Object`, and `Object` is a supertype of every reference type. We also say, trivially, that every type is a subtype of itself.

The Substitution Principle tells us that wherever a value of one type is expected, one may provide a value of any subtype of that type:

> *Substitution Principle*: a variable of a given type may be assigned a value of any subtype of that type, and a method with a parameter of a given type may be invoked with an argument of any subtype of that type.

Consider the interface Collection<E>. One of its methods is add, which takes a parameter of type E:

```
interface Collections<E> {
  public boolean add(E elt);
  ...
}
```

According to the Substitution Principle, if we have a collection of numbers, we may add an integer or a double to it, because Integer and Double are subtypes of Number.

```
List<Number> nums = new ArrayList<Number>();
nums.add(2);
nums.add(3.14);
assert nums.toString().equals("[2, 3.14]");
```

Here, subtyping is used in two ways for each method call. The first call is permitted because nums has type List<Number>, which is a subtype of Collection<Number>, and 2 has type Integer (thanks to boxing), which is a subtype of Number. The second call is similarly permitted. In both calls, the E in List<E> is taken to be Number.

It may seem reasonable to expect that since Integer is a subtype of Number, it follows that List<Integer> is a subtype of List<Number>. But this is *not* the case, because the Substitution Principle would rapidly get us into trouble. It is not always safe to assign a value of type List<Integer> to a variable of type List<Number>. Consider the following code fragment:

```
List<Integer> ints = Arrays.asList(1,2);
List<Number> nums = ints; // compile-time error
nums.add(3.14);
assert ints.toString().equals("[1, 2, 3.14]"); // uh oh!
```

This code assigns variable ints to point at a list of integers, and then assigns nums to point at the *same* list of integers; hence the call in the third line adds a double to this list, as shown in the fourth line. This must not be allowed! The problem is prevented by observing that here the Substitution Principle does *not* apply: the assignment on the second line is not allowed because List<Integer> is not a subtype of List<Number>, and the compiler reports that the second line is in error.

What about the reverse? Can we take List<Number> to be a subtype of List<Integer>? No, that doesn't work either, as shown by the following code:

```
List<Number> nums = Arrays.<Number>asList(2.78, 3.14);
List<Integer> ints = nums; // compile-time error
assert ints.toString().equals("[2.78, 3.14]"); // uh oh!
```

The problem is prevented by observing that here the Substitution Principle does *not* apply: the assignment on the second line is *not* allowed because List<Integer> is *not* a subtype of List<Number>, and the compiler reports that the second line is in error.

So List<Integer> is not a subtype of List<Number>, nor is List<Number> a subtype of List<Integer>; all we have is the trivial case, where List<Integer> is a subtype of itself, and we also have that List<Integer> is a subtype of Collection<Integer>.

Arrays behave quite differently; with them, Integer[] *is* a subtype of Number[]. We will compare the treatment of lists and arrays later (see Section 2.5).

Sometimes we would like lists to behave more like arrays, in that we want to accept not only a list with elements of a given type, but also a list with elements of any subtype of a given type. For this purpose, we use *wildcards*.

2.2 Wildcards with extends

Another method in the Collection interface is addAll, which adds all of the members of one collection to another collection:

```
interface Collection<E> {
    ...
    public boolean addAll(Collection<? extends E> c);
    ...
}
```

Clearly, given a collection of elements of type E, it is OK to add all members of another collection with elements of type E. The quizzical phrase "? extends E" means that it is also OK to add all members of a collection with elements of any type that is a *subtype* of E. The question mark is called a *wildcard*, since it stands for some type that is a subtype of E.

Here is an example. We create an empty list of numbers, and add to it first a list of integers and then a list of doubles:

```
List<Number> nums = new ArrayList<Number>();
List<Integer> ints = Arrays.asList(1, 2);
List<Double> dbls = Arrays.asList(2.78, 3.14);
nums.addAll(ints);
nums.addAll(dbls);
assert nums.toString().equals("[1, 2, 2.78, 3.14]");
```

The first call is permitted because nums has type List<Number>, which is a subtype of Collection<Number>, and ints has type List<Integer>, which is a subtype of Collection<? extends Number>. The second call is similarly permitted. In both calls, E is taken to be Number. If the method signature for addAll had been written without the wildcard, then the calls to add lists of integers and doubles to a list of numbers would not have been permitted; you would only have been able to add a list that was explicitly declared to be a list of numbers.

We can also use wildcards when declaring variables. Here is a variant of the example at the end of the preceding section, changed by adding a wildcard to the second line:

```
List<Integer> ints = Arrays.asList(1,2);
List<? extends Number> nums = ints;
```

```
nums.add(3.14);  // compile-time error
assert ints.toString().equals("[1, 2, 3.14]");  // uh oh!
```

Before, the second line caused a compile-time error (because List<Integer> is not a subtype of List<Number>), but the third line was fine (because a double is a number, so you can add a double to a List<Number>). Now, the second line is fine (because List<Integer> is a subtype of List<? extends Number>), but the third line causes a compile-time error (because you cannot add a double to a List<? extends Number>, since it might be a list of some other subtype of number). As before, the fourth line shows why one of the preceding lines is illegal!

In general, if a structure contains elements with a type of the form ? extends E, we can get elements out of the structure, but we cannot put elements into the structure. To put elements into the structure we need another kind of wildcard, as explained in the next section.

2.3 Wildcards with super

Here is a method that copies into a destination list all of the elements from a source list, from the convenience class Collections:

```
public static <T> void copy(List<? super T> dst, List<? extends T> src) {
  for (int i = 0; i < src.size(); i++) {
    dst.set(i, src.get(i));
  }
}
```

The quizzical phrase ? super T means that the destination list may have elements of any type that is a *supertype* of T, just as the source list may have elements of any type that is a *subtype* of T.

Here is a sample call.

```
List<Object> objs = Arrays.<Object>asList(2, 3.14, "four");
List<Integer> ints = Arrays.asList(5, 6);
Collections.copy(objs, ints);
assert objs.toString().equals("[5, 6, four]");
```

As with any generic method, the type parameter may be inferred or may be given explicitly. In this case, there are four possible choices, all of which type-check and all of which have the same effect:

```
Collections.copy(objs, ints);
Collections.<Object>copy(objs, ints);
Collections.<Number>copy(objs, ints);
Collections.<Integer>copy(objs, ints);
```

The first call leaves the type parameter implicit; it is taken to be Integer, since that is the most specific choice that works. In the third line, the type parameter T is taken to be

---

Number. The call is permitted because objs has type List<Object>, which is a subtype of List<? super Number> (since Object is a supertype of Number, as required by the super) and ints has type List<Integer>, which is a subtype of List<? extends Number> (since Integer is a subtype of Number, as required by the extends wildcard).

We could also declare the method with several possible signatures.

```
public static <T> void copy(List<T> dst, List<T> src)
public static <T> void copy(List<T> dst, List<? extends T> src)
public static <T> void copy(List<? super T> dst, List<T> src)
public static <T> void copy(List<? super T> dst, List<? extends T> src)
```

The first of these is too restrictive, as it only permits calls when the destination and source have exactly the same type. The remaining three are equivalent for calls that use implicit type parameters, but differ for explicit type parameters. For the example calls above, the second signature works only when the type parameter is Object, the third signature works only when the type parameter is Integer, and the last signature works (as we have seen) for all three type parameters—i.e., Object, Number, and Integer. Always use wildcards where you can in a signature, since this permits the widest range of calls.

2.4 The Get and Put Principle

It may be good practice to insert wildcards whenever possible, but how do you decide *which* wildcard to use? Where should you use extends, where should you use super, and where is it inappropriate to use a wildcard at all?

Fortunately, a simple principle determines which is appropriate.

> *The Get and Put Principle*: use an extends wildcard when you only *get* values out of a structure, use a super wildcard when you only *put* values into a structure, and don't use a wildcard when you *both* get and put.

We already saw this principle at work in the signature of the copy method:

```
public static <T> void copy(List<? super T> dest, List<? extends T> src)
```

The method gets values out of the source src, so it is declared with an extends wildcard, and it puts values into the destination dst, so it is declared with a super wildcard.

Whenever you use an iterator, you get values out of a structure, so use an extends wildcard. Here is a method that takes a collection of numbers, converts each to a double, and sums them up:

```
public static double sum(Collection<? extends Number> nums) {
  double s = 0.0;
  for (Number num : nums) s += num.doubleValue();
  return s;
}
```

Since this uses extends, all of the following calls are legal:

```
List<Integer> ints = Arrays.asList(1,2,3);
assert sum(ints) == 6.0;

List<Double> doubles = Arrays.asList(2.78,3.14);
assert sum(doubles) == 5.92;

List<Number> nums = Arrays.<Number>asList(1,2,2.78,3.14);
assert sum(nums) == 8.92;
```

The first two calls would not be legal if extends was not used.

Whenever you use the add method, you put values into a structure, so use a super wildcard. Here is a method that takes a collection of numbers and an integer n, and puts the first n integers, starting from zero, into the collection:

```
public static void count(Collection<? super Integer> ints, int n) {
  for (int i = 0; i < n; i++) ints.add(i);
}
```

Since this uses super, all of the following calls are legal:

```
List<Integer> ints = new ArrayList<Integer>();
count(ints, 5);
assert ints.toString().equals("[0, 1, 2, 3, 4]");

List<Number> nums = new ArrayList<Number>();
count(nums, 5);   nums.add(5.0);
assert nums.toString().equals("[0, 1, 2, 3, 4, 5.0]");

List<Object> objs = new ArrayList<Object>();
count(objs, 5);   objs.add("five");
assert objs.toString().equals("[0, 1, 2, 3, 4, five]");
```

The last two calls would not be legal if super was not used.

Whenever you both put values into and get values out of the same structure, you should not use a wildcard.

```
public static double sumCount(Collection<Number> nums, int n) {
  count(nums, n);
  return sum(nums);
}
```

The collection is passed to both sum and count, so its element type must both extend Number (as sum requires) and be super to Integer (as count requires). The only two classes that satisfy both of these constraints are Number and Integer, and we have picked the first of these. Here is a sample call:

```
List<Number> nums = new ArrayList<Number>();
double sum = sumCount(nums,5);
assert sum == 10;
```

Since there is no wildcard, the argument must be a collection of Number.

If you don't like having to choose between Number and Integer, it might occur to you that if Java let you write a wildcard with both extends and super, you would not need to choose. For instance, we could write the following:

```
double sumCount(Collection<? extends Number super Integer> coll, int n)
// not legal Java!
```

Then we could call sumCount on either a collection of numbers or a collection of integers. But Java *doesn't* permit this. The only reason for outlawing it is simplicity, and conceivably Java might support such notation in the future. But, for now, if you need to both get and put then don't use wildcards.

The Get and Put Principle also works the other way around. If an extends wildcard is present, pretty much all you will be able to do is get but not put values of that type; and if a super wildcard is present, pretty much all you will be able to do is put but not get values of that type.

For example, consider the following code fragment, which uses a list declared with an extends wildcard:

```
List<Integer> ints = Arrays.asList(1,2,3);
List<? extends Number> nums = ints;
double dbl = sum(nums);  // ok
nums.add(3.14);  // compile-time error
```

The call to sum is fine, because it gets values from the list, but the call to add is not, because it puts a value into the list. This is just as well, since otherwise we could add a double to a list of integers!

Conversely, consider the following code fragment, which uses a list declared with a super wildcard:

```
List<Object> objs = Arrays.<Object>asList(1,"two");
List<? super Integer> ints = objs;
ints.add(3);  // ok
double dbl = sum(ints);  // compile-time error
```

Now the call to add is fine, because it puts a value into the list, but the call to sum is not, because it gets a value from the list. This is just as well, because the sum of a list containing a string makes no sense!

The exception proves the rule, and each of these rules has one exception. You cannot put anything into a type declared with an extends wildcard—except for the value null, which belongs to every reference type:

```
List<Integer> ints = Arrays.asList(1,2,3);
List<? extends Number> nums = ints;
nums.add(null);    // ok
assert nums.toString().equals("[1,2,3,null]");
```

Similarly, you cannot get anything out from a type declared with an extends wildcard—except for a value of type Object, which is a supertype of every reference type:

```
List<Object> objs = Arrays.<Object>asList(1,"two");
List<? super Integer> ints = objs;
String str = "";
for (Object obj : ints) str += obj.toString();
assert str.equals("1two");
```

You may find it helpful to think of ? extends T as containing every type in an interval bounded by the type of null below and by T above (where the type of null is a subtype of every reference type). Similarly, you may think of ? super T as containing every type in an interval bounded by T below and by Object above.

It is tempting to think that an extends wildcard ensures immutability, but it does not. As we saw earlier, given a list of type List<? extends Number>, you may still add null values to the list. You may also remove list elements (using remove, removeAll, or retainAll) or permute the list (using swap, sort, or shuffle in the convenience class Collections; see Section 17.1.1). If you want to ensure that a list cannot be changed, use the method unmodifiableList in the class Collections; similar methods exist for other collection classes (see Section 17.3.2). If you want to ensure that list elements cannot be changed, consider following the rules for making a class immutable given by Joshua Bloch in his book *Effective Java* (Addison-Wesley) in "Item 13: Favor immutability"; for example, in Part II, the classes CodingTask and PhoneTask in Section 12.1 are immutable, as is the class PriorityTask in Section 13.2.

Because String is final and can have no subtypes, you might expect that List<String> is the same type as List<? extends String>. But in fact the former is a subtype of the latter, but not the same type, as can be seen by an application of our principles. The Substitution Principle tells us it is a subtype, because it is fine to pass a value of the former type where the latter is expected. The Get and Put Principle tells us that it is not the same type, because we can add a string to a value of the former type but not the latter.

2.5 Arrays

It is instructive to compare the treatment of lists and arrays in Java, keeping in mind the Substitution Principle and the Get and Put Principle.

In Java, array subtyping is *covariant*, meaning that type S[] is considered to be a subtype of T[] whenever S is a subtype of T. Consider the following code fragment, which allocates an array of integers, assigns it to an array of numbers, and then attempts to assign a double into the array:

```
Integer[] ints = new Integer[] {1,2,3};
Number[] nums = ints;
nums[2] = 3.14;  // array store exception
assert Arrays.toString(ints).equals("[1, 2, 3.14]");  // uh oh!
```

Something is wrong with this program, since it puts a double into an array of integers! Where is the problem? Since `Integer[]` is considered a subtype of `Number[]`, according to the Substitution Principle the assignment on the second line must be legal. Instead, the problem is caught on the third line, and it is caught at run time. When an array is allocated (as on the first line), it is tagged with its reified type (a run-time representation of its component type, in this case, `Integer`), and every time an array is assigned into (as on the third line), an array store exception is raised if the reified type is not compatible with the assigned value (in this case, a double cannot be stored into an array of `Integer`).

In contrast, the subtyping relation for generics is *invariant*, meaning that type `List<S>` is *not* considered to be a subtype of `List<T>`, except in the trivial case where S and T are identical. Here is a code fragment analogous to the preceding one, with lists replacing arrays:

```
List<Integer> ints = Arrays.asList(1,2,3);
List<Number> nums = ints;  // compile-time error
nums.put(2, 3.14);
assert ints.toString().equals("[1, 2, 3.14]");  // uh oh!
```

Since `List<Integer>` is not considered to be a subtype of `List<Number>`, the problem is detected on the second line, not the third, and it is detected at compile time, not run time.

Wildcards reintroduce covariant subtyping for generics, in that type `List<S>` *is* considered to be a subtype of `List<? extends T>` when S is a subtype of T. Here is a third variant of the fragment:

```
List<Integer> ints = Arrays.asList(1,2,3);
List<? extends Number> nums = ints;
nums.put(2, 3.14);  // compile-time error
assert ints.toString().equals("[1, 2, 3.14]");  // uh oh!
```

As with arrays, the third line is in error, but, in contrast to arrays, the problem is detected at compile time, not run time. The assignment violates the Get and Put Principle, because you cannot put a value into a type declared with an `extends` wildcard.

Wildcards also introduce *contravariant* subtyping for generics, in that type `List<S>` is considered to be a *subtype* of `List<? super T>` when S is a *supertype* of T (as opposed to a subtype). Arrays do not support contravariant subtyping. For instance, recall that the method `count` accepted a parameter of type `Collection<? super Integer>` and filled it with integers. There is no equivalent way to do this with an array, since Java does not permit you to write `(? super Integer)[]`.

Detecting problems at compile time rather than at run time brings two advantages, one minor and one major. The minor advantage is that it is more efficient. The system does not need to carry around a description of the element type at run time, and the system does not need to check against this description every time an assignment into an array is performed. The major advantage is that a common family of errors is detected by the compiler. This improves every aspect of the program's life cycle: coding, debugging, testing, and maintenance are all made easier, quicker, and less expensive.

Apart from the fact that errors are caught earlier, there are many other reasons to prefer collection classes to arrays. Collections are far more flexible than arrays. The only operations supported on arrays are to get or set a component, and the representation is fixed. Collections support many additional operations, including testing for containment, adding and removing elements, comparing or combining two collections, and extracting a sublist of a list. Collections may be either lists (where order is significant and elements may be repeated) or sets (where order is not significant and elements may not be repeated), and a number of representations are available, including arrays, linked lists, trees, and hash tables. Finally, a comparison of the convenience classes Collections and Arrays shows that collections offer many operations not provided by arrays, including operations to rotate or shuffle a list, to find the maximum of a collection, and to make a collection unmodifiable or synchronized.

Nonetheless, there are a few cases where arrays are preferred over collections. Arrays of primitive type are much more efficient since they don't involve boxing; and assignments into such an array need not check for an array store exception, because primitive types don't have subtypes. And despite the check for array store exceptions, even arrays of reference type may be more efficient than collection classes with the current generation of compilers, so you may want to use arrays in crucial inner loops. As always, you should measure performance to justify such a design, especially since future compilers may optimize collection classes specially. Finally, in some cases arrays may be preferable for reasons of compatibility.

To summarize, it is better to detect errors at compile time rather than run time, but Java arrays are forced to detect certain errors at run time by the decision to make array subtyping covariant. Was this a good decision? Before the advent of generics, it was absolutely necessary. For instance, look at the following methods, which are used to sort any array or to fill an array with a given value:

```
public static void sort(Object[] a);
public static void fill(Object[] a, Object val);
```

Thanks to covariance, these methods can be used to sort or fill arrays of any reference type. Without covariance and without generics, there would be no way to declare methods that apply for all types. However, now that we have generics, covariant arrays are no longer necessary. Now we can give the methods the following signatures, directly stating that they work for all types:

```
public static <T> void sort(T[] a);
public static <T> void fill(T[] a, T val);
```

In some sense, covariant arrays are an artifact of the lack of generics in earlier versions of Java. Once you have generics, covariant arrays are probably the wrong design choice, and the only reason for retaining them is backward compatibility.

Sections 6.4–6.8 discuss inconvenient interactions between generics and arrays. For many purposes, it may be sensible to consider arrays a deprecated type. We return to this point in Section 6.9.

2.6 Wildcards Versus Type Parameters

The `contains` method checks whether a collection contains a given object, and its generalization, `containsAll`, checks whether a collection contains every element of another collection. This section presents two alternate approaches to giving generic signatures for these methods. The first approach uses wildcards and is the one used in the Java Collections Framework. The second approach uses type parameters and is often a more appropriate alternative.

Wildcards Here are the types that the methods have in Java with generics:

```
interface Collection<E> {
  ...
  public boolean contains(Object o);
  public boolean containsAll(Collection<?> c);
  ...
}
```

The first method does not use generics at all! The second method is our first sight of an important abbreviation. The type `Collection<?>` stands for:

```
Collection<? extends Object>
```

Extending `Object` is one of the most common uses of wildcards, so it makes sense to provide a short form for writing it.

These methods let us test for membership and containment:

```
Object obj = "one";
List<Object> objs = Arrays.<Object>asList("one", 2, 3.14, 4);
List<Integer> ints = Arrays.asList(2, 4);
assert objs.contains(obj);
assert objs.containsAll(ints);
assert !ints.contains(obj);
assert !ints.containsAll(objs);
```

The given list of objects contains both the string `"one"` and the given list of integers, but the given list of integers does not contain the string `"one"`, nor does it contain the given list of objects.

The tests `ints.contains(obj)` and `ints.containsAll(objs)` might seem silly. Of course, a list of integers won't contain an arbitrary object, such as the string `"one"`. But it is permitted because sometimes such tests might succeed:

```
Object obj = 1;
List<Object> objs = Arrays.<Object>asList(1, 3);
```

```
List<Integer> ints = Arrays.asList(1, 2, 3, 4);
assert ints.contains(obj);
assert ints.containsAll(objs);
```

In this case, the object may be contained in the list of integers because it happens to be an integer, and the list of objects may be contained within the list of integers because every object in the list happens to be an integer.

Type Parameters You might reasonably choose an alternative design for collections—a design in which you can only test containment for subtypes of the element type:

```
interface MyCollection<E> {  // alternative design
  ...
  public boolean contains(E o);
  public boolean containsAll(Collection<? extends E> c);
  ...
}
```

Say we have a class MyList that implements MyCollection. Now the tests are legal only one way around:

```
Object obj = "one";
MyList<Object> objs = MyList.<Object>asList("one", 2, 3.14, 4);
MyList<Integer> ints = MyList.asList(2, 4);
assert objs.contains(obj);
assert objs.containsAll(ints)
assert !ints.contains(obj);       // compile-time error
assert !ints.containsAll(objs);   // compile-time error
```

The last two tests are illegal, because the type declarations require that we can only test whether a list contains an element of a subtype of that list. So we can check whether a list of objects contains a list of integers, but not the other way around.

Which of the two styles is better is a matter of taste. The first permits more tests, and the second catches more errors at compile time (while also ruling out some sensible tests). The designers of the Java libraries chose the first, more liberal, alternative, because someone using the Collections Framework *before* generics might well have written a test such as ints.containsAll(objs), and that person would want that test to remain valid *after* generics were added to Java. However, when designing a new generic library, such as MyCollection, when backward compatibility is less important, the design that catches more errors at compile time might make more sense.

Arguably, the library designers made the wrong choice. Only rarely will a test such as ints.containsAll(objs) be required, and such a test can still be permitted by declaring ints to have type List<Object> rather than type List<Integer>. It might have been better to catch more errors in the common case rather than to permit more-precise typing in an uncommon case.

The same design choice applies to other methods that contain `Object` or `Collection<?>` in their signature, such as `remove`, `removeAll`, and `retainAll`.

2.7 Wildcard Capture

When a generic method is invoked, the type parameter may be chosen to match the unknown type represented by a wildcard. This is called *wildcard capture*.

Consider the method `reverse` in the convenience class `java.util.Collections`, which accepts a list of any type and reverses it. It can be given either of the following two signatures, which are equivalent:

```
public static void reverse(List<?> list);
public static void <T> reverse(List<T> list);
```

The wildcard signature is slightly shorter and clearer, and is the one used in the library.

If you use the second signature, it is easy to implement the method:

```
public static void <T> reverse(List<T> list) {
  List<T> tmp = new ArrayList<T>(list);
  for (int i = 0; i < list.size(); i++) {
    list.set(i, tmp.get(list.size()-i-1));
  }
}
```

This copies the argument into a temporary list, and then writes from the copy back into the original in reverse order.

If you try to use the first signature with a similar method body, it won't work:

```
public static void reverse(List<?> list) {
  List<Object> tmp = new ArrayList<Object>(list);
  for (int i = 0; i < list.size(); i++) {
    list.set(i, tmp.get(list.size()-i-1));  // compile-time error
  }
}
```

Now it is not legal to write from the copy back into the original, because we are trying to write from a list of objects into a list of unknown type. Replacing `List<Object>` with `List<?>` won't fix the problem, because now we have two lists with (possibly different) unknown element types.

Instead, you can implement the method with the first signature by implementing a private method with the second signature, and calling the second from the first:

```
public static void reverse(List<?> list) { rev(list); }
private static <T> void rev(List<T> list) {
  List<T> tmp = new ArrayList<T>(list);
```

```
  for (int i = 0; i < list.size(); i++) {
    list.set(i, tmp.get(list.size()-i-1));
  }
}
```

Here we say that the type variable T has *captured* the wildcard. This is a generally useful technique when dealing with wildcards, and it is worth knowing.

Another reason to know about wildcard capture is that it can show up in error messages, even if you don't use the above technique. In general, each occurrence of a wildcard is taken to stand for some unknown type. If the compiler prints an error message containing this type, it is referred to as `capture of ?`. For instance, with Sun's current compiler, the incorrect version of `reverse` generates the following error message:

```
Capture.java:6: set(int,capture of ?) in java.util.List<capture of ?>
cannot be applied to (int,java.lang.Object)
            list.set(i, tmp.get(list.size()-i-1));
            ^
```

Hence, if you see the quizzical phrase `capture of ?` in an error message, it will come from a wildcard type. Even if there are two distinct wildcards, the compiler will print the type associated with each as `capture of ?`. Bounded wildcards generate names that are even more long-winded, such as `capture of ? extends Number`.

2.8 Restrictions on Wildcards

Wildcards may not appear at the top level in class instance creation expressions (`new`), in explicit type parameters in generic method calls, or in supertypes (`extends` and `implements`).

Instance Creation   In a class instance creation expression, if the type is a parameterized type, then none of the type parameters may be wildcards. For example, the following are illegal:

```
List<?> list = new ArrayList<?>();  // compile-time error
Map<String, ? extends Number> map
  = new HashMap<String, ? extends Number>();  // compile-time error
```

This is usually not a hardship. The Get and Put Principle tells us that if a structure contains a wildcard, we should only get values out of it (if it is an `extends` wildcard) or only put values into it (if it is a `super` wildcard). For a structure to be useful, we must do both. Therefore, we usually create a structure at a precise type, even if we use wildcard types to put values into or get values from the structure, as in the following example:

```
List<Number> nums = new ArrayList<Number>();
List<? super Number> sink = nums;
List<? extends Number> source = nums;
for (int i=0; i<10; i++) sink.add(i);
double sum=0; for (Number num : source) sum+=num.doubleValue();
```

Here wildcards appear in the second and third lines, but not in the first line that creates the list.

Only top-level parameters in instance creation are prohibited from containing wildcards. Nested wildcards are permitted. Hence, the following is legal:

```
List<List<?>> lists = new ArrayList<List<?>>();
lists.add(Arrays.asList(1,2,3));
lists.add(Arrays.asList("four","five"));
assert lists.toString().equals("[[1, 2, 3], [four, five]]");
```

Even though the list of lists is created at a wildcard type, each individual list within it has a specific type: the first is a list of integers and the second is a list of strings. The wildcard type prohibits us from extracting elements from the inner lists at any type other than Object, but since that is the type used by toString, this code is well typed.

One way to remember the restriction is that the relationship between wildcards and ordinary types is similar to the relationship between interfaces and classes—wildcards and interfaces are more general, ordinary types and classes are more specific, and instance creation requires the more specific information. Consider the following three statements:

```
List<?> list = new ArrayList<Object>();   // ok
List<?> list = new List<Object>()   // compile-time error
List<?> list = new ArrayList<?>()   // compile-time error
```

The first is legal; the second is illegal because an instance creation expression requires a class, not an interface; and the third is illegal because an instance creation expression requires an ordinary type, not a wildcard.

You might wonder why this restriction is necessary. The Java designers had in mind that every wildcard type is shorthand for some ordinary type, so they believed that ultimately every object should be created with an ordinary type. It is not clear whether this restriction is necessary, but it is unlikely to be a problem. (We tried hard to contrive a situation in which it was a problem, and we failed!)

Generic Method Calls   If a generic method call includes explicit type parameters, those type parameters must not be wildcards. For example, say we have the following generic method:

```
class Lists {
  public static <T> List<T> factory() { return new ArrayList<T>(); }
}
```

You may choose for the type parameters to be inferred, or you may pass an explicit type parameter. Both of the following are legal:

```
List<?> list = Lists.factory();
List<?> list = Lists.<Object>factory();
```

If an explicit type parameter is passed, it must not be a wildcard:

```
List<?> list = Lists.<?>factory();   // compile-time error
```

As before, nested wildcards are permitted:

```
List<List<?>> = Lists.<List<?>>factory();   // ok
```

The motivation for this restriction is similar to the previous one. Again, it is not clear whether it is necessary, but it is unlikely to be a problem.

Supertypes When a class instance is created, it invokes the initializer for its supertype. Hence, any restriction that applies to instance creation must also apply to supertypes. In a class declaration, if the supertype or any superinterface has type parameters, these types must not be wildcards.

For example, this declaration is illegal:

```
class AnyList extends ArrayList<?> {...} // compile-time error
```

And so is this:

```
class AnotherList implements List<?> {...} // compile-time error
```

But, as before, nested wildcards are permitted:

```
class NestedList implements ArrayList<List<?>> {...}  // ok
```

The motivation for this restriction is similar to the previous two. As before, it is not clear whether it is necessary, but it is unlikely to be a problem.

CHAPTER 3

Comparison and Bounds

Now that we have the basics, let's look at some more-advanced uses of generics. This chapter describes the interfaces Comparable<T> and Comparator<T>, which are used to support comparison on elements. These interfaces are useful, for instance, if you want to find the maximum element of a collection or sort a list. Along the way, we will introduce bounds on type variables, an important feature of generics that is particularly useful in combination with the Comparable<T> interface.

3.1 Comparable

The interface Comparable<T> contains a single method that can be used to compare one object to another:

```
interface Comparable<T> {
  public int compareTo(T o);
}
```

The compareTo method returns a value that is negative, zero, or positive depending upon whether the argument is less than, equal to, or greater than the given object. When a class implements Comparable, the ordering specified by this interface is called the *natural ordering* for that class.

Typically, an object belonging to a class can only be compared with an object belonging to the same class. For instance, Integer implements Comparable<Integer>:

```
Integer int0 = 0;
Integer int1 = 1;
assert int0.compareTo(int1) < 0;
```

The comparison returns a negative number, since 0 precedes 1 under numerical ordering. Similarly, String implements Comparable<String>:

```
String str0 = "zero";
String str1 = "one";
assert str0.compareTo(str1) > 0;
```

This comparison returns a positive number, since "zero" follows "one" under alphabetic ordering.

The type parameter to the interface allows nonsensical comparisons to be caught at compile time:

```
Integer i = 0;
String s = "one";
assert i.compareTo(s) < 0;  // compile-time error
```

You can compare an integer with an integer or a string with a string, but attempting to compare an integer with a string signals a compile-time error.

Comparison is not supported between arbitrary numerical types:

```
Number m = new Integer(2);
Number n = new Double(3.14);
assert m.compareTo(n) < 0;  // compile-time error
```

Here the comparison is illegal, because the Number class does not implement the Comparable interface.

Consistent with Equals   Usually, we require that two objects are equal if and only if they compare as the same:

x.equals(y) *if and only if* x.compareTo(y) == 0

In this case, we say that the natural ordering is *consistent with equals*.

It is recommended that when designing a class you choose a natural ordering that is consistent with equals. This is particularly important if you use the interfaces SortedSet or SortedMap in the Collections Framework, both of which compare items using natural ordering. If two items that compare as the same are added to a sorted set, then only one will be stored, even if the two items are not equal; the same is true for a sorted map. (You may also specify a different ordering for use with a sorted set or sorted map, using a comparator as described in Section 3.4; but in that case the specified ordering should again be consistent with equals.)

Almost every class in the Java core libraries that has a natural ordering is consistent with equals. An exception is java.math.BigDecimal, which compares as the same two decimals that have the same value but different precisions, such as 4.0 and 4.00. Section 3.3 gives another example of a class with a natural ordering that is not consistent with equals.

Comparison differs from equality in that is does not accept a null argument. If x is not null, x.equals(null) must return false, while x.compareTo(null) must throw a NullPointerException.

We use standard idioms for comparison, writing x.compareTo(y) < 0 instead of x < y, and writing x.compareTo(y) <= 0 instead of x <= y. It is perfectly sensible to use the last of these even on types such as `java.math.BigDecimal`, where the natural ordering is not consistent with equals.

Contract for Comparable The contract for the `Comparable<T>` interface specifies three properties. The properties are defined using the sign function, which is defined such that `sgn(x)` returns -1, 0, or 1, depending on whether x is negative, zero, or positive.

First, comparison is anti-symmetric. Reversing the order of arguments reverses the result:

`sgn(x.compareTo(y)) == -sgn(y.compareTo(x))`

This generalizes the property for numbers: x < y if and only if y < x. It is also required that `x.compareTo(y)` raises an exception if and only if `y.compareTo(x)` raises an exception.

Second, comparison is transitive. If one value is smaller than a second, and the second is smaller than a third, then the first is smaller than the third:

if `x.compareTo(y) < 0` *and* `y.compareTo(z) < 0` *then* `x.compareTo(z) < 0`

This generalizes the property for integers: if x < y and y < z then x < z.

Third, comparison is a congruence. If two values compare as the same then they compare the same way with any third value:

if `x.compareTo(y) == 0` *then* `sgn(x.compareTo(z)) == sgn(y.compareTo(z))`

This generalizes the property for integers: if x == y then x < z if and only if y < z. Presumably, it is also required that if `x.compareTo(y) == 0` then `x.compareTo(z)` raises an exception if and only if `y.compareTo(z)` raises an exception, although this is not explicitly stated.

It is strongly recommended that comparison be compatible with equality:

`x.equals(y)` *if and only if* `x.compareTo(y) == 0`

As we saw earlier, a few exceptional classes, such as `java.math.BigDecimal`, violate this constraint.

However, it is always required that comparison be reflexive. Every value is compares as the same as itself:

`x.compareTo(x) == 0`

This follows from the first requirement, since taking x and y to be the same gives us `sgn(x.compareTo(x)) == -sgn(x.compareTo(x))`.

Look Out for This! It's worth pointing out a subtlety in the definition of comparison. Here is the right way to compare two integers:

```
class Integer implements Comparable<Integer> {
    ...
```

```
  public int compareTo(Integer that) {
    return this.value < that.value ? -1 :
           this.value == that.value ? 0 : 1 ;
  }
  ...
}
```

The conditional expression returns −1, 0, or 1 depending on whether the receiver is less than, equal to, or greater than the argument. You might think the following code would work just as well, since the method is permitted to return any negative integer if the receiver is less than the argument:

```
class Integer implements Comparable<Integer> {
  ...
  public int compareTo(Integer that) {
    // bad implementation -- don't do it this way!
    return this.value - that.value;
  }
  ...
}
```

But this code may give the wrong answer when there is overflow. For instance, when comparing a large negative value to a large positive value, the difference may be more than the largest value that can be stored in an integer, Integer.MAX_VALUE.

3.2 Maximum of a Collection

In this section, we show how to use the Comparable<T> interface to find the maximum element in a collection. We begin with a simplified version. The actual version found in the Collections Framework has a type signature that is a bit more complicated, and later we will see why.

Here is code to find the maximum element in a nonempty collection, from the class Collections:

```
public static <T extends Comparable<T>> T max(Collection<T> coll) {
    T candidate = coll.iterator().next();
    for (T elt : coll) {
        if (candidate.compareTo(elt) < 0) candidate = elt;
    }
    return candidate;
}
```

We first saw generic methods that declare new type variables in the signature in Section 1.4. For instance, the method asList takes an array of type E[] and returns a result of type List<E>, and does so for *any* type E. Here we have a generic method that declares a *bound* on the type variable. The method max takes a collection of type Collection<T> and returns a T, and it does this for *any* type T such that T is a subtype of Comparable<T>.

The highlighted phrase in angle brackets at the beginning of the type signature declares the type variable T, and we say that T is *bounded* by Comparable<T>. As with wildcards, bounds for type variables are always indicated by the keyword extends, even when the bound is an interface rather than a class, as is the case here. Unlike wildcards, type variables must always be bounded using extends, never super.

In this case, the bound is *recursive*, in that the bound on T itself depends upon T. It is even possible to have mutually recursive bounds, such as:

```
<T extends C<T,U>, U extends D<T,U>>
```

An example of mutually recursive bounds appears in Section 9.5.

The method body chooses the first element in the collection as a candidate for the maximum, and then compares the candidate with each element in the collection, setting the candidate to the element when the element is larger. We use iterator().next() rather than get(0) to get the first element, because get is not defined on collections other than lists. The method raises a NoSuchElement exception when the collection is empty.

When calling the method, T may be chosen to be Integer (since Integer implements Comparable<Integer>) or String (since String implements Comparable<String>):

```
List<Integer> ints = Arrays.asList(0,1,2);
assert Collections.max(ints) == 2;

List<String> strs = Arrays.asList("zero","one","two");
assert Collections.max(strs).equals("zero");
```

But we may not choose T to be Number (since Number does not implement Comparable):

```
List<Number> nums = Arrays.asList(0,1,2,3.14);
assert Collections.max(nums) == 3.14;   // compile-time error
```

As expected, here the call to max is illegal.

Here's an efficiency tip. The preceding implementation used a *foreach* loop to increase brevity and clarity. If efficiency is a pressing concern, you might want to rewrite the method to use an explicit iterator, as follows:

```
public static <T extends Comparable<T>> T max(Collection<T> coll) {
  Iterator<T> it = coll.iterator();
  T candidate = it.next();
  while (it.hasNext()) {
    T elt = it.next();
    if (candidate.compareTo(elt) < 0) candidate = elt;
  }
  return candidate;
}
```

This allocates an iterator once instead of twice and performs one less comparison.

Signatures for methods should be as general as possible to maximize utility. If you can replace a type parameter with a wildcard then you should do so. We can improve the signature of max by replacing:

```
<T extends Comparable<T>> T max(Collection<T> coll)
```

with:

```
<T extends Comparable<? super T>> T max(Collection<? extends T> coll)
```

Following the Get and Put Principle, we use extends with Collection because we *get* values of type T from the collection, and we use super with Comparable because we *put* value of type T into the compareTo method. In the next section, we'll see an example that would not type-check if the super clause above was omitted.

If you look at the signature of this method in the Java library, you will see something that looks even worse than the preceding code:

```
<T extends Object & Comparable<? super T>>
  T max(Collection<? extends T> coll)
```

This is there for backward compatibility, as we will explain at the end of Section 3.6.

3.3 A Fruity Example

The Comparable<T> interface gives fine control over what can and cannot be compared. Say that we have a Fruit class with subclasses Apple and Orange. Depending on how we set things up, we may *prohibit* comparison of apples with oranges or we may *permit* such comparison.

Example 3.2 prohibits comparison of apples with oranges. Here are the three classes it declares:

```
class Fruit {...}
class Apple extends Fruit implements Comparable<Apple> {...}
class Orange extends Fruit implements Comparable<Orange> {...}
```

Each fruit has a name and a size, and two fruits are equal if they have the same name and the same size. Following good practice, we have also defined a hash method, to ensure that equal objects have the same hash code. Apples are compared by comparing their sizes, and so are oranges. Since Apple implements Comparable<Apple>, it is clear that you can compare apples with apples, but not with oranges. The test code builds three lists, one of apples, one of oranges, and one containing mixed fruits. We may find the maximum of the first two lists, but attempting to find the maximum of the mixed list signals an error at compile time.

Example 3.1 permits comparison of apples with oranges. Compare these three class declarations with those given previously (all differences between Examples 3.2 and 3.1 are highlighted):

```
class Fruit implements Comparable<Fruit> {...}
class Apple extends Fruit {...}
class Orange extends Fruit {...}
```

As before, each fruit has a name and a size, and two fruits are equal if they have the same name and the same size. Now any two fruits are compared by ignoring their names and comparing their sizes. Since Fruit implements Comparable<Fruit>, any two fruits may be compared. Now the test code can find the maximum of all three lists, including the one that mixes apples with oranges.

Recall that at the end of the previous section we extended the type signature of compareTo to use super:

```
<T extends Comparable<? super T>> T max(Collection<? extends T> coll)
```

The second example shows why this wildcard is needed. If we want to compare two oranges, we take T in the preceding code to be Orange:

```
Orange extends Comparable<? super Orange>
```

And this is true because both of the following hold:

```
Orange extends Comparable<Fruit>   and   Fruit super Orange
```

Without the super wildcard, finding the maximum of a List<Orange> would be illegal, even though finding the maximum of a List<Fruit> is permitted.

Also note that the natural ordering used here is not consistent with equals (see Section 3.1). Two fruits with different names but the same size compare as the same, but they are not equal.

3.4 Comparator

Sometimes we want to compare objects that do not implement the Comparable interface, or to compare objects using a different ordering from the one specified by that interface. The ordering provided by the Comparable interface is called the *natural ordering*, so the Comparator interface provides, so to speak, an unnatural ordering.

We specify additional orderings using the Comparator interface, which contains a single method:

```
interface Comparator<T> {
  public int compare(T o1, T o2);
}
```

The compare method returns a value that is negative, zero, or positive depending upon whether the first object is less than, equal to, or greater than the second object—just as with compareTo.

Example 3.1. Permitting comparison of apples with oranges

```java
abstract class Fruit implements Comparable<Fruit> {
  protected String name;
  protected int size;
  protected Fruit(String name, int size) {
    this.name = name; this.size = size;
  }
  public boolean equals(Object o) {
    if (o instanceof Fruit) {
      Fruit that = (Fruit)o;
      return this.name.equals(that.name) && this.size == that.size;
    } else return false;
  }
  public int hash() {
    return name.hash()*29 + size;
  }
  public int compareTo(Fruit that) {
    return this.size < that.size ? - 1 :
           this.size == that.size ? 0 : 1 ;
  }
}
class Apple extends Fruit {
  public Apple(int size) { super("Apple", size); }
}
class Orange extends Fruit {
  public Orange(int size) { super("Orange", size); }
}
class Test {
  public static void main(String[] args) {

    Apple a1 = new Apple(1);  Apple a2 = new Apple(2);
    Orange o3 = new Orange(3);  Orange o4 = new Orange(4);

    List<Apple> apples = Arrays.asList(a1,a2);
    assert Collections.max(apples).equals(a2);

    List<Orange> oranges = Arrays.asList(o3,o4);
    assert Collections.max(oranges).equals(o4);

    List<Fruit> mixed = Arrays.<Fruit>asList(a1,o3);
    assert Collections.max(mixed).equals(o3);  // ok
  }
}
```

Example 3.2. Prohibiting comparison of apples with oranges

```
abstract class Fruit {
  protected String name;
  protected int size;
  protected Fruit(String name, int size) {
    this.name = name; this.size = size;
  }
  public boolean equals(Object o) {
    if (o instanceof Fruit) {
      Fruit that = (Fruit)o;
      return this.name.equals(that.name) && this.size == that.size;
    } else return false;
  }
  public int hash() {
    return name.hash()*29 + size;
  }
  protected int compareTo(Fruit that) {
    return this.size < that.size ? -1 :
           this.size == that.size ? 0 : 1 ;
  }
}
class Apple extends Fruit implements Comparable<Apple> {
  public Apple(int size) { super("Apple", size); }
  public int compareTo(Apple a) { return super.compareTo(a); }
}
class Orange extends Fruit implements Comparable<Orange> {
  public Orange(int size) { super("Orange", size); }
  public int compareTo(Orange o) { return super.compareTo(o); }
}
class Test {
  public static void main(String[] args) {

    Apple a1 = new Apple(1);  Apple a2 = new Apple(2);
    Orange o3 = new Orange(3);  Orange o4 = new Orange(4);

    List<Apple> apples = Arrays.asList(a1,a2);
    assert Collections.max(apples).equals(a2);

    List<Orange> oranges = Arrays.asList(o3,o4);
    assert Collections.max(oranges).equals(o4);

    List<Fruit> mixed = Arrays.<Fruit>asList(a1,o3);
    assert Collections.max(mixed).equals(o3);  // compile-time error
  }
}
```

Here is a comparator that considers the shorter of two strings to be smaller. Only if two strings have the same length are they compared using the natural (alphabetic) ordering.

```
Comparator<String> sizeOrder =
  new Comparator<String>() {
    public int compare(String s1, String s2) {
      return
        s1.length() < s2.length() ? -1 :
        s1.length() > s2.length() ? 1 :
        s1.compareTo(s2) ;
      }
  };
```

Here is an example:

```
assert "two".compareTo("three") > 0;
assert sizeOrder.compare("two","three") < 0;
```

In the natural alphabetic ordering, `"two"` is greater than `"three"`, whereas in the size ordering it is smaller.

The Java libraries always provide a choice between `Comparable` and `Comparator`. For every generic method with a type variable bounded by `Comparable`, there is another generic method with an additional argument of type `Comparator`. For instance, corresponding to:

```
public static <T extends Comparable<? super T>>
  T max(Collection<? extends T> coll)
```

we also have:

```
public static <T>
  T max(Collection<? extends T> coll, Comparator<? super T> cmp)
```

There are similar methods to find the minimum. For example, here is how to find the maximum and minimum of a list using the natural ordering and using the size ordering:

```
Collection<String> strings = Arrays.asList("from","aaa","to","zzz");
assert max(strings).equals("zzz");
assert min(strings).equals("aaa");
assert max(strings,sizeOrder).equals("from");
assert min(strings,sizeOrder).equals("to");
```

The string `"from"` is the maximum using the size ordering because it is longest, and `"to"` is minimum because it is shortest.

Here is the code for a version of max using comparators:

```
public static <T>
  T max(Collection<? extends T> coll, Comparator<? super T> cmp)
{
```

```
  T candidate = coll.iterator().next();
  for (T elt : coll) {
    if (cmp.compare(candidate, elt) < 0) { candidate = elt; }
  }
  return candidate;
}
```

Compared to the previous version, the only change is that where before we wrote candidate.compareTo(elt), now we write cmp.compare(candidate,elt).

It is easy to define a comparator that provides the natural ordering:

```
public static <T extends Comparable<? super T>>
  Comparator<T> naturalOrder()
{
  return new Comparator<T> {
    public int compare(T o1, T o2) { return o1.compareTo(o2); }
  }
}
```

Using this, it is easy to define the version of max that uses the natural ordering in terms of the version that uses a given comparator:

```
public static <T extends Comparable<? super T>>
  T max(Collection<? extends T> coll)
{
  return max(coll, Comparators.<T>naturalOrder());
}
```

A type parameter must be explicitly supplied for the invocation of the generic method naturalOrder, since the algorithm that infers types would fail to work out the correct type otherwise.

It is also easy to define a method that takes a comparator and returns a new comparator with the reverse of the given ordering:

```
public static <T> Comparator<T>
  reverseOrder(final Comparator<T> cmp)
{
  return new Comparator<T>() {
    public int compare(T o1, T o2) { return cmp.compare(o2,o1); }
  };
}
```

This simply reverses the order of arguments to the comparator. (By the contract for comparators, it would be equivalent to leave the arguments in the original order but negate the result.) And here is a method that returns the reverse of the natural ordering:

```
public static <T extends Comparable<? super T>>
  Comparator<T> reverseOrder()
```

```
{
  return new Comparator<T>() {
    public int compare(T o1, T o2) { return o2.compareTo(o1); }
  };
}
```

Similar methods are provided in `java.util.Collections`, see Section 17.4.

Finally, we can define the two versions of `min` in terms of the two versions of `max` by using the two versions of `reverseOrder`:

```
public static <T>
  T min(Collection<? extends T> coll, Comparator<? super T> cmp)
{
  return max(coll, reverseOrder(cmp));
}
public static <T extends Comparable<? super T>>
  T min(Collection<? extends T> coll)
{
  return max(coll, Comparators.<T>reverseOrder());
}
```

For easy reference, the code we have presented here is summarized in Example 3.3.

The Collections Framework does provide two versions each of `min` and `max` with the signatures given here, see Section 17.1. However, if you examine the source code of the library, you will see that none of the four is defined in terms of any of the others; instead, each is defined directly. The more direct version is longer and harder to maintain, but faster. With Sun's current JVM, measurements show a speedup of around 30 percent. Whether such a speedup is worth the code duplication depends on the situation in which the code is used. Since the Java utilities might well be used in a critical inner loop, the designers of the library were right to prefer speed of execution over economy of expression. But this is not always the case. An improvement of 30 percent may sound impressive, but it's insignificant unless the total time of the program is large and the routine appears in a heavily-used inner loop. Don't make your own code needlessly prolix just to eke out a small improvement.

As a final example of comparators, here is a method that takes a comparator on elements and returns a comparator on lists of elements:

```
public static <E>
  Comparator<List<E>> listComparator(final Comparator<E> comp) {
  return new Comparator<List<E>>() {
    public int compare(List<E> list1, List<E> list2) {
      int n1 = list1.size();
      int n2 = list2.size();
```

```
      for (int i = 0; i < Math.min(n1,n2); i++) {
        int k = comp.compare(list1.get(i), list2.get(i));
        if (k != 0) return k;
      }
      return (n1 < n2) ? -1 : (n1 == n2) ? 0 : 1;
    }
  };
}
```

The loop compares corresponding elements of the two lists, and terminates when corresponding elements are found that are not equal (in which case, the list with the smaller element is considered smaller) or when the end of either list is reached (in which case, the shorter list is considered smaller). This is the usual ordering for lists; if we convert a string to a list of characters, it gives the usual ordering on strings.

3.5 Enumerated Types

Java 5 includes support for enumerated types. Here is a simple example:

```
enum Season { WINTER, SPRING, SUMMER, FALL }
```

Each enumerated type declaration can be expanded into a corresponding class in a stylized way. The corresponding class is designed so that it has exactly one instance for each of the enumerated constants, bound to a suitable static final variable. For example, the enum declaration above expands into a class called Season. Exactly four instances of this class exist, bound to four static final variables with the names WINTER, SPRING, SUMMER, and FALL.

Each class that corresponds to an enumerated type is a subclass of java.lang.Enum. Its definition in the Java documentation begins like this:

```
class Enum<E extends Enum<E>>
```

You may find this frightening at first sight—both of us certainly did! But don't panic. Actually, we've already seen something similar. The worrying phrase E extends Enum<E> is a lot like the phrase T extends Comparable<T> that we encountered in the definition of max (see Section 3.2), and we'll see that they appear for related reasons.

To understand what's going on, we need to take a look at the code. Example 3.4 shows the base class Enum and Example 3.5 shows the class Season that corresponds to the enumerated type declaration above. (The code for Enum follows the source in the Java library, but we have simplified a few points.)

Here is the first line of the declaration for the Enum class:

```
public abstract class Enum<E extends Enum<E>> implements Comparable<E>
```

And here is the first line of the declaration for the Season class:

```
class Season extends Enum<Season>
```

Example 3.3. Comparators

```
class Comparators {
  public static <T>
    T max(Collection<? extends T> coll, Comparator<? super T> cmp)
  {
    T candidate = coll.iterator().next();
    for (T elt : coll) {
      if (cmp.compare(candidate, elt) < 0) { candidate = elt; }
    }
    return candidate;
  }
  public static <T extends Comparable<? super T>>
    T max(Collection<? extends T> coll)
  {
    return max(coll, Comparators.<T>naturalOrder());
  }
  public static <T>
    T min(Collection<? extends T> coll, Comparator<? super T> cmp)
  {
    return max(coll, reverseOrder(cmp));
  }
  public static <T extends Comparable<? super T>>
    T min(Collection<? extends T> coll)
  {
    return max(coll, Comparators.<T>reverseOrder());
  }
  public static <T extends Comparable<? super T>>
    Comparator<T> naturalOrder()
  {
    return new Comparator<T>() {
      public int compare(T o1, T o2) { return o1.compareTo(o2); }
    };
  }
  public static <T> Comparator<T>
    reverseOrder(final Comparator<T> cmp)
  {
    return new Comparator<T>() {
      public int compare(T o1, T o2) { return cmp.compare(o2,o1); }
    };
  }
  public static <T extends Comparable<? super T>>
    Comparator<T> reverseOrder()
  {
    return new Comparator<T>() {
      public int compare(T o1, T o2) { return o2.compareTo(o1); }
    };
  }
}
```

Example 3.4. Base class for enumerated types

```java
public abstract class Enum<E extends Enum<E>> implements Comparable<E> {
  private final String name;
  private final int ordinal;
  protected Enum(String name, int ordinal) {
    this.name = name; this.ordinal = ordinal;
  }
  public final String name() { return name; }
  public final int ordinal() { return ordinal; }
  public String toString() { return name; }
  public final int compareTo(E o) {
    return ordinal - o.ordinal;
  }
}
```

Example 3.5. Class corresponding to an enumerated type

```java
// corresponds to
// enum Season { WINTER, SPRING, SUMMER, FALL }
final class Season extends Enum<Season> {
  private Season(String name, int ordinal) { super(name,ordinal); }
  public static final Season WINTER = new Season("WINTER",0);
  public static final Season SPRING = new Season("SPRING",1);
  public static final Season SUMMER = new Season("SUMMER",2);
  public static final Season FALL   = new Season("FALL",3);
  private static final Season[] VALUES = { WINTER, SPRING, SUMMER, FALL };
  public static Season[] values() { return VALUES.clone(); }
  public static Season valueOf(String name) {
    for (Season e : VALUES) if (e.name().equals(name)) return e;
    throw new IllegalArgumentException();
  }
}
```

Matching things up, we can begin to see how this works. The type variable E stands for the subclass of Enum that implements a particular enumerated type, such as Season. Every E must satisfy:

```java
E extends Enum<E>
```

So we can take E to be Season, since:

```java
Season extends Enum<Season>
```

Furthermore, the declaration of Enum tells us that:

```java
Enum<E> implements Comparable<E>
```

So it follows that:

```
Enum<Season> implements Comparable<Season>
```

Hence, we are allowed to compare two values of type Season with each other, but we cannot compare a value of type Season with a value of any other type.

Without the type variable, the declaration of the Enum class would begin like this:

```
class Enum implements Comparable<Enum>
```

And the declaration for the Season class would begin like this:

```
class Season extends Enum
```

This is simpler, but it is *too* simple. With this definition, Season would implement Comparable<Enum> rather than Comparable<Season>, which would mean that we could compare a value of type Season with a value of *any* enumerated type, which is certainly *not* what we want!

In general, patterns like T extends Comparable<T> and E extends Enum<E> often arise when you want to pin down types precisely. We'll see further examples of this when we look at the Strategy and Subject-Observer design patterns, in Sections 9.4 and 9.5.

The rest of the definition is a straightforward application of the *typesafe enum* pattern described by Joshua Bloch in *Effective Java* (Addison-Wesley), which in turn is an instance of the *singleton* pattern described by Gamma, Helm, Johnson, and Vlissides in *Design Patterns* (Addison-Wesley).

The base class Enum defines two fields, a string name and an integer ordinal, that are possessed by every instance of an enumerated type; the fields are final because once they are initialized, their value never changes. The constructor for the class is protected, to ensure that it is used only within subclasses of this class. Each enumeration class makes the constructor private, to ensure that it is used only to create the enumerated constants. For instance, the Season class has a private constructor that is invoked exactly four times in order to initialize the final variables WINTER, SPRING, SUMMER, and FALL.

The base class defines accessor methods for the name and ordinal fields. The toString method returns the name, and the compareTo method just returns the difference of the ordinals for the two enumerated values. (Unlike the definition of Integer in Section 3.1, this is safe because there is no possibility of overflow.) Hence, constants have the same ordering as their ordinals—for example, WINTER precedes SUMMER.

Lastly, there are two static methods in every class that corresponds to an enumerated type. The values method returns an array of all the constants of the type. It returns a (shallow) clone of the internal array. Cloning is vital to ensure that the client cannot alter the internal array. Note that you don't need a cast when calling the clone method, because cloning for arrays now takes advantage of covariant return types (see Section 3.8). The valueOf method takes a string and returns the corresponding constant, found by searching the internal array. It returns an IllegalArgumentException if the string does not name a value of the enumeration.

3.6 Multiple Bounds

We have seen many examples where a type variable or wildcard is bounded by a single class or interface. In rare situations, it may be desirable to have multiple bounds, and we show how to do so here.

To demonstrate, we use three interfaces from the Java library. The Readable interface has a read method to read into a buffer from a source, the Appendable interface has an append method to copy from a buffer into a target, and the Closeable interface has a close method to close a source or target. Possible sources and targets include files, buffers, streams, and so on.

For maximum flexibility, we might want to write a copy method that takes any source that implements both Readable and Closeable and any target that implements both Appendable and Closeable:

```
public static <S extends Readable & Closeable,
               T extends Appendable & Closeable>
  void copy(S src, T trg, int size)
  throws IOException
{
  CharBuffer buf = CharBuffer.allocate(size);
  int i = src.read(buf);
  while (i >= 0) {
    buf.flip();  // prepare buffer for writing
    trg.append(buf);
    buf.clear();  // prepare buffer for reading
    i = src.read(buf);
  }
  src.close();
  trg.close();
}
```

This method repeatedly reads from the source into a buffer and appends from the buffer into a target. When the source is empty, it closes both the source and the target. The first line specifies that S ranges over any type that implements both Readable and Closeable, and that T ranges over any type that implements Appendable and Closeable. When multiple bounds on a type variable appear, they are separated by ampersands. (You cannot use a comma, since that is already used to separate declarations of type variables.)

For example, this method may be called with two files as source and target, or with the same two files wrapped in buffers as source and target:

```
int size = 32;
FileReader r = new FileReader("file.in");
FileWriter w = new FileWriter("file.out");
copy(r,w,size);
BufferedReader br = new BufferedReader(new FileReader("file.in"));
BufferedWriter bw = new BufferedWriter(new FileWriter("file.out"));
copy(br,bw,size);
```

Other possible sources include `FilterReader`, `PipedReader`, and `StringReader`, and other possible targets include `FilterWriter`, `PipedWriter`, and `PrintStream`. But you could not use `StringBuffer` as a target, since it implements `Appendable` but not `Closeable`.

If you are picky, you may have spotted that all classes that implement both `Readable` and `Closeable` are subclasses of `Reader`, and almost all classes that implement `Appendable` and `Closeable` are subclasses of `Writer`. So you might wonder why we don't simplify the method signature like this:

```
public static void copy(Reader src, Writer trg, int size)
```

This will indeed admit most of the same classes, but not all of them. For instance, `PrintStream` implements `Appendable` and `Closeable` but is not a subclass of `Writer`. Furthermore, you can't rule out the possibility that some programmer using your code might have his or her own custom class that, say, implements `Readable` and `Closeable` but is not a subclass of `Reader`.

When multiple bounds appear, the first bound is used for erasure. We saw a use of this earlier in Section 3.2:

```
public static <T extends Object & Comparable<? super T>>
  T max(Collection<? extends T> coll)
```

Without the highlighted text, the erased type signature for `max` would have `Comparable` as the return type, whereas in legacy libraries the return type is `Object`. Maintaining compatibility with legacy libraries is further discussed in Chapter 5 and Section 8.4.

3.7 Bridges

As we mentioned earlier, generics are implemented by erasure: when you write code with generics, it compiles in almost exactly the same way as the code you would have written without generics. In the case of a parameterized interface such as `Comparable<T>`, this may cause additional methods to be inserted by the compiler; these additional methods are called *bridges*.

Example 3.6 shows the `Comparable` interface and a simplified version of the `Integer` class in Java before generics. In the nongeneric interface, the `compareTo` method takes an argument of type `Object`. In the nongeneric class, there are two `compareTo` methods. The first is the naïve method you might expect, to compare an integer with another integer. The second compares an integer with an arbitrary object: it casts the object to an integer and calls the first method. The second method is necessary in order to override the `compareTo` method in the `Comparable` interface, because overriding occurs only when the method signatures are identical. This second method is called a *bridge*.

Example 3.7 shows what happens when the `Comparable` interface and the `Integer` class are generified. In the generic interface, the `compareTo` method takes an argument of type T. In the generic class, a single `compareTo` method takes an argument of type `Integer`. The

Example 3.6. Legacy code for comparable integers

```
interface Comparable {
  public int compareTo(Object o);
}
class Integer implements Comparable {
  private final int value;
  public Integer(int value) { this.value = value; }
  public int compareTo(Object o) {
    return compareTo((Integer)o);
  }
  public int compareTo(Integer i) {
    return (value < i.value) ? -1 : (value == i.value) ? 0 : 1;
  }
}
```

Example 3.7. Generic code for comparable integers

```
interface Comparable<T> {
  public int compareTo(T o);
}
class Integer implements Comparable<Integer> {
  private final int value;
  public Integer(int value) { this.value = value; }
  public int compareTo(Integer i) {
    return (value < i.value) ? -1 : (value == i.value) ? 0 : 1;
  }
}
```

bridge method is generated automatically by the compiler. Indeed, the compiled version of the code for both examples is essentially identical.

You can see the bridge if you apply reflection. Here is code that finds all methods with the name compareTo in the class Integer, using toGenericString to print the generic signature of a method (see Section 7.5).

```
for (Method m : Integer.class.getMethods())
    if (m.getName().equals("compareTo"))
        System.out.println(m.toGenericString());
```

Running this code on the generic version of the Integer class produces the following output:

```
public int Integer.compareTo(Integer)
public bridge int Integer.compareTo(java.lang.Object)
```

This indeed contains two methods, both the declared method that takes an argument of type `Integer` and the bridge method that takes an argument of type `Object`. (As of this writing, the Sun JVM prints `volatile` instead of `bridge`, because the bit used in Java bytecode to indicate bridge methods is also used to indicate volatile fields; this bug is expected to be fixed in a future release.)

Bridges can play an important role when converting legacy code to use generics; see Section 8.4.

3.8   Covariant Overriding

Java 5 supports covariant method overriding. This feature is not directly related to generics, but we mention it here because it is worth knowing, and because it is implemented using a bridging technique like that described in the previous section.

In Java 1.4 and earlier, one method can override another only if the signatures match exactly. In Java 5, a method can override another if the arguments match exactly but the return type of the overriding method is a subtype of the return type of the other method.

The `clone` method of class `Object` illustrates the advantages of covariant overriding:

```
class Object {
  ...
  public Object clone() { ... }
}
```

In Java 1.4, any class that overrides `clone` must give it exactly the same return type, namely `Object`:

```
class Point {
  public int x;
  public int y;
  public Point(int x, int y) { this.x=x; this.y=y; }
  public Object clone() { return new Point(x,y); }
}
```

Here, even though `clone` always returns a `Point`, the rules require it to have the return type `Object`. This is annoying, since every invocation of `clone` must cast its result.

```
Point p = new Point(1,2);
Point q = (Point)p.clone();
```

In Java 5, it is possible to give the `clone` method a return type that is more to the point:

```
class Point {
  public int x;
  public int y;
```

```
  public Point(int x, int y) { this.x=x; this.y=y; }
  public Point clone() { return new Point(x,y); }
}
```

Now we may clone without a cast:

```
Point p = new Point(1,2);
Point q = p.clone();
```

Covariant overriding is implemented using the bridging technique described in the previous section. As before, you can see the bridge if you apply reflection. Here is code that finds all methods with the name clone in the class Point:

```
for (Method m : Point.class.getMethods())
  if (m.getName().equals("clone"))
    System.out.println(m.toGenericString());
```

Running this code on the covariant version of the Point class produces the following output:

```
public Point Point.clone()
public bridge java.lang.Object Point.clone()
```

Here the bridging technique exploits the fact that in a class file two methods of the same class may have the same argument signature, even though this is not permitted in Java source. The bridge method simply calls the first method. (Again, as of this writing, the Sun JVM prints volatile instead of bridge.)

CHAPTER 4

Declarations

This chapter discusses how to declare a generic class. It describes constructors, static members, and nested classes, and it fills in some details of how erasure works.

4.1 Constructors

In a generic class, type parameters appear in the header that declares the class, but not in the constructor:

```
class Pair<T, U> {
  private final T first;
  private final U second;
  public Pair(T first, U second) { this.first=first; this.second=second; }
  public T getFirst() { return first; }
  public U getSecond() { return second; }
}
```

The type parameters T and U are declared at the beginning of the class, not in the constructor. However, actual type parameters are passed to the constructor whenever it is invoked:

```
Pair<String, Integer> pair = new Pair<String, Integer>("one",2);
assert pair.getFirst().equals("one") && pair.getSecond() == 2;
```

Look Out for This! A common mistake is to forget the type parameters when invoking the constructor:

```
Pair<String, Integer> pair = new Pair("one",2);
```

This mistake produces a warning, but not an error. It is taken to be legal, because Pair is treated as a raw type, but conversion from a raw type to the corresponding parameterized type generates an unchecked warning; see Section 5.3, which explains how the -Xlint:unchecked flag can help you spot errors of this kind.

4.2 Static Members

Because generics are compiled by erasure, at run time the classes List<Integer>, List<String>, and List<List<String>> are all implemented by a single class, namely List. You can see this using reflection:

```
List<Integer> ints = Arrays.asList(1,2,3);
List<String> strings = Arrays.asList("one","two");
assert ints.getClass() == strings.getClass();
```

Here the class associated with a list of integers at run time is the same as the class associated with a list of strings.

One consequence is that static members of a generic class are shared across all instantiations of that class, including instantiations at different types. Static members of a class cannot refer to the type parameter of a generic class, and when accessing a static member the class name should not be parameterized.

For example, here is a class, Cell<T>, in which each cell has an integer identifier and a value of type T:

```
class Cell<T> {
  private final int id;
  private final T value;
  private static int count = 0;
  private static synchronized int nextId() { return count++; }
  public Cell(T value) { this.value=value; id=nextId(); }
  public T getValue() { return value; }
  public int getId() { return id; }
  public static int getCount() { return count; }
}
```

A static field, count, is used to allocate a distinct identifier to each cell. The static nextId method is synchronized to ensure that unique identifiers are generated even in the presence of multiple threads. The static getCount method returns the current count.

Here is code that allocates a cell containing a string and a cell containing an integer, which are allocated the identifiers 0 and 1, respectively:

```
Cell<String> a = new Cell<String>("one");
Cell<Integer> b = new Cell<Integer>(2);
assert a.getId() == 0 && b.getId() == 1 && Cell.getCount() == 2;
```

Static members are shared across all instantiations of a class, so the same count is incremented when allocating either a string or an integer cell.

Because static members are independent of any type parameters, we are not permitted to follow the class name with type parameters when accessing a static member:

```
Cell.getCount();           // ok
Cell<Integer>.getCount();  // compile-time error
Cell<?>.getCount();        // compile-time error
```

The count is static, so it is a property of the class as a whole, not any particular instance.

For the same reason, you may not refer to a type parameter anywhere within a static member. Here is a second version of Cell, which attempts to use a static variable to keep a list of all values stored in any cell:

```
class Cell2<T> {
  private final T value;
  private static List<T> values = new ArrayList<T>(); // illegal
  public Cell(T value) { this.value=value; values.add(value); }
  public T getValue() { return value; }
  public static List<T> getValues() { return values; } // illegal
}
```

Since the class may be used with different type parameters at different places, it makes no sense to refer to T in the declaration of the static field values or the static method getValues(), and these lines are reported as errors at compile time. If we want a list of all values kept in cells, then we need to use a list of objects, as in the following variant:

```
class Cell2<T> {
  private final T value;
  private static List<Object> values = new ArrayList<Object>();  // ok
  public Cell(T value) { this.value=value; values.add(value); }
  public T getValue() { return value; }
  public static List<Object> getValues() { return values; }  // ok
}
```

This code compiles and runs with no difficulty:

```
Cell2<String> a = new Cell2<String>("one");
Cell2<Integer> b = new Cell2<Integer>(2);
assert Cell2.getValues().toString().equals("[one, 2]");
```

4.3 Nested Classes

Java permits nesting one class inside another. If the outer class has type parameters and the inner class is not static, then type parameters of the outer class are visible within the inner class.

Example 4.1 shows a class implementing collections as a singly-linked list. The class extends java.util.AbstractCollection, so it only needs to define the methods size, add, and iterator. The class contains an inner class, Node, for the list nodes, and an anonymous inner class implementing Iterator<E>. The type parameter E is in scope within both of these classes.

Example 4.1. Type parameters are *in scope for nested,* nonstatic *classes*

```
public class LinkedCollection<E> extends AbstractCollection<E> {
  private class Node {
    private E element;
    private Node next = null;
    private Node(E elt) { element = elt; }
  }
  private Node first = new Node(null);
  private Node last = first;
  private int size = 0;
  public LinkedCollection() {}
  public LinkedCollection(Collection<? extends E> c) { addAll(c); }
  public int size() { return size; }
  public boolean add(E elt) {
    last.next = new Node(elt); last = last.next; size++;
    return true;
  }
  public Iterator<E> iterator() {
    return new Iterator<E>() {
      private Node current = first;
      public boolean hasNext() {
        return current.next != null;
      }
      public E next() {
        if (current.next != null) {
          current = current.next;
          return current.element;
        } else throw new NoSuchElementException();
      }
      public void remove() {
        throw new UnsupportedOperationException();
      }
    };
  }
}
```

For contrast, Example 4.2 shows a similar implementation, but this time the nested Node class is static, and so the type parameter E is *not* in scope for this class. Instead, the nested class is declared with its own type parameter, T. Where the previous version referred to Node, the new version refers to Node<E>. The anonymous iterator class in the preceding example has also been replaced by a nested static class, again with its own type parameter.

If the node classes had been made public rather than private, you would refer to the node class in the first example as LinkedCollection<E>.Node, whereas you would refer to the node class in the second example as LinkedCollection.Node<E>.

Example 4.2. Type parameters are not *in scope for nested,* static *classes*

```
class LinkedCollection<E> extends AbstractCollection<E> {
  private static class Node<T> {
    private T element;
    private Node<T> next = null;
    private Node(T elt) { element = elt; }
  }
  private Node<E> first = new Node<E>(null);
  private Node<E> last = first;
  private int size = 0;
  public LinkedCollection() {}
  public LinkedCollection(Collection<? extends E> c) { addAll(c); }
  public int size() { return size; }
  public boolean add(E elt) {
    last.next = new Node<E>(elt); last = last.next; size++;
    return true;
  }
  private static class LinkedIterator<T> implements Iterator<T> {
    private Node<T> current;
    public LinkedIterator(Node<T> first) { current = first; }
    public boolean hasNext() {
      return current.next != null;
    }
    public T next() {
      if (current.next != null) {
        current = current.next;
        return current.element;
      } else throw new NoSuchElementException();
    }
    public void remove() {
      throw new UnsupportedOperationException();
    }
  }
  public Iterator<E> iterator() {
    return new LinkedIterator<E>(first);
  }
}
```

Of the two alternatives described here, the second is preferable. Nested classes that are not static are implemented by including a reference to the enclosing instance, since they may, in general, access components of that instance. Static nested classes are usually both simpler and more efficient.

4.4 How Erasure Works

The erasure of a type is defined as follows: drop all type parameters from parameterized types, and replace any type variable with the erasure of its bound, or with Object if it has no bound, or with the erasure of the leftmost bound if it has multiple bounds. Here are some examples:

- The erasure of List<Integer>, List<String>, and List<List<String>> is List.
- The erasure of List<Integer>[] is List[].
- The erasure of List is itself, similarly for any raw type (see Section 5.3 for an explanation of raw types).
- The erasure of int is itself, similarly for any primitive type.
- The erasure of Integer is itself, similarly for any type without type parameters.
- The erasure of T in the definition of asList (see Section 1.4) is Object, because T has no bound.
- The erasure of T in the definition of max (see Section 3.2) is Comparable, because T has bound Comparable<? super T>.
- The erasure of T in the final definition of max (see Section 3.6) is Object, because T has bound Object & Comparable<T> and we take the erasure of the leftmost bound.
- The erasures of S and T in the definition of copy (see Section 3.6) are Appendable and Readable, because S has bound Appendable & Closeable and T has bound Readable & Closeable.
- The erasure of LinkedCollection<E>.Node or LinkedCollection.Node<E> (see Section 4.3) is LinkedCollection.Node.

In Java, two distinct methods cannot have the same signature. Since generics are implemented by erasure, it also follows that two distinct methods cannot have signatures with the same erasure. A class cannot overload two methods whose signatures have the same erasure, and a class cannot implement two interfaces that have the same erasure.

For example, here is a class with two convenience methods. One adds together every integer in a list of integers, and the other concatenates together every string in a list of strings:

```
class Overloaded {
  public static int sum(List<Integer> ints) {
    int sum = 0;
    for (int i : ints) sum += i;
    return sum;
  }
  public static String sum(List<String> strings) {
    StringBuffer sum = new StringBuffer();
    for (String s : strings) sum.append(s);
```

```
    return sum.toString();
  }
}
```

This works as intended:

```
assert sum(Arrays.asList(1,2,3)) == 6;
assert sum(Arrays.asList("a","b")).equals("ab");
```

Here are the erasures of the signatures of the two methods:

```
int sum(List)
String sum(List)
```

The two methods have different return types, which is sufficient for Java to distinguish them.

However, say we change the methods so that each appends its result to the end of the argument list rather than returning a value:

```
class Overloaded2 {
  // compile-time error, cannot overload two methods with same erasure
  public static boolean allZero(List<Integer> ints) {
    for (int i : ints) if (i != 0) return false;
    return true;
  }
  public static boolean allZero(List<String> strings) {
    for (String s : strings) if (s.length() != 0) return false;
    return true;
  }
}
```

We intend this code to work as follows:

```
assert allZero(Arrays.asList(0,0,0));
assert allZero(Arrays.asList("","",""));
```

However, in this case the erasures of the signatures of both methods are identical:

```
boolean allZero(List)
```

Therefore, a name clash is reported at compile time. It is not possible to give both methods the same name and try to distinguish between them by overloading, because after erasure it is impossible to distinguish one method call from the other.

For another example, here is a bad version of the integer class, that tries to make it possible to compare an integer with either an integer or a long:

```
class Integer implements Comparable<Integer>, Comparable<Long> {
    // compile-time error, cannot implement two interfaces with same erasure
    private final int value;
    public Integer(int value) { this.value = value; }
```

```
public int compareTo(Integer i) {
    return (value < i.value) ? -1 : (value == i.value) ? 0 : 1;
}
public int compareTo(Long 1) {
    return (value < 1.value) ? -1 : (value == 1.value) ? 0 : 1;
}
}
```

If this were supported, it would, in general, require a complex and confusing definition of bridge methods (see Section 3.7). By far, the simplest and most understandable option is to ban this case.

CHAPTER 5

Evolution, Not Revolution

One motto underpinning the design of generics for Java is *evolution, not revolution*. It must be possible to migrate a large, existing body of code to use generics gradually (evolution) without requiring a radical, all-at-once change (revolution). The generics design ensures that old code compiles against the new Java libraries, avoiding the unfortunate situation in which half of your code needs old libraries and half of your code needs new libraries.

The requirements for evolution are much stronger than the usual *backward compatibility*. With simple backward compatibility, one would supply both legacy and generic versions for each application; this is exactly what happens in C#, for example. If you are building on top of code supplied by multiple suppliers, some of whom use legacy collections and some of whom use generic collections, this might rapidly lead to a versioning nightmare.

What we require is that the *same* client code works with both the legacy and generic versions of a library. This means that the supplier and clients of a library can make completely independent choices about when to move from legacy to generic code. This is a much stronger requirement than backward compatibility; it is called *migration compatibility* or *platform compatibility*.

Java implements generics via erasure, which ensures that legacy and generic versions usually generate identical class files, save for some auxiliary information about types. It is possible to replace a legacy class file by a generic class file without changing, or even recompiling, any client code; this is called *binary compatibility*.

We summarize this with the motto *binary compatibility ensures migration compatibility—* or, more concisely, *erasure eases evolution*.

This section shows how to add generics to existing code; it considers a small example, a library for stacks that extends the Collections Framework, together with an associated client. We begin with the legacy stack library and client (written for Java before generics), and then present the corresponding generic library and client (written for Java with generics). Our example code is small, so it is easy to update to generics all in one go, but in practice the library and client will be much larger, and we may want to evolve them separately. This is aided by *raw types*, which are the legacy counterpart of parameterized types.

The parts of the program may evolve in either order. You may have a generic library with a legacy client; this is the common case for anyone that uses the Collections Framework in Java 5 with legacy code. Or you may have a legacy library with a generic client; this is the case where you want to provide generic signatures for the library without the need to rewrite the entire library. We consider three ways to do this: minimal changes to the source, stub files, and wrappers. The first is useful when you have access to the source and the second when you do not; we recommend against the third.

In practice, the library and client may involve many interfaces and classes, and there may not even be a clear distinction between library and client. But the same principles discussed here still apply, and may be used to evolve any part of a program independently of any other part.

5.1 Legacy Library with Legacy Client

We begin with a simple library of stacks and an associated client, as presented in Example 5.1. This is *legacy* code, written for Java 1.4 and its version of the Collections Framework. Like the Collections Framework, we structure the library as an interface Stack (analogous to List), an implementation class ArrayStack (analogous to ArrayList), and a utility class Stacks (analogous to Collections). The interface Stack provides just three methods: empty, push, and pop. The implementation class ArrayStack provides a single constructor with no arguments, and implements the methods empty, push, and pop using methods size, add, and remove on lists. The body of pop could be shorter—instead of assigning the value to the variable, it could be returned directly—but it will be interesting to see how the type of the variable changes as the code evolves. The utility class provides just one method, reverse, which repeatedly pops from one stack and pushes onto another.

The client allocates a stack, pushes a few integers onto it, pops an integer off, and then reverses the remainder into a fresh stack. Since this is Java 1.4, integers must be explicitly boxed when passed to push, and explicitly unboxed when returned by pop.

5.2 Generic Library with Generic Client

Next, we update the library and client to use generics, as presented in Example 5.2. This is *generic* code, written for Java 5 and its version of the Collections Framework. The interface now takes a type parameter, becoming Stack<E> (analogous to List<E>), and so does the implementing class, becoming ArrayStack<E> (analogous to ArrayList<E>), but no type parameter is added to the utility class Stacks (analogous to Collections). The type Object in the signatures and bodies of push and pop is replaced by the type parameter E. Note that the constructor in ArrayStack does not require a type parameter. In the utility class, the reverse method becomes a generic method with argument and result of type Stack<T>. Appropriate type parameters are added to the client, and boxing and unboxing are now implicit.

In short, the conversion process is straightforward: just add a few type parameters and replace occurrences of Object by the appropriate type variable. All differences between

Example 5.1. Legacy library with legacy client

```
1/Stack.java:
  interface Stack {
    public boolean empty();
    public void push(Object elt);
    public Object pop();
  }

1/ArrayStack.java:
  import java.util.*;
  class ArrayStack implements Stack {
    private List list;
    public ArrayStack() { list = new ArrayList(); }
    public boolean empty() { return list.size() == 0; }
    public void push(Object elt) { list.add(elt); }
    public Object pop() {
      Object elt = list.remove(list.size()-1);
      return elt;
    }
    public String toString() { return "stack"+list.toString(); }
  }

1/Stacks.java:
  class Stacks {
    public static Stack reverse(Stack in) {
      Stack out = new ArrayStack();
      while (!in.empty()) {
        Object elt = in.pop();
        out.push(elt);
      }
      return out;
    }
  }

1/Client.java:
  class Client {
    public static void main(String[] args) {
      Stack stack = new ArrayStack();
      for (int i = 0; i<4; i++) stack.push(new Integer(i));
      assert stack.toString().equals("stack[0, 1, 2, 3]");
      int top = ((Integer)stack.pop()).intValue();
      assert top == 3 && stack.toString().equals("stack[0, 1, 2]");
      Stack reverse = Stacks.reverse(stack);
      assert stack.empty();
      assert reverse.toString().equals("stack[2, 1, 0]");
    }
  }
```

the legacy and generic versions can be spotted by comparing the highlighted portions of the two examples. The implementation of generics is designed so that the two versions generate essentially equivalent class files. Some auxiliary information about the types may differ, but the actual bytecodes to be executed will be identical. Hence, executing the legacy and generic versions yields the same results. The fact that legacy and generic sources yield identical class files eases the process of evolution, as we discuss next.

5.3 Generic Library with Legacy Client

Now let's consider the case where the library is updated to generics while the client remains in its legacy version. This may occur because there is not enough time to convert everything all at once, or because the library and client are controlled by different organizations. This corresponds to the most important case of backward compatibility, where the generic Collections Framework of Java 5 must still work with legacy clients written against the Collections Framework in Java 1.4.

In order to support evolution, whenever a parameterized type is defined, Java also recognizes the corresponding unparameterized version of the type, called a *raw type*. For instance, the parameterized type Stack<E> corresponds to the raw type Stack, and the parameterized type ArrayStack<E> corresponds to the raw type ArrayStack.

Every parameterized type is a subtype of the corresponding raw type, so a value of the parameterized type can be passed where a raw type is expected. Usually, it is an error to pass a value of a supertype where a value of its subtype is expected, but Java does permit a value of a raw type to be passed where a parameterized type is expected—however, it flags this circumstance by generating an *unchecked conversion* warning. For instance, you can assign a value of type Stack<E> to a variable of type Stack, since the former is a subtype of the latter. You can also assign a value of type Stack to a variable of type Stack<E>, but this will generate an unchecked conversion warning.

To be specific, consider compiling the generic source for Stack<E>, ArrayStack<E>, and Stacks from Example 5.2 (say, in directory g) with the legacy source for Client from Example 5.1 (say, in directory l). Sun's Java 5 compiler yields the following message:

```
% javac g/Stack.java g/ArrayStack.java g/Stacks.java l/Client.java
Note: Client.java uses unchecked or unsafe operations.
Note: Recompile with -Xlint:unchecked for details.
```

The unchecked warning indicates that the compiler cannot offer the same safety guarantees that are possible when generics are used uniformly throughout. However, when the generic code is generated by updating legacy code, we know that equivalent class files are produced from both, and hence (despite the unchecked warning) running a legacy client with the generic library will yield the same result as running the legacy client with the legacy library. Here we assume that the only change in updating the library was to introduce generics, and that no change to the behavior was introduced, either on purpose or by mistake.

Example 5.2. Generic library with generic client

g/Stack.java:
```
interface Stack<E> {
  public boolean empty();
  public void push(E elt);
  public E pop();
}
```

g/ArrayStack.java:
```
import java.util.*;
class ArrayStack<E> implements Stack<E> {
  private List<E> list;
  public ArrayStack() { list = new ArrayList<E>(); }
  public boolean empty() { return list.size() == 0; }
  public void push(E elt) { list.add(elt); }
  public E pop() {
    E elt = list.remove(list.size()-1);
    return elt;
  }
  public String toString() { return "stack"+list.toString(); }
}
```

g/Stacks.java:
```
class Stacks {
  public static <T> Stack<T> reverse(Stack<T> in) {
    Stack<T> out = new ArrayStack<T>();
    while (!in.empty()) {
      T elt = in.pop();
      out.push(elt);
    }
    return out;
  }
}
```

g/Client.java:
```
class Client {
  public static void main(String[] args) {
    Stack<Integer> stack = new ArrayStack<Integer>();
    for (int i = 0; i<4; i++) stack.push(i);
    assert stack.toString().equals("stack[0, 1, 2, 3]");
    int top = stack.pop();
    assert top == 3 && stack.toString().equals("stack[0, 1, 2]");
    Stack<Integer> reverse = Stacks.reverse(stack);
    assert stack.empty();
    assert reverse.toString().equals("stack[2, 1, 0]");
  }
}
```

If we follow the suggestion above and rerun the compiler with the appropriate switch enabled, we get more details:

```
% javac -Xlint:unchecked g/Stack.java g/ArrayStack.java \
%    g/Stacks.java l/Client.java
l/Client.java:4: warning: [unchecked] unchecked call
to push(E) as a member of the raw type Stack
      for (int i = 0; i<4; i++) stack.push(new Integer(i));
                                           ^
l/Client.java:8: warning: [unchecked] unchecked conversion
found   : Stack
required: Stack<E>
      Stack reverse = Stacks.reverse(stack);
                                     ^
l/Client.java:8: warning: [unchecked] unchecked method invocation:
<E>reverse(Stack<E>) in Stacks is applied to (Stack)
      Stack reverse = Stacks.reverse(stack);
                                     ^

3 warnings
```

Not every use of a raw type gives rise to a warning. Because every parameterized type is a subtype of the corresponding raw type, but not conversely, passing a parameterized type where a raw type is expected is safe (hence, no warning for getting the result from reverse), but passing a raw type where a parameterized type is expected issues a warning (hence, the warning when passing an argument to reverse); this is an instance of the Substitution Principle. When we invoke a method on a receiver of a raw type, the method is treated as if the type parameter is a wildcard, so getting a value from a raw type is safe (hence, no warning for the invocation of pop), but putting a value into a raw type issues a warning (hence, the warning for the invocation of push); this is an instance of the Get and Put Principle.

Even if you have not written any generic code, you may still have an evolution problem because others have generified their code. This will affect everyone with legacy code that uses the Collections Framework, which has been generified by Sun. So the most important case of using generic libraries with legacy clients is that of using the Java 5 Collections Framework with legacy code written for the Java 1.4 Collections Framework.

In particular, applying the Java 5 compiler to the legacy code in Example 5.1 also issues unchecked warnings, because of the uses of the generified class ArrayList from the legacy class ArrayStack. Here is what happens when we compile legacy versions of all the files with the Java 5 compiler and libraries:

```
% javac -Xlint:unchecked l/Stack.java l/ArrayStack.java \
%    l/Stacks.java l/Client.java
l/ArrayStack.java:6: warning: [unchecked] unchecked call to add(E)
as a member of the raw type java.util.List
    public void push(Object elt)  list.add(elt);
                                          ^

1 warning
```

Here the warning for the use of the generic method add in the legacy method push is issued for reasons similar to those for issuing the previous warning for use of the generic method push from the legacy client.

It is poor practice to configure the compiler to repeatedly issue warnings that you intend to ignore. It is distracting and, worse, it may lead you to ignore warnings that require attention—just as in the fable of the little boy who cried wolf. In the case of pure legacy code, such warnings can be turned off by using the -source 1.4 switch:

```
% javac -source 1.4 1/Stack.java 1/ArrayStack.java \
%     1/Stacks.java 1/Client.java
```

This compiles the legacy code and issues no warnings or errors. This method of turning off warnings is only applicable to true legacy code, with none of the features introduced in Java 5, generic or otherwise. One can also turn off unchecked warnings by using annotations, as described in the next section, and this works even with features introduced in Java 5.

5.4 Legacy Library with Generic Client

It usually makes sense to update the library before the client, but there may be cases when you wish to do it the other way around. For instance, you may be responsible for maintaining the client but not the library; or the library may be large, so you may want to update it gradually rather than all at once; or you may have class files for the library, but no source.

In such cases, it makes sense to update the library to use parameterized types in its method signatures, but not to change the method bodies. There are three ways to do this: by making minimal changes to the source, by creating stub files, or by use of wrappers. We recommend use of minimal changes when you have access to source and use of stubs when you have access only to class files, and we recommend against use of wrappers.

5.4.1 Evolving a Library using Minimal Changes

The minimal changes technique is shown in Example 5.3. Here the source of the library has been edited, but only to change method signatures, not method bodies. The exact changes required are highlighted in boldface. This is the recommended technique for evolving a library to be generic when you have access to the source.

To be precise, the changes required are:

- Adding type parameters to interface or class declarations as appropriate (for interface Stack<E> and class ArrayStack<E>)

- Adding type parameters to any newly parameterized interface or class in an extends or implements clause (for Stack<E> in the implements clause of ArrayStack<E>),

- Adding type parameters to each method signature as appropriate (for push and pop in Stack<E> and ArrayStack<E>, and for reverse in Stacks)

- Adding an unchecked cast to each return where the return type contains a type parameter (for pop in `ArrayStack<E>`, where the return type is E)—without this cast, you will get an error rather than an unchecked warning

- Optionally adding annotations to suppress unchecked warnings (for `ArrayStack<E>` and `Stacks`)

It is worth noting a few changes that we do *not* need to make. In method bodies, we can leave occurrences of `Object` as they stand (see the first line of pop in `ArrayStack`), and we do not need to add type parameters to any occurrences of raw types (see the first line of `reverse` in `Stacks`). Also, we need to add a cast to a return clause only when the return type is a type parameter (as in pop) but not when the return type is a parameterized type (as in `reverse`).

With these changes, the library will compile successfully, although it will issue a number of unchecked warnings. Following best practice, we have commented the code to indicate which lines trigger such warnings:

```
% javac -Xlint:unchecked m/Stack.java m/ArrayStack.java m/Stacks.java
m/ArrayStack.java:7: warning: [unchecked] unchecked call to add(E)
as a member of the raw type java.util.List
    public void push(E elt) list.add(elt);   // unchecked call
                                    ^
m/ArrayStack.java:10: warning: [unchecked] unchecked cast
found    : java.lang.Object
required: E
       return (E)elt; // unchecked cast
              ^
m/Stacks.java:7: warning: [unchecked] unchecked call to push(T)
as a member of the raw type Stack
          out.push(elt); // unchecked call
              ^
m/Stacks.java:9: warning: [unchecked] unchecked conversion
found    : Stack
required: Stack<T>
       return out; // unchecked conversion
              ^
4 warnings
```

To indicate that we expect unchecked warnings when compiling the library classes, the source has been annotated to suppress such warnings.

```
@SuppressWarnings("unchecked");
```

(The suppress warnings annotation does not work in early versions of Sun's compiler for Java 5.) This prevents the compiler from crying wolf—we've told it not to issue unchecked warnings that we expect, so it will be easy to spot any that we *don't* expect. In particular,

Example 5.3. Evolving a library using minimal changes

m/Stack.java:
```
interface Stack<E> {
  public boolean empty();
  public void push(E elt);
  public E pop();
}
```

m/ArrayStack.java:
```
@SuppressWarnings("unchecked")
class ArrayStack<E> implements Stack<E> {
  private List list;
  public ArrayStack() { list = new ArrayList(); }
  public boolean empty() { return list.size() == 0; }
  public void push(E elt) { list.add(elt); }  // unchecked call
  public E pop() {
    Object elt = list.remove(list.size()-1);
    return (E)elt;  // unchecked cast
  }
  public String toString() { return "stack"+list.toString(); }
}
```

m/Stacks.java:
```
@SuppressWarnings("unchecked")
class Stacks {
  public static <T> Stack<T> reverse(Stack<T> in) {
    Stack out = new ArrayStack();
    while (!in.empty()) {
      Object elt = in.pop();
      out.push(elt); // unchecked call
    }
    return out;  // unchecked conversion
  }
}
```

once we've updated the library, we should not see any unchecked warnings from the client. Note as well that we've suppressed warnings on the library classes, but *not* on the client.

The only way to eliminate (as opposed to suppress) the unchecked warnings generated by compiling the library is to update the entire library source to use generics. This is entirely reasonable, as unless the entire source is updated there is no way the compiler can check that the declared generic types are correct. Indeed, unchecked warnings are warnings—rather than errors—largely because they support the use of this technique. Use this technique only if you are sure that the generic signatures are in fact correct. The best practice is to use this technique only as an intermediate step in evolving code to use generics throughout.

Example 5.4. Evolving a library using stubs

```
s/Stack.java:
  interface Stack<E> {
    public boolean empty();
    public void push(E elt);
    public E pop();
  }

s/StubException.java:
  class StubException extends UnsupportedOperationException {}

s/ArrayStack.java:
  class ArrayStack<E> implements Stack<E> {
    public boolean empty() { throw new StubException(); }
    public void push(E elt) { throw new StubException(); }
    public E pop() { throw new StubException(); }
    public String toString() { throw new StubException(); }
  }

s/Stacks.java:
  class Stacks {
    public static <T> Stack<T> reverse(Stack<T> in) {
      throw new StubException();
    }
  }
```

5.4.2 Evolving a Library using Stubs

The stubs technique is shown in Example 5.4. Here we write stubs with generic signatures but no bodies. We compile the generic client against the generic signatures, but run the code against the legacy class files. This technique is appropriate when the source is not released, or when others are responsible for maintaining the source.

To be precise, we introduce the same modifications to interface and class declarations and method signatures as with the minimal changes technique, except we completely delete all executable code, replacing each method body with code that throws a StubException (a new exception that extends UnsupportedOperationException).

When we compile the generic client, we do so against the class files generated from the stub code, which contain appropriate generic signatures (say, in directory s). When we run the client, we do so against the original legacy class files (say, in directory l).

```
% javac -classpath s g/Client.java
% java -ea -classpath l g/Client
```

Again, this works because the class files generated for legacy and generic files are essentially identical, save for auxiliary information about the types. In particular, the generic signatures that the client is compiled against match the legacy signatures (apart from auxiliary information about type parameters), so the code runs successfully and gives the same answer as previously.

5.4.3 Evolving a Library using Wrappers

The wrappers technique is shown in Example 5.5. Here we leave the legacy source and class files unchanged, and provide a generic wrapper class that accesses the legacy class via delegation. We present this technique mainly in order to warn you *against* its use—it is usually better to use minimal changes or stubs.

This techique creates a parallel hierarchy of generic interfaces and wrapper classes. To be precise, we create a new interface GenericStack corresponding to the legacy interface Stack, we create a new class GenericWrapperClass to access the legacy implementation ArrayStack, and we create a new class GenericStacks corresponding to the legacy convenience class Stacks.

The generic interface GenericStack is derived from the legacy interface Stack by the same method used in the previous sections to update the signatures to use generics. In addition, a new method unwrap is added, that extracts the legacy implementation from a wrapper.

The wrapper class GenericStackWrapper<E> implements GenericStack<E> by delegation to a Stack. The constructor takes an instance that implements the legacy interface Stack, which is stored in a private field, and the unwrap method returns this instance. Because delegation is used, any updates made to the underlying legacy stack will be seen through the generic stack view offered by the wrapper.

The wrapper implements each method in the interface (empty, push, pop) by a call to the corresponding legacy method; and it implements each method in Object that is overridden in the legacy class (toString) similarly. As with minimal changes, we add an unchecked cast to the return statement when the return type contains a type parameter (as in pop); without this cast you will get an error rather than an unchecked warning.

A single wrapper will suffice for multiple implementations of the same interface. For instance, if we had both ArrayStack and LinkedStack implementations of Stack, we could use GenericStackWrapper<E> for both.

The new convenience class GenericStacks is implemented by delegation to the legacy class Stacks. The generic reverse method unwraps its argument, calls the legacy reverse method, and wraps its result.

Required changes to the client in Example 5.5 are shown in boldface.

Wrappers have a number of disadvantages compared to minimal changes or stubs. Wrappers require maintaining two parallel hierarchies, one of legacy interfaces and classes and one of generic interfaces and classes. Conversion by wrapping and unwrapping between these can become tedious. If and when the legacy classes are generified properly, further work will be required to remove the redundant wrappers.

Example 5.5. Evolving a library using wrappers

```
// Don't do this---use of wrappers is not recommended!

1/Stack.java, 1/Stacks.java, 1/ArrayStack.java:
  // As in Example 5.1

w/GenericStack.java:
  interface GenericStack<E> {
    public Stack unwrap();
    public boolean empty();
    public void push(E elt);
    public E pop();
  }

w/GenericStackWrapper.java:
  @SuppressWarnings("unchecked")
  class GenericStackWrapper<E> implements GenericStack<E> {
    private Stack stack;
    public GenericStackWrapper(Stack stack) { this.stack = stack; }
    public Stack unwrap() { return stack; }
    public boolean empty() { return stack.empty(); }
    public void push(E elt) { stack.push(elt); }
    public E pop() { return (E)stack.pop(); }  // unchecked cast
    public String toString() { return stack.toString(); }
  }

w/GenericStacks.java:
  class GenericStacks {
    public static <T> GenericStack<T> reverse(GenericStack<T> in) {
      Stack rawIn = in.unwrap();
      Stack rawOut = Stacks.reverse(rawIn);
      return new GenericStackWrapper<T>(rawOut);
    }
  }

w/Client.java:
  class Client {
    public static void main(String[] args) {
      GenericStack<Integer> stack
        = new GenericStackWrapper<Integer>(new ArrayStack());
      for (int i = 0; i<4; i++) stack.push(i);
      assert stack.toString().equals("stack[0, 1, 2, 3]");
      int top = stack.pop();
      assert top == 3 && stack.toString().equals("stack[0, 1, 2]");
      GenericStack<Integer> reverse = GenericStacks.reverse(stack);
      assert stack.empty();
      assert reverse.toString().equals("stack[2, 1, 0]");
    }
  }
```

Wrappers also present deeper and subtler problems. If the code uses object identity, problems may appear because the legacy object and the wrapped object are distinct. Further, complex structures will require multiple layers of wrappers. Imagine applying this technique to a stack of stacks! You would need to define a two-level wrapper, that wraps or unwraps each second-level stack as it is pushed onto or popped from the top-level stack. Because wrapped and legacy objects are distinct, it may be hard or even impossible to always ensure that the wrapped objects view all changes to the legacy objects.

The design of Java generics, by ensuring that legacy objects and generic objects are the same, avoids all of these problems with wrappers. The design of generics for C# is very different: legacy classes and generic classes are completely distinct, and any attempt to combine legacy collections and generic collections will bump into the difficulties with wrappers discussed here.

5.5 Conclusions

To review, we have seen both generic and legacy versions of a library and client. These generate equivalent class files, which greatly eases evolution. You can use a generic library with a legacy client, or a legacy library with a generic client. In the latter case, you can update the legacy library with generic method signatures, either by minimal changes to the source or by use of stub files.

The foundation stone that supports all this is the decision to implement generics by erasure, so that generic code generates essentially the same class files as legacy code—a property referred to as binary compatibility. Usually, adding generics in a natural way causes the legacy and generic versions to be binary compatible. However, there are some corner cases where caution is required; these are discussed in Section 8.4.

It is interesting to compare the design of generics in Java and in C#. In Java, generic types do not carry information about type parameters at run time, whereas arrays do contain information about the array element type at run time. In C#, both generic types and arrays contain information about parameter and element types at run time. Each approach has advantages and disadvantages. In the next chapter, we will discuss problems with casting and arrays that arise because Java does not reify information about type parameters, and these problems do not arise in C#. On the other hand, evolution in C# is much more difficult. Legacy and generic collection classes are completely distinct, and any attempt to combine legacy collections and generic collections will encounter the difficulties with wrappers discussed earlier. In contrast, as we've seen, evolution in Java is straightforward.

CHAPTER 6

Reification

The Oxford English Dictionary defines *reify* thus: "To convert mentally into a thing; to materialize." A plainer word with the same meaning is *thingify*. In computing, *reification* has come to mean an explicit representation of a type—that is, run-time type information. In Java, arrays reify information about their component types, while generic types do not reify information about their type parameters.

The previous chapter was, in a sense, about the advantages of *not* reifying parameter types. Legacy code makes no distinction between List<Integer> and List<String> and List<List<String>>, so not reifying parameter types is essential to easing evolution and promoting compatibility between legacy code and new code.

But now the time has come to pay the piper. Reification plays a critical role in certain aspects of Java, and the absence of reification that is beneficial for evolution also necessarily leads to some rough edges. This chapter warns you of the limitations and describes some workarounds. The chapter deals almost entirely with things you might wish you didn't need to know—and, indeed, if you never use generic types in casts, instance tests, exceptions, or arrays then you are unlikely to need the material covered here.

We begin with a precise definition of what it means for a type in Java to be *reifiable*. We then consider corner cases related to reification, including instance tests and casts, exceptions, and arrays. The fit between arrays and generics is the worst rough corner in the language, and we encapsulate how to avoid the worst pitfalls with the Principle of Truth in Advertising and the Principle of Indecent Exposure.

6.1 Reifiable Types

In Java, the type of an array is reified *with* its component type, while the type of a parameterized type is reified *without* its type parameters. For instance, an array of numbers will carry the reified type Number[], while a list of numbers will carry the reified type ArrayList, not ArrayList<Number>; the raw type, not the parameterized type, is reified. Of course, each element of the list will have a reified type attached to it—say Integer or Double—but this is not the same as reifying the parameter type. If every element in the list was an integer, we would not be able to tell whether we had an ArrayList<Integer>, ArrayList<Number>, or `ArrayList<Object>`; if the list was empty, we would not be able to tell what kind of empty list it was.

In Java, we say that a type is *reifiable* if the type is completely represented at run time — that is, if erasure does not remove any useful information. To be precise, a type is reifiable if it is one of the following:

- A primitive type
  (such as `int`)
- A nonparameterized class or interface type
  (such as `Number`, `String`, or `Runnable`)
- A parameterized type in which all type arguments are unbounded wildcards
  (such as `List<?>`, `ArrayList<?>`, or `Map<?, ?>`)
- A raw type
  (such as `List`, `ArrayList`, or `Map`)
- An array whose component type is reifiable
  (such as `int[]`, `Number[]`, `List<?>[]`, `List[]`, or `int[][]`)

A type is *not* reifiable if it is one of the following:

- A type variable
  (such as `T`)
- A parameterized type with actual parameters
  (such as `List<Number>`, `ArrayList<String>`, or `Map<String, Integer>`)
- A parameterized type with a bound
  (such as `List<? extends Number>` or `Comparable<? super String>`)

So the type `List<? extends Object>` is *not* reifiable, even though it is equivalent to `List<?>`. Defining reifiable types in this way makes them easy to identify syntactically.

6.2 Instance Tests and Casts

Instance tests and casts depend on examining types at run time, and hence depend on reification. For this reason, an instance test against a type that is not reifiable reports an error, and a cast to a type that is not reifiable usually issues a warning.

As an example, consider the use of instance tests and casts in writing equality. Here is a fragment of the definition of the class `Integer` in `java.lang` (slightly simplified from the actual source):

```
public class Integer extends Number {
  private final int value;
  public Integer(int value) { this.value=value; }
  public int intValue() { return value; }
  public boolean equals(Object o) {
```

```
      if (o instanceof Integer) {
        return value == ((Integer)o).intValue();
      } else return false;
  }
  ...
}
```

The equality method takes an argument of type `Object`, checks whether the object is an instance of class `Integer`, and, if so, casts it to `Integer` and compares the values of the two integers. This code works because `Integer` is a reifiable type: all of the information needed to check whether an object is an instance of `Integer` is available at run time.

Now consider how one might define equality on lists, as in the class `AbstractList` in `java.util`. A natural—but incorrect—way to define this is as follows:

```
import java.util.*;
public abstract class AbstractList<E>
  extends AbstractCollection<E> implements List<E>
{
  public boolean equals(Object o) {
    if (o instanceof List<E>) { // compile-time error
      Iterator<E> it1 = iterator();
      Iterator<E> it2 = ((List<E>)o).iterator(); // unchecked cast
      while (it1.hasNext() && it2.hasNext()) {
        E e1 = it1.next();
        E e2 = it2.next();
        if (!(e1 == null ? e2 == null : e1.equals(e2)))
          return false;
      }
      return !it1.hasNext() && !it2.hasNext();
    } else return false;
  }
  ...
}
```

Again, the equality method takes an argument of type `Object`, checks whether the object is an instance of type `List<E>`, and, if so, casts it to `List<E>` and compares corresponding elements of the two lists. This code does *not* work because `List<E>` is *not* a reifiable type: some of the information needed to check whether an object is an instance of `List<E>` is not available at run time. You can test whether an object implements the interface `List`, but not whether its type parameter is E. Indeed, information on E is missing doubly, as it is not available for either the receiver or the argument of the `equals` method.

(Even if this code worked, there is a further problem. The contract for equality on lists doesn't mention types. A `List<Integer>` may be equal to a `List<Object>` if they contain the same values in the same order. For instance, [1,2,3] should be equal to itself, regardless of whether it is regarded as a list of integers or a list of objects.)

Compiling the preceding code reports two problems, an error for the instance test and an unchecked warning for the cast:

```
% javac -Xlint:unchecked AbstractList.java
AbstractList.java:6: illegal generic type for instanceof
    if (!(o instanceof List<E>)) return false;  // compile-time error
              ^
AbstractList.java:8: warning: [unchecked] unchecked cast
found    : java.lang.Object
required: List<E>
    Iterator<E> it2 = ((List<E>)o).iterator();  // unchecked cast
                       ^

1 error
1 warning
```

The instance check reports an error because there is no possible way to test whether the given object belongs to the type List<E>. The cast reports an unchecked warning; it will perform the cast, but it cannot check that the list elements are, in fact, of type E.

To fix the problem, we replace the nonreifiable type List<E> with the reifiable type List<?>. Here is a corrected definition (again, slightly simplified from the actual source):

```
import java.util.*;
public abstract class AbstractList<E>
extends AbstractCollection<E> implements List<E> {
  public boolean equals(Object o) {
    if (o instanceof List<?>) {
      Iterator<E> it1 = iterator();
      Iterator<?> it2 = ((List<?>)o).iterator();
      while (it1.hasNext() && it2.hasNext()) {
        E e1 = it1.next();
        Object e2 = it2.next();
        if (!(e1 == null ? e2 == null : e1.equals(e2)))
          return false;
      }
      return !it1.hasNext() && !it2.hasNext();
    } else return false;
  }
  ...
}
```

In addition to changing the type of the instance test and the cast, the type of the second iterator is changed from Iterator<E> to Iterator<?>, and the type of the second element is changed from E to Object. The code type-checks, because even though the element type of the second iterator is unknown, it is guaranteed that it must be a subtype of Object, and the nested call to equals requires only that its second argument be an object.

(This code properly satisfies the contract for equality on lists. Now a List<Integer> will be equal to a List<Object> if they contain the same values in the same order.)

Alternative fixes are possible. Instead of the wildcard types List<?> and Iterator<?>, you could use the raw types List and Iterator, which are also reifiable. We recommend using unbounded wildcard types in preference to raw types because they provide stronger static typing guarantees; many mistakes that are caught as an error when you use unbounded wildcards will only be flagged as a warning if you use raw types. Also, you could change the declaration of the first iterator to Iterator<?> and of the first element to Object, so that they match the second iterator, and the code will still type-check. We recommend always using type declarations that are as specific as possible; this helps the compiler to catch more errors and to compile more-efficient code.

Nonreifiable Casts   An instance test against a type that is not reifiable is always an error. However, in some circumstances a cast to a type that is not reifiable is permitted.

For example, the following method converts a collection to a list:

```
public static <T> List<T> asList(Collection<T> c)
  throws InvalidArgumentException
{
  if (c instanceof List<?>) {
    return (List<T>)c;
  } else throw new InvalidArgumentException("Argument not a list");
}
```

Compiling this code succeeds with no errors or warnings. The instance test is not in error because List<?> is a reifiable type. The cast does not report a warning because the source of the cast has type Collection<T>, and any object with this type that implements the interface List must, in fact, have type List<T>.

Unchecked casts   Only rarely will the compiler be able to determine that if a cast to a nonreifiable type succeeds then it must yield a value of that type. In the remaining cases, a cast to a type that is not reifiable is flagged with an unchecked warning, whereas an instance test against a type that is not reifiable is always caught as an error. This is because there is never any point to an instance test that cannot be performed, but there may be a point to a cast that cannot be checked.

Type systems deduce facts about programs—for instance, that a certain variable always contains a list of strings. But no type system is perfect; there will always be some facts that a programmer can deduce but that the type system does not. To permit the programmer a workaround in such circumstances, the compiler issues warnings rather than errors when performing some casts.

For example, here is code that promotes a list of objects into a list of strings, if the list of objects contains only strings, and throws a class cast exception otherwise:

```
class Promote {
  public static List<String> promote(List<Object> objs) {
    for (Object o : objs)
      if (!(o instanceof String))
        throw new ClassCastException();
```

```
    return (List<String>)(List<?>)objs; // unchecked cast
  }
  public static void main(String[] args) {
    List<Object> objs1 = Arrays.<Object>asList("one","two");
    List<Object> objs2 = Arrays.<Object>asList(1,"two");
    List<String> strs1 = promote(objs1);
    assert (List<?>)strs1 == (List<?>)objs1;
    boolean caught = false;
    try {
      List<String> strs2 = promote(objs2);
    } catch (ClassCastException e) { caught = true; }
    assert caught;
  }
}
```

The method promote loops over the list of objects and throws a class cast exception if any object is not a string. Hence, when the last line of the method is reached, it is safe to cast the list of objects to a list of strings.

But the compiler cannot deduce this, so the programmer must use an unchecked cast. It is illegal to cast a list of objects to a list of strings, so the cast must take place in two steps. First, cast the list of objects into a list of wildcard type; this cast is safe. Second, cast the list of wildcard type into a list of strings; this cast is permitted but generates an unchecked warning:

```
% javac -Xlint:unchecked Promote.java
Promote.java:7: warning: [unchecked] unchecked cast
found    : java.util.List
required: java.util.List<java.lang.String>
      return (List<String>)(List<?>)objs; // unchecked cast
                           ^
1 warning
```

The test code applies the method to two lists, one containing only strings (so it succeeds) and one containing an integer (so it raises an exception). In the first assertion, to compare the object list and the string list, we must first cast both to the type List<?> (this cast is safe), because attempting to compare a list of objects with a list of strings raises a type error.

Exactly the same technique can be used to promote a raw list to a list of strings if the raw list contains only strings. This technique is important for fitting together legacy and generic code, and is one of the chief reasons for using erasure to implement generics. A related technique is discussed in Section 8.1.

Another example of the use of unchecked casts to interface legacy and generic code occurred in Section 5.4.1, where we needed an unchecked cast to the element type (E) to make the type of the value returned by the legacy add method match its generic signature.

You should minimize the number of unchecked casts in your code, but sometimes, as in the case above, they cannot be avoided. In this book, we follow the convention that we always

---

place the comment `unchecked cast` on the line containing the cast, to document that this is an intentional workaround rather than an unintended slip; and we recommend you do the same. It is important to put the comment on the same line as the cast, so that when scanning the warnings issued by the compiler it is easy to confirm that each line contains the comment. If it does not, then you should regard the warning as equivalent to an error!

If a method deliberately contains unchecked casts, you may wish to precede it with the annotation `@SuppressWarnings("unchecked")` in order to avoid spurious warnings. We saw an application of this technique in Section 5.4.1.

As another example of the use of unchecked casts, in Section 6.5 we will see code that uses an unchecked cast from type `Object[]` to type `T[]`. Because of the way the object array is created, it is, in fact, guaranteed that the array will always have the correct type.

Unchecked casts in C (and in its descendants C++ and C#) are much more dangerous than unchecked casts in Java. Unlike C, the Java runtime guarantees important security properties even in the presence of unchecked casts; for instance, it is never permitted to access an array with an index outside of the array bounds. Nonetheless, unchecked casts in Java are a workaround that should be used with caution.

6.3 Exception Handling

In a `try` statement, each `catch` clause checks whether the thrown exception matches a given type. This is the same as the check performed by an instance test, so the same restriction applies: the type must be reifiable. Further, the type in a `catch` clause is required to be a subclass of `Throwable`. Since there is little point in creating a subclass of `Throwable` that cannot appear in a `catch` clause, the Java compiler complains if you attempt to create a parameterized subclass of `Throwable`.

For example, here is a permissible definition of a new exception, which contains an integer value:

```
class IntegerException extends Exception {
  private final int value;
  public IntegerException(int value) { this.value = value; }
  public int getValue() { return value; }
}
```

And here is a simple example of how to use the exception:

```
class IntegerExceptionTest {
  public static void main(String[] args) {
    try {
      throw new IntegerException(42);
    } catch (IntegerException e) {
      assert e.getValue() == 42;
    }
  }
}
```

The body of the try statement throws the exception with a given value, which is caught by the catch clause.

In contrast, the following definition of a new exception is prohibited, because it creates a parameterized type:

```
class ParametricException<T> extends Exception {  // compile-time error
  private final T value;
  public ParametricException(T value) { this.value = value; }
  public T getValue() { return value; }
}
```

An attempt to compile the above reports an error:

```
% javac ParametricException.java
ParametricException.java:1: a generic class may not extend
java.lang.Throwable
class ParametricException<T> extends Exception {  // compile-time error
      ^
1 error
```

This restriction is sensible because almost any attempt to catch such an exception must fail, because the type is not reifiable. One might expect a typical use of the exception to be something like the following:

```
class ParametricExceptionTest {
  public static void main(String[] args) {
    try {
      throw new ParametricException<Integer>(42);
    } catch (ParametricException<Integer> e) {  // compile-time error
      assert e.getValue()==42;
    }
  }
}
```

This is not permitted, because the type in the catch clause is not reifiable. At the time of this writing, the Sun compiler reports a cascade of syntax errors in such a case:

```
% javac ParametricExceptionTest.java
ParametricExceptionTest.java:5: <identifier> expected
    } catch (ParametricException<Integer> e) {
                                ^
ParametricExceptionTest.java:8: ')' expected
  }
  ^
ParametricExceptionTest.java:9: '}' expected
}
 ^
3 errors
```

Because exceptions cannot be parametric, the syntax is restricted so that the type must be written as an identifier, with no following parameter.

Type Variable in a Throws Clause Although subclasses of Throwable cannot be parametric, it is possible to use a type variable in the throws clause of a method declaration. This technique is illustrated in Section 9.3.

6.4 Array Creation

Arrays reify their component types, meaning that they carry run-time information about the type of their components. This reified type information is used in instance tests and casts, and also used to check whether assignments into array components are permitted. Recall this example from Section 2.5.

```
Integer[] ints = new Integer[] {1,2,3};
Number[] nums = ints;
nums[2] = 3.14;  // array store exception
```

The first line allocates a new array, with reified type information indicating that it is an array of integers. The second line assigns this array to a variable containing an array of numbers; this is permitted because arrays, unlike generic types, are covariant. The assignment on the third line raises an array store exception at run time because the assigned value is of type double, and this is not compatible with the reified type attached to the array.

Because arrays must reify their component types, it is an error to create a new array unless its component type is reifiable. The two main problems you are likely to encounter are when the type of the array is a type variable, and when the type of the array is a parameterized type.

Consider the following (incorrect) code to convert a collection to an array:

```
import java.util.*;
class Annoying {
  public static <T> T[] toArray(Collection<T> c) {
    T[] a = new T[c.size()];  // compile-time error
    int i=0; for (T x : c) a[i++] = x;
    return a;
  }
}
```

This is an error, because a type variable is not a reifiable type. An attempt to compile this code reports a *generic array creation* error:

```
% javac Annoying.java
Annoying.java:4: generic array creation
    T[] a = new T[c.size()];  // compile-time error
          ^
1 error
```

We discuss workarounds for this problem shortly.

As a second example, consider the following (incorrect) code that returns an array containing two lists:

```
import java.util.*;
class AlsoAnnoying {
  public static List<Integer>[] twoLists() {
    List<Integer> a = Arrays.asList(1,2,3);
    List<Integer> b = Arrays.asList(4,5,6);
    return new List<Integer>[] {a, b};  // compile-time error
  }
}
```

This is an error, because a parameterized type is not a reifiable type. An attempt to compile this code also reports a generic array creation error:

```
% javac AlsoAnnoying.java
AlsoAnnoying.java:6: generic array creation
    return new List<Integer>[] {a, b};  // compile-time error
                   ^
1 error
```

We also discuss workarounds for this problem shortly.

Inability to create generic arrays is one of the most serious restrictions in Java. Because it is so annoying, it is worth reiterating the reason it occurs: generic arrays are problematic because generics are implemented via erasure, but erasure is beneficial because it eases evolution.

The best workaround is to use ArrayList or some other class from the Collections Framework in preference to an array. We discussed the tradeoffs between collection classes and arrays in Section 2.5, and we noted that in many cases collections are preferable to arrays: because they catch more errors at compile time, because they provide more operations, and because they offer more flexibility in representation. By far, the best solution to the problems offered by arrays is to "just say no": use collections in preference to arrays.

Sometimes this won't work, because you need an array for reasons of compatibility or efficiency. Examples of this occur in the Collections Framework: for compatibility, the method toArray converts a collection to an array; and, for efficiency, the class ArrayList is implemented by storing the list elements in an array. We discuss both of these cases in detail in the following sections, together with associated pitfalls and principles that help you avoid them: the Principle of Truth in Advertising and the Principle of Indecent Exposure. We also consider problems that arise with *varargs* and generic array creation.

6.5 The Principle of Truth in Advertising

We saw in the previous section that a naïve method to convert a collection to an array will not work. The first fix we might try is to add an unchecked cast, but we will see shortly that this leads to even more perplexing problems. The correct fix will require us to resort to reflection. Since the same issues arise when converting any generic structure to an array, it is worth understanding the problems and their solution. We will study variations of the static toArray method from the previous section; the same ideas apply to the toArray method in the Collection interface of the Collections Framework.

Here is a second attempt to convert a collection to an array, this time using an unchecked cast, and with test code added:

```
import java.util.*;
class Wrong {
  public static <T> T[] toArray(Collection<T> c) {
    T[] a = (T[])new Object[c.size()];  // unchecked cast
    int i=0; for (T x : c) a[i++] = x;
    return a;
  }
  public static void main(String[] args) {
    List<String> strings = Arrays.asList("one","two");
    String[] a = toArray(strings);  // class cast error
  }
}
```

The code in the previous section used the phrase new T[c.size()] to create the array, causing the compiler to report a generic array creation error. The new code instead allocates an array of objects and casts it to type T[], which causes the compiler to issue an unchecked cast warning:

```
% javac -Xlint Wrong.java
Wrong.java:4: warning: [unchecked] unchecked cast
found    : java.lang.Object[]
required: T[]
        T[] a = (T[])new Object[c.size()];  // unchecked cast
                ^
1 warning
```

As you might guess from the name chosen for this program, this warning should not be ignored. Indeed, running this program gives the following result:

```
% java Wrong
Exception in thread "main" java.lang.ClassCastException: [Ljava.lang.Object;
        at Wrong.main(Wrong.java:11)
```

The obscure phrase [Ljava.lang.Object is the reified type of the array, where [L indicates that it is an array of reference type, and java.lang.Object is the component type of the array. The class cast error message refers to the line containing the call to toArray. This error message may be confusing, since that line does not appear to contain a cast!

In order to see what went wrong with this program, let's look at how the program is translated using erasure. Erasure drops type parameters on Collection and List, replaces occurrences of the type variable T with Object, and inserts an appropriate cast on the call to toArray, yielding the following equivalent code:

```java
import java.util.*;
class Wrong {
  public static Object[] toArray(Collection c) {
    Object[] a = (Object[])new Object[c.size()];  // unchecked cast
    int i=0; for (Object x : c) a[i++] = x;
    return a;
  }
  public static void main(String[] args) {
    List strings = Arrays.asList(args);
    String[] a = (String[])toArray(strings);  // class cast error
  }
}
```

Erasure converts the unchecked cast to T[] into a cast to Object[], and inserts a cast to String[] on the call to toArray. When run, the first of these casts succeeds. But even though the array contains only strings, its reified type indicates that it is an array of Object, so the second cast fails.

In order to avoid this problem, you must stick to the following principle:

> *The Principle of Truth in Advertising*: the reified type of an array must be a subtype of the erasure of its static type.

The principle is obeyed within the body of toArray itself, where the erasure of T is Object, but not within the main method, where T has been bound to String but the reified type of the array is still Object.

Before we see how to create arrays in accordance with this principle, there is one more point worth stressing. Recall that generics for Java are accompanied by a cast-iron guarantee: no cast inserted by erasure will fail, so long as there are no unchecked warnings. The preceding principle illustrates the converse: if there are unchecked warnings, then casts inserted by erasure may fail. Further, *the cast that fails may be in a different part of the source code than was responsible for the unchecked warning!* This is why code that generates unchecked warnings must be written with extreme care.

Array Begets Array "Tis money that begets money," said Thomas Fuller in 1732, observing that one way to get money is to already have money. Similarly, one way to get a new array of a generic type is to already have an array of that type. Then the reified type information for the new array can be copied from the old.

We therefore alter the previous method to take two arguments, a collection and an array. If the array is big enough to hold the collection, then the collection is copied into the array. Otherwise, reflection is used to allocate a new array with the same reified type as the old, and then the collection is copied into the new array.

Here is code to implement the alternative:

```
import java.util.*;
class Right {
  public static <T> T[] toArray(Collection<T> c, T[] a) {
    if (a.length < c.size())
      a = (T[])java.lang.reflect.Array.  // unchecked cast
          newInstance(a.getClass().getComponentType(), c.size());
    int i=0; for (T x : c) a[i++] = x;
    if (i < a.length) a[i] = null;
    return a;
  }
  public static void main(String[] args) {
    List<String> strings = Arrays.asList("one", "two");
    String[] a = toArray(strings, new String[0]);
    assert Arrays.toString(a).equals("[one, two]");
    String[] b = new String[] { "x","x","x","x" };
    toArray(strings, b);
    assert Arrays.toString(b).equals("[one, two, null, x]");
  }
}
```

This uses three methods from the reflection library to allocate a new array with the same component type as the old array: the method getClass (in java.lang.Object) returns a Class object representing the array type, T[]; the method getComponentType (from java.lang.Class) returns a second Class object representing the array's component type, T; and the method newInstance (in java.lang.reflect.Array) allocates a new array with the given component type and size, again of type T[]. The result type of the call to newInstance is Object, so an unchecked cast is required to cast the result to the correct type T[].

In Java 5, the class Class has been updated to a generic class Class<T>; more on this shortly.

(A subtle point: in the call to newInstance, why is the result type Object rather than Object[]? Because, in general, newInstance may return an array of a primitive type such as int[], which is a subtype of Object but not of Object[]. However, that won't happen here because the type variable T must stand for a reference type.)

The size of the new array is taken to be the size of the given collection. If the old array is big enough to hold the collection and there is room left over, a null is written just after the collection to mark its end.

The test code creates a list of strings of length two and then performs two demonstration calls. Neither encounters the problem described previously, because the returned array has the reified type String[], in accordance with the Principle of Truth in Advertising. The first call is passed an array of length zero, so the list is copied into a freshly allocated array of length two. The second call is passed an array of length four, so the list is copied into the existing array, and a null is written past the end; the original array content after the null is not affected. The utility method toString (in java.util.Arrays) is used to convert the array to a string in the assertions.

The Collections Framework contains two methods for converting collections to arrays, similar to the one we just discussed:

```
interface Collection<E> {
  ...
  public Object[] toArray();
  public <T> T[] toArray(T[] a)
}
```

The first method returns an array with the reified component type Object, while the second copies the reified component type from the argument array, just as in the static method above. Like that method, it copies the collection into the array if there is room (and writes a null past the end of the collection if there is room for that), and allocates a fresh array otherwise. A call to the first method, c.toArray(), returns the same result as a call to the second method with an empty array of objects, c.toArray(new Object[0]). These methods are discussed further at the beginning of Chapter 12.

Often on encountering this design, programmers presume that the array argument exists mainly for reasons of efficiency, in order to minimize allocations by reusing the array. This is indeed a benefit of the design, but its main purpose is to get the reified types correct! Most calls to toArray will be with an argument array of length zero.

A Classy Alternative   Some days it may seem that the only way to get money is to have money. Not quite the same is true for arrays. An alternative to using an array to create an array is to use an instance of class Class.

Instances of the class Class represent information about a class at run time; there are also instances of this class that represent primitive types and arrays. In this text, we will refer to instances of the Class class as *class tokens*.

In Java 5, the class Class has been made generic, and now has the form Class<T>. What does the T stand for? An instance of type Class<T> represents the type T. For example, String.class has type Class<String>.

We can define a variant of our previous method that accepts a class token of type Class<T> rather than an array of type T[]. Applying newInstance to a class token of type Class<T> returns a new array of type T[], with the component type specified by the class token. The newInstance method still has a return type of Object (because of the same problem with primitive arrays), so an unchecked cast is still required.

```
import java.util.*;
class RightWithClass {
  public static <T> T[] toArray(Collection<T> c, Class<T> k) {
    T[] a = (T[])java.lang.reflect.Array.  // unchecked cast
            newInstance(k, c.size());
    int i=0; for (T x : c) a[i++] = x;
    return a;
  }
  public static void main(String[] args) {
```

```
    List<String> strings = Arrays.asList("one", "two");
    String[] a = toArray(strings, String.class);
    assert Arrays.toString(a).equals("[one, two]");
  }
}
```

The conversion method is now passed the class token String.class rather than an array of strings.

The type Class<T> represents an interesting use of generics, quite different from collections or comparators. If you still find this use of generics confusing, don't worry—we'll cover this subject in greater detail in Chapter 7.

6.6 The Principle of Indecent Exposure

Although it is an error to create an array with a component type that is not reifiable, it is *possible* to declare an array with such a type and to perform an unchecked cast to such a type. These features must be used with extreme caution, and it is worthwhile to understand what can go wrong if they are not used properly. In particular, a library should *never* publicly expose an array with a nonreifiable type.

Recall that Section 2.5 presents an example of why reification is necessary:

```
Integer[] ints = new Integer[] {1};
Number[] nums = ints;
nums[0] = 1.01;  // array store exception
int n = ints[0];
```

This assigns an array of integers to an array of numbers, and then attempts to store a double into the array of numbers. The attempt raises an array store exception because of the check against the reified type. This is just as well, since otherwise the last line would attempt to store a double into an integer variable.

Here is a similar example, where arrays of numbers are replaced by arrays of *lists of numbers*:

```
List<Integer>[] intLists
  = (List<Integer>[])new List[] {Arrays.asList(1)}; // unchecked cast
List<? extends Number>[] numLists = intLists;
numLists[0] = Arrays.asList(1.01);
int n = intLists[0].get(0);  // class cast exception!
```

This assigns an array of lists of integers to an array of lists of numbers, and then attempts to store a list of doubles into the array of lists of numbers. This time the attempted store does not fail, even though it should, because the check against the reified type is inadequate: the reified information contains only the erasure of the type, indicating that it is an array of List, not an array of List<Integer>. Hence the store succeeds, and the program fails unexpectedly elsewhere.

Example 6.1. Avoid arrays of nonreifiable type

```
DeceptiveLibrary.java:
import java.util.*;
public class DeceptiveLibrary {
  public static List<Integer>[] intLists(int size) {
    List<Integer>[] intLists =
      (List<Integer>[]) new List[size];  // unchecked cast
    for (int i = 0; i < size; i++)
      intLists[i] = Arrays.asList(i+1);
    return ints;
  }
}
```

```
InnocentClient.java:
import java.util.*;
public class InnocentClient {
  public static void main(String[] args) {
    List<Integer>[] intLists = DeceptiveLibrary.intLists(1);
    List<? extends Number>[] numLists = intLists;
    numLists[0] = Arrays.asList(1.01);
    int i = intLists[0].get(0);  // class cast error!
  }
}
```

Example 6.1 presents a similar example, divided into two classes in order to demonstrate how a poorly designed library can create problems for an innocent client. The first class, called DeceptiveLibrary, defines a static method that returns an array of lists of integers of a given size. Since generic array creation is not permitted, the array is created with components of the raw type List, and a cast is used to give the components the parameterized type List<Integer>. The cast generates an unchecked warning:

```
%javac -Xlint:unchecked DeceptiveLibrary.java
DeceptiveLibrary.java:5: warning: [unchecked] unchecked cast
found    : java.util.List[]
required: java.util.List<java.lang.Integer>[]
      (List<Integer>[]) new List[size];  // unchecked cast
                        ^
1 warning
```

Since the array really is an array of lists of integers, the cast appears reasonable, and you might think that this warning could be safely ignored. As we shall see, you ignore this warning at your peril!

The second class, called InnocentClient, has a main method similar to the previous example. Because the unchecked cast appears in the library, no unchecked warning is issued when compiling this code. However, running the code overwrites a list of integers with a list of doubles. Attempting to extract an integer from the array of lists of integers causes the cast implicitly inserted by erasure to fail:

```
%java InnocentClient
Exception in thread "main" java.lang.ClassCastException: java.lang.Double
        at InnocentClient.main(InnocentClient.java:7)
```

As in the previous section, this error message may be confusing, since that line does not appear to contain a cast!

In order to avoid this problem, you must stick to the following principle:

> *Principle of Indecent Exposure*: never publicly expose an array where the components do not have a reifiable type.

Again, this is a case where an unchecked cast in one part of the program may lead to a class cast error in a completely different part, where the cast does not appear in the source code but is instead introduced by erasure. Since such errors can be extremely confusing, unchecked casts must be used with extreme caution.

The Principle of Truth in Advertising and the Principle of Indecent Exposure are closely linked. The first requires that the run-time type of an array is properly reified, and the second requires that the compile-time type of an array must be reifiable.

It has taken some time for the importance of the Principle of Indecent Exposure to be understood, even among the designers of generics for Java. For example, the following two methods in the reflection library violate the principle:

```
TypeVariable<Class<T>>[] java.lang.Class.getTypeParameters()
TypeVariable<Method>[] java.lang.Reflect.Method.getTypeParameters()
```

Following the preceding model, it is not hard to create your own version of InnocentClient that throws a class cast error at a point where there is no cast, where in this case the role of DeceptiveLibrary is played by the official Java library! (At the time of going to press, remedies for this bug are under consideration. Possible fixes are to delete the type parameter from TypeVariable so that the methods return an array of reified type, or to replace the arrays with lists.)

Don't get caught out in the same way—be sure to follow the Principle of Indecent Exposure rigorously in your own code!

6.7 How to Define ArrayList

We have argued elsewhere that it is usually preferable to use a list than to use an array. There are a few places where this is not appropriate. In rare circumstances, you will need to use an array for reasons of efficiency or compatibility. Also, of course, you need to use arrays to implement ArrayList itself. Here we present the implementation of ArrayList as a model of what to do in the rare circumstance where you do need to use an array. Such implementations need to be written with care, as they necessarily involve use of unchecked casts. We will see how the Principles of Indecent Exposure and of Truth in Advertising figure in the implementation.

Example 6.2 shows the implementation. We have derived `ArrayList` by subclassing from `AbstractList`. Classes derived from this class need to define only four methods, namely `get`, `set`, `add`, and `remove`; the other methods are defined in terms of these. We also indicate that the class implements `RandomAccess`, indicating that clients of the class will have more efficient access using `get` than using the list iterator.

The class represents a list with elements of type E by two private fields: `size` of type `int` containing the length of the list, and `arr` of type `E[]` containing the elements of the list. The array must have a length at least equal to `size`, but it may have additional unused elements at the end.

There are two places where new instances of the array are allocated, one in the initializer for the class and one in the method that increases the array capacity (which in turn is called from the `add` method). In both places, the array is allocated as an `Object[]` and an unchecked cast is made to type `E[]`.

It is essential that the field containing the array is private; otherwise, it would violate both the Principle of Truth in Advertising and the Principle of Indecent Exposure. It would violate the Principle of Truth in Advertising because E might be bound to a type (such as `String`) other than `Object`. It would violate the Principle of Indecent Exposure because E might be bound to a type (such as `List<Integer>`) that is not a reifiable type. However, neither of these principles is violated because the array is not public: it is stored in a private field, and no pointer to the array escapes from the class. We might call this the Principle of Anything Goes Behind Closed Doors.

The way we've defined `ArrayList` here is close to the actual definition in the source released by Sun. Recently, Neal Gafter, the coauthor of that library, has argued that he used bad style—that it would have been better to declare the private array to have type `Object[]` and use casts to type `(E)` when retrieving elements from the array. There is something to be said for this point, although there is also something to be said for the style we have used here, which minimizes the need for unchecked casts.

The method `toArray` does return an array in public, but it uses the techniques described in Section 6.5 in accordance with the Principle of Truth in Advertising. As before, there is an argument array, and if it is not big enough to hold the collection, then reflection is used to allocate a new array with the same reified type. The implementation is similar to the one we saw earlier, except that the more efficient `arraycopy` routine can be used to copy the private array into the public array to be returned.

6.8   Array Creation and Varargs

The convenient *vararg* notation allows methods to accept a variable number of arguments and packs them into an array, as discussed in Section 1.4. This notation is not as convenient

---

Example 6.2. How to define ArrayList

```java
import java.util.*;
class ArrayList<E> extends AbstractList<E> implements RandomAccess {
  private E[] arr;
  private int size = 0;
  public ArrayList(int cap) {
    if (cap < 0)
      throw new IllegalArgumentException("Illegal Capacity: "+cap);
    arr = (E[])new Object[cap];   // unchecked cast
  }
  public ArrayList() { this(10); }
  public ArrayList(Collection<? extends E> c) { this(c.size()); addAll(c); }
  public void ensureCapacity(int mincap) {
    int oldcap = arr.length;
    if (mincap > oldcap) {
      int newcap = Math.max(mincap, (oldcap*3)/2+1);
      E[] oldarr = arr;
      arr = (E[])new Object[newcap];   // unchecked cast
      System.arraycopy(oldarr,0,arr,0,size);
    }
  }
  public int size() { return size; }
  private void checkBounds(int i, int size) {
    if (i < 0 || i >= size)
      throw new IndexOutOfBoundsException("Index: "+i+", Size: "+size);
  }
  public E get(int i) { checkBounds(i,size); return arr[i]; }
  public E set(int i, E elt) {
    checkBounds(i,size); E old = arr[i]; arr[i] = elt; return old;
  }
  public void add(int i, E elt) {
    checkBounds(i,size+1); ensureCapacity(size+1);
    System.arraycopy(arr,i,arr,i+1,size-i); arr[i] = elt;  size++;
  }
  public E remove(int i) {
    checkBounds(i,size); E old = arr[i];  arr[i] = null;  size--;
    System.arraycopy(arr,i+1,arr,i,size-i); return old;
  }
  public <T> T[] toArray(T[] a) {
    if (a.length < size)
      a = (T[])java.lang.reflect.Array.   // unchecked cast
             newInstance(a.getClass().getComponentType(), c.size());
    System.arraycopy(arr,0,a,0,size);
    if (size < a.length) a[size] = null;
    return a;
  }
  public Object[] toArray() { return toArray(new Object[0]); }
}
```

as you might like, because the arrays it creates suffer from the same issues involving reification as other arrays.

In Section 1.4 we discussed the method java.util.Arrays.asList, which is declared as follows:

```
public static <E> List<E> asList(E... arr)
```

For instance, here are three calls to this method:

```
List<Integer> a = Arrays.asList(1, 2, 3);
List<Integer> b = Arrays.asList(4, 5, 6);
List<List<Integer>> x = Arrays.asList(a, b);  // generic array creation
```

Recall that an argument list of variable length is implemented by packing the arguments into an array and passing that. Hence these three calls are equivalent to the following:

```
List<Integer> a = Arrays.asList(new Integer[] { 1, 2, 3 });
List<Integer> b = Arrays.asList(new Integer[] { 4, 5, 6 });
List<List<Integer>> x
  = Arrays.asList(new List<Integer>[] { a, b });  // generic array creation
```

The first two calls are fine, but since List<Integer> is not a reifiable type, the third warns of an unchecked generic array creation at compile time.

```
VarargError.java:6: warning: [unchecked] unchecked generic array creation
of type java.util.List<java.lang.Integer>[] for varargs parameter
        List<List<Integer>> x = Arrays.asList(a, b);
```

This warning can be confusing, particularly since that line of source code does not contain an explicit instance of array creation!

A similar problem occurs if one attempts to create a list of a generic type. Here is a method that uses Arrays.asList to create a list of length one containing a given element:

```
public static List<E> singleton(E elt) {
  return Arrays.asList(elt);  // generic array creation
}
```

This also generates a warning, which can be confusing for the same reasons.

Normally, generic array creation reports an error. As a workaround, one can create the array at a reifiable type and perform an unchecked cast. That workaround is not available for the array creation that is implicit in the use of *varargs*, so in this case generic array creation issues a warning rather than an error. A generic array creation warning is just like an unchecked warning, in that it invalidates the cast-iron guarantee that accompanies generics. It is not too difficult to take each of the previous examples where a mishap occurs as the result of an unchecked warning, and create a similar example using *varargs* where a generic array creation warning is issued instead.

In our opinion, the convenience offered by *varargs* is outweighed by the danger inherent in unchecked warnings, and we recommend that you never use *varargs* when the argument

---

is of a nonrefiable type. For instance, in both of the preceding examples, instead of using `Arrays.asList`, we would have created a new `ArrayList` and used the `add` method, even though this is less convenient and less efficient.

The need for generic array creation warnings and the associated workarounds would not have arisen if the *vararg* notation had been defined to pack arguments into a list rather than an array, taking `T...` to be equivalent to `List<T>` rather than `T[]`. Unfortunately, the *vararg* notation was designed before this problem was fully understood.

6.9 Arrays as a Deprecated Type?

We have seen that collections are superior to arrays in a number of ways:

- Collections provide more precise typing than arrays. With lists, one can write `List<T>`, `List<? extends T>`, or `List<? super T>`; whereas with arrays, one can only write `T[]`, which corresponds to the second of the three options for lists. More-precise typing enables more errors to be detected at compile time rather than run time. This makes coding, debugging, testing, and maintenance easier, and also improves efficiency. (See Section 2.5.)

- Collections are more flexible than arrays. Collections offer a variety of representations, including arrays, linked lists, trees, and hash tables, whereas arrays have a fixed representation, and the libraries offer a larger variety of methods and convenience algorithms on collections than on arrays. (See Section 2.5.)

- Collections may have elements of any type, whereas arrays should only have components of reifiable type. When creating an array, one must adhere to the Principle of Truth in Advertising—the reified type must conform to the static type—and the Principle of Indecent Exposure—never publicly expose an array where the components do not have reifiable type. (See Sections 6.5 and 6.6.)

In retrospect, there are several places in Java 5 where avoiding the use of arrays might have improved the design:

- Variable-length arguments (*varargs*) are represented by an array, and so are subject to the same restrictions. If a *vararg* is bound to actual arguments of nonreifiable type then a generic array creation warning is issued (which raises the same concerns as an unchecked warning). For instance, the function `Arrays.asList` takes a *vararg*. There is no difficulty in applying this function to return a result of type `List<Integer>`, but it is problematic to create a result of type `List<List<Integer>>` or of type `List<E>`. This problem would not arise if lists had been used in preference to arrays. (See Section 6.8.)

- Some methods in the Java library have signatures that violate the Principle of Indecent Exposure:

```
TypeVariable<Class<T>>[] java.lang.Class.getTypeParameters()
TypeVariable<Method>[] java.lang.Reflect.Method.getTypeParameters()
```

It is possible for code that invokes these methods to violate the cast-iron guarantee that accompanies generics: it may raise a class cast exception where there is no explicit cast in the code, even though no unchecked warning is issued by the compiler. (A warning was issued—and wrongly ignored—when the library was compiled.) Again, this problem would not arise if lists had been used in preference to arrays. (See Section 6.6.)

One reason for some of the complexities in the Java 5 design was to provide good support for the use of arrays. In retrospect, it might have been better to choose a design that was simpler, but made arrays not quite as convenient to use:

- Arrays must be created with components of reifiable type, so some attempt was made to make the notion of reifiable type as general as possible in order to minimize this restriction. If the designers had been willing to restrict the notion of reified type, they could have simplified it by including raw types (such as `List`), but excluding types with unbounded wildcards (such as `List<?>`). Had they done so, reifiable types would have become synonymous with unparameterized types (that is, primitive types, raw types, and types declared without a type parameter).

  This change would simplify the types permitted in an instance test. Consider the following three tests:

  ```
  obj instanceof List
  obj instanceof List<?>
  obj instanceof List<? extends Object>
  ```

  Currently, the first two are permitted, but the third is not. With the proposed restriction, only the first would be permitted. Arguably, this might be easier to understand. It would also be consistent with the treatment of class tokens, since currently `List.class` is permitted but `List<?>.class` is illegal.

- Currently, array creation is restricted to arrays of reifiable type. But it is permitted to declare an array of nonreifiable type or to cast to an array type that is not reifiable, at the cost of an unchecked warning somewhere in the code. As we have seen, such warnings violate the cast-iron guarantee that accompanies generics, and may lead to class cast errors even when the source code contains no casts.

  A simpler and safer design would be to outlaw any reference to an array of nonreifiable type (using the simpler form of reifiable type just described). This design would mean that one could never declare an array of type `E[]`, where `E` is a type variable.

  This change would make it more complicated to implement `ArrayList<E>` (or similar classes). The type of the private variable must change from `E[]` to `Object[]`, and you must add an unchecked cast `(E)` to the result of `get` and similar methods. But the complication is small, and arises only for the implementor of `ArrayList` (or similar classes), not for the clients.

  This change would also mean that you could not assign a generic type to the `toArray` method for collections (or similar methods). Instead of:

  ```
  public <T> T[] toArray(T[] arr)
  ```

  we would have:

  ```
  public Object[] toArray(Object[] arr)
  ```

and many uses of this method would require an explicit cast of the result. This does make life more awkward for users, but arguably the improvement to simplicity and safety would be worth it.

- The preceding changes would mean that often one would use lists in preference to arrays. Use of lists could be made easier by permitting Java programmers to write `l[i]` as an abbreviation for `l.get(i)`, and `l[i] = v` as an abbreviation for `l.put(i,v)`. (Some people like this sort of "syntactic sugar," while others think of it as "syntactic rat poison.")

Some of these changes can still be adapted in a backward compatible manner. We mentioned in Section 6.8 that it may be desirable to add a second form of *vararg* based on lists rather than arrays. Permitting abbreviations to make list indexing look like array indexing could easily be incorporated in a future version of Java.

But the window for some of these changes has closed. Too many users have written code with generic `toArrays` to permit reverting to the nongeneric version. Nonetheless, it seems worthwhile to record this alternate design. Perhaps understanding how the current design might have been simpler can lead to better insight and a better future design.

Just as the Java 5 design might have been improved if it had put less emphasis on arrays, your own code designs may be improved if you use collections and lists in preference to arrays. Perhaps the time has come to regard arrays as a deprecated type?

6.10 Summing Up

We conclude by giving a checklist of places where reifiable types are required or recommended.

- An instance test must be against a reifiable type.
- A cast should usually be to a reifiable type. (A cast to a nonreifiable type usually issues an unchecked warning.)
- A class that extends `Throwable` must not be parameterized.
- An array instance creation must be at a reifiable type.
- The reified type of an array must be a subtype of the erasure of its static type (see the Principle of Truth in Advertising), and a publicly exposed array should be of a reifiable type (see the Principle of Indecent Exposure).
- *Varargs* should be of a reifiable type. (A *vararg* of a nonreifiable type will issue an unchecked warning.)

These restrictions arise from the fact that generics are implemented via erasure, and they should be regarded as the price one pays for the ease of evolution that we explored in the previous chapter.

For completeness, we also list restrictions connected with reflection:

- Class tokens correspond to reifiable types, and the type parameter in `Class<T>` should be a reifiable type. (See Section 7.2.)

These are discussed in the next chapter.

CHAPTER 7

Reflection

Reflection is the term for a set of features that allows a program to examine its own definition. Reflection in Java plays a role in class browsers, object inspectors, debuggers, interpreters, services such as JavaBeans^{TM} and object serialization, and any tool that creates, inspects, or manipulates arbitrary Java objects on the fly.

Reflection has been present in Java since the beginning, but the advent of generics changes reflection in two important ways, introducing both *generics for reflection* and *reflection for generics*.

By *generics for reflection* we mean that some of the types used for reflection are now generic types. In particular, the class `Class` becomes the generic class `Class<T>`. This may seem confusing at first, but once understood it can make programs using reflection much clearer. Class literals and the method `Object.getClass` use special tricks to return more-precise type information. Generics are used to especially good effect in the reflection of annotations. We observe that the type parameter `T` in `Class<T>` should always be bound to a reifiable type, and we present a short library that can help you avoid many common cases of unchecked casts.

By *reflection for generics* we mean that reflection now returns information about generic types. There are new interfaces to represent generic types, including type variables, parameterized types, and wildcard types, and there are new methods that get the generic types of fields, constructors, and methods.

We explain each of these points in turn. We don't assume any previous knowledge of reflection, but we focus on the aspects tied to generics.

7.1 Generics for Reflection

Java has supported facilities for *reflection* since version 1.0 and class literals since version 1.1. Central to these is the class `Class`, which represents information about the type of an object at run time. You may write a type followed by `.class` as a literal that denotes the class token corresponding to that type, and the method `getClass` is defined on every object and returns a class token that represents the reified type information carried by that object at run-time. Here is an example:

```
Class ki = Integer.class;
Number n = new Integer(42);
Class kn = n.getClass();
assert ki == kn;
```

For a given class loader, the same type is always represented by the same class token. To emphasize this point, here we compare class tokens using identity (the == operator). However, in practice, it often is more robust to use equality (the equals method).

One of the changes in Java 5 is that the class Class now takes a type parameter, so Class<T> is the type of the class token for the type T. The preceding code is now written as follows:

```
Class<Integer> ki = Integer.class;
Number n = new Integer(42);
Class<? extends Number> kn = n.getClass();
assert ki == kn;
```

Class tokens and the getClass method are treated specially by the compiler. In general, if T is a type without type parameters, then T.class has type Class<T>, and if e is an expression of type T then e.getClass() has type Class<? extends T>. (We'll see what happens when T does have type parameters in the next section.) The wildcard is needed because the type of the object referred to by the variable may be a subtype of the type of the variable, as in this case, where a variable of type Number contains an object of type Integer.

For many uses of reflection, you won't know the exact type of the class token (if you did, you probably wouldn't need to use reflection), and in those cases you can write Class<?> for the type, using an unbounded wildcard. However, in some cases the type information provided by the type parameter is invaluable, as in the variant of toArray that we discussed in Section 6.5:

```
public static <T> T[] toArray(Collection<T> c, Class<T> k)
```

Here the type parameter lets the compiler check that the type represented by the class token matches the type of the collection and of the array.

Further Examples of Generics for Reflection   The class Class<T> contains just a few methods that use the type parameter in an interesting way:

```
class Class<T> {
  public T newInstance();
  public T cast(Object o);
  public Class<? super T> getSuperclass();
  public <U> Class<? extends U> asSubclass(Class<U> k);
  public <A extends Annotation> A getAnnotation(Class<A> k);
  public boolean isAnnotationPresent(Class<? extends Annotation> k);
  ...
}
```

The first returns a new instance of the class, which will, of course, have type T. The second casts an arbitrary object to the receiver class, and so it either throws a class cast exception or returns a result of type T. The third returns the superclass, which must have the specified type. The fourth checks that the receiver class is a subclass of the argument class, and either throws a class cast exception or returns the receiver with its type suitably changed.

The fifth and sixth methods are part of the new annotation facility. The methods are interesting, because they show how the type parameter for classes can be used to good effect. For example, Retention is a subclass of Annotation, so you can extract the retention annotation on a class k as follows:

```
Retention r = k.getAnnotation(Retention.class);
```

Here the generic type gains two advantages. First, it means that no cast is required on the result of the call, because the generic type system can assign it precisely the correct type. Second, it means that if you accidentally call the method with a class token for a class that is not a subclass of Annotation, then this is detected at compile time rather than at run time.

Another use of class tokens, similar to that for annotations, appears in the getListeners method of the class Component in the package java.awt:

```
public <T extends EventListener>
  T[] getListeners(Class<T> listenerType);
```

Again, this means that the code of getListeners requires no cast, and it means that the compiler can check that the method is called with a class token of an appropriate type.

As a final example of an interesting use of class tokens, the convenience class Collections contains a method that builds a wrapper that checks whether every element added to or extracted from the given list belongs to the given class. (There are similar methods for other collection classes, such as sets and maps.) It has the following signature:

```
public static <T> List<T> checkedList(List<T> l, Class<T> k)
```

The wrapper supplements static checking at compile time with dynamic checking at run time, which can be useful for improving security or interfacing with legacy code (see Section 8.1). The implementation calls the method cast in the class Class described earlier, where the receiver is the class token passed into the method, and the cast is applied to any element read from or written into the list using get, set, or add. Yet again, the type parameter on Class<T> means that the code of checkedList requires no additional casts (beyond calls to the cast method in the class Class), and that the compiler can check that the method is called with a class token of an appropriate type.

7.2 Reflected Types are Reifiable Types

Reflection makes reified type information available to the program. Of necessity, therefore, each class token corresponds to a reifiable type. If you try to reflect a parameterized type, you get the reified information for the corresponding raw type:

```
List<Integer> ints = new ArrayList<Integer>();
List<String> strs  = new ArrayList<String>();
assert ints.getClass() == strs.getClass();
assert ints.getClass() == ArrayList.class;
```

Here the type list of integers and the type list of strings are both represented by the same class token, the class literal for which is written `ArrayList.class`.

Because the class always represents a reifiable type, there is no point in parameterizing the class `Class` with a type that is not reifiable. Hence, the two main methods for producing a class with a type parameter, namely the `getClass` method and class literals, are both designed to yield a reifiable type for the type parameter in all cases.

Recall that the `getClass` method is treated specially by the compiler. In general, if expression e has type T, then the expression `e.getClass()` has type `Class<? extends |T|>`, where $|T|$ is the erasure of the type T. Here's an example:

```
List<Integer> ints = new ArrayList<Integer>();
Class<? extends List> k = ints.getClass();
assert k == ArrayList.class;
```

Here the expression `ints` has type `List<Integer>`, so the expression `int.getClass()` has type `Class<? extends List>`; this is the case because erasing `List<Integer>` yields the raw type `List`. The actual value of k is `ArrayList.class`, which has type `Class<ArrayList>`, which is indeed a subtype of `Class<? extends List>`.

Class literals are also restricted; it is not even syntactically valid to supply a type parameter to the type in a class literal. Thus, the following fragment is illegal:

```
class ClassLiteral {
  public Class<?> k = List<Integer>.class;  // syntax error
}
```

Indeed, Java's grammar makes a phrase such as the preceding one difficult to parse, and it may trigger a cascade of syntax errors:

```
% javac ClassLiteral.java
ClassLiteral.java:2: illegal start of expression
  public Class<?> k = List<Integer>.class;  // syntax error
                          ^
ClassLiteral.java:2: ';' expected
  public Class<?> k = List<Integer>.class;  // syntax error
                                 ^
ClassLiteral.java:2: <identifier> expected
  public Class<?> k = List<Integer>.class;  // syntax error
                                       ^
ClassLiteral.java:4: '}' expected
^
4 errors
```

The parser has so much trouble with this phrase that it is still confused when it reaches the end of the file!

This syntax problem leads to an irregularity. Everywhere else that a reifiable type is required, you may supply either a raw type (such as List) or a parameterized type with unbounded wildcards (such as List<?>). However, for class tokens, you must supply a raw type; not even unbounded wildcards may appear. Replacing List<Integer> with List<?> in the preceding code leads to a similar error cascade.

The restrictions on class tokens lead to a useful property. Wherever a type of the form Class<T> appears, the type T should be a reifiable type. The same is true for types of the form T[].

7.3 Reflection for Primitive Types

Every type in Java, including primitive types and array types, has a class literal and a corresponding class token.

For instance, int.class denotes the class token for the primitive type for integers (this token is also the value of the static field Integer.TYPE). The type of this class token cannot be Class<int>, since int is not a reference type, so it is taken to be Class<Integer>. Arguably, this is an odd choice, since according to this type you might expect the calls int.class.cast(o) and int.class.newInstance() to return values of type Integer, but in fact these calls raise an exception. Similarly, you might expect the call

```
java.lang.reflect.array.newInstance(int.class,size)
```

to return a value of type Integer[], but in fact the call returns a value of type int[]. These examples suggest that it might have made more sense to give the class token int.class the type Class<?>.

On the other hand, int[].class denotes the class token for arrays with components of the primitive type integer, and the type of this class token is Class<int[]>, which is permitted since int[] is a reference type.

7.4 A Generic Reflection Library

As we've seen, careless use of unchecked casts can lead to problems, such as violating the Principle of Truth in Advertising or the Principle of Indecent Exposure (see Sections 6.5 and 6.6). One technique to minimize the use of unchecked casts is to encapsulate these within a library. The library can be carefully scrutinized to ensure that its use of unchecked casts is safe, while code that calls the library can be free of unchecked casts. Sun is considering adding library methods similar to the ones described here.

Example 7.1 provides a library of generic functions that use reflection in a type-safe way. It defines a convenience class GenericReflection containing the following methods:

```
public static <T> T newInstance(T object)
public static <T> Class<? extends T> getComponentType(T[] a)
public static <T> T[] newArray(Class<? extends T> k, int size)
public static <T> T[] newArray(T[] a, int size)
```

The first takes an object, finds the class of that object, and returns a new instance of the class; this must have the same type as the original object. The second takes an array and returns a class token for its component type, as carried in its run-time type information. Conversely, the third allocates a new array with its component type specified by a given class token and a specified size. The fourth takes an array and a size, and allocates a new array with the same component type as the given array and the given size; it simply composes calls to the previous two methods. The code for each of the first three methods consists of a call to one or two corresponding methods in the Java reflection library and an unchecked cast to the appropriate return type.

Unchecked casts are required because the methods in the Java reflection library cannot return sufficiently accurate types, for various reasons. The method getComponentType is in the class Class<T>, and Java provides no way to restrict the receiver type to be Class<T[]> in the signature of the method (though the call raises an exception if the receiver is not a class token for an array type). The method newInstance in java.lang.reflect.Array must

Example 7.1. A type-safe library for generic reflection

```
class GenericReflection {
  public static <T> T newInstance(T obj)
  throws InstantiationException,
         IllegalAccessException,
         InvocationTargetException,
         NoSuchMethodException
  {
    Object newobj = obj.getClass().getConstructor().newInstance();
    return (T)newobj;  // unchecked cast
  }
  public static <T> Class<? extends T> getComponentType(T[] a) {
    Class<?> k = a.getClass().getComponentType();
    return (Class<? extends T>)k;  // unchecked cast
  }
  public static <T> T[] newArray(Class<? extends T> k, int size) {
    if (k.isPrimitive())
      throw new IllegalArgumentException
                ("Argument cannot be primitive: "+k);
    Object a = java.lang.reflect.Array.newInstance(k, size);
    return (T[])a;  // unchecked cast
  }
  public static <T> T[] newArray(T[] a, int size) {
    return newArray(getComponentType(a), size);
  }
}
```

have the return type `Object` rather than the return type `T[]`, because it may return an array of a primitive type. The method `getClass`, when called on a receiver of type `T`, returns a token not of type `Class<? extends T>` but of type `Class<?>`, because of the erasure that is required to ensure that class tokens always have a reifiable type. However, in each case the unchecked cast is safe, and users can call on the four library routines defined here without violating the cast-iron guarantee.

The first method uses `Constructor.newInstance` (in `java.lang.reflect`) in preference to `Class.newInstance`, in order to avoid a known problem with the latter. To quote from Sun's documentation for `Class.newInstance`: "Note that this method propagates any exception thrown by the nullary constructor, including a checked exception. Use of this method effectively bypasses the compile-time exception checking that would otherwise be performed by the compiler. The `Constructor.newInstance` method avoids this problem by wrapping any exception thrown by the constructor in a (checked) `InvocationTargetException`."

The second method is guaranteed to be well typed in any program that obeys the Principle of Indecent Exposure and the Principle of Truth in Advertising. The first principle guarantees that the component type at compile time will be a reifiable type, and then the second principle guarantees that the reified component type returned at run time must be a subtype of the reifiable component type declared at compile time.

The third method raises an illegal argument exception if its class argument is a primitive type. This catches the following tricky case: if the first argument is, say, `int.class` then its type is `Class<Integer>`, but the new array will have type `int[]`, which is not a subtype of `Integer[]`. This problem would not have arisen if `int.class` had the type `Class<?>` rather than `Class<Integer>`, as discussed in the preceding section.

As an example of the use of the first method, here is a method that copies a collection into a fresh collection of the same kind, preserving the type of the argument:

```
public static <T, C extends Collection<T>> C copy(C coll) {
  C copy = GenericReflection.newInstance(coll);
  copy.addAll(coll);  return copy;
}
```

Calling `copy` on an `ArrayList<Integer>` returns a new `ArrayList<Integer>`, while calling `copy` on a `HashSet<String>` returns a new `HashSet<String>`.

As an example of the use of the last method, here is the `toArray` method of Section 6.5, rewritten to replace its unchecked casts by a call to the generic reflection library:

```
public static <T> T[] toArray(Collection<T> c, T[] a) {
  if (a.length < c.size())
    a = GenericReflection.newArray(a, c.size());
  int i=0; for (T x : c) a[i++] = x;
  if (i < a.length) a[i] = null;
  return a;
}
```

In general, we recommend that if you need to use unchecked casts then you should encapsulate them into a small number of library methods, as we've done here. Don't let unchecked code proliferate through your program!

7.5 Reflection for Generics

Generics change the reflection library in two ways. We have discussed *generics for reflection*, where Java added a type parameter to the class Class<T>. We now discuss *reflection for generics*, where Java adds methods and classes that support access to generic types.

Example 7.2 shows a simple demonstration of the use of reflection for generics. It uses reflection to find the class associated with a given name, and it prints out the fields,

Example 7.2. Reflection for generics

```
import java.lang.reflect.*;
import java.util.*;
class ReflectionForGenerics {
  public static void toString(Class<?> k) {
    System.out.println(k + " (toString)");
    for (Field f : k.getDeclaredFields())
      System.out.println(f.toString());
    for (Constructor c : k.getDeclaredConstructors())
      System.out.println(c.toString());
    for (Method m : k.getDeclaredMethods())
      System.out.println(m.toString());
    System.out.println();
  }
  public static void toGenericString(Class<?> k) {
    System.out.println(k + " (toGenericString)");
    for (Field f : k.getDeclaredFields())
      System.out.println(f.toGenericString());
    for (Constructor c : k.getDeclaredConstructors())
      System.out.println(c.toGenericString());
    for (Method m : k.getDeclaredMethods())
      System.out.println(m.toGenericString());
    System.out.println();
  }
  public static void main (String[] args)
  throws ClassNotFoundException {
    for (String name : args) {
      Class<?> k = Class.forName(name);
      toString(k);
      toGenericString(k);
    }
  }
}
```

Example 7.3. A sample class

```
class Cell<E> {
  private E value;
  public Cell(E value) { this.value=value; }
  public E getValue() { return value; }
  public void setValue(E value) { this.value=value; }
  public static <T> Cell<T> copy(Cell<T> cell) {
    return new Cell<T>(cell.getValue());
  }
}
```

Example 7.4. A sample run

```
% java ReflectionForGenerics Cell
class Cell (toString)
private java.lang.Object Cell.value
public Cell(java.lang.Object)
public java.lang.Object Cell.getValue()
public static Cell Cell.copy(Cell)
public void Cell.setValue(java.lang.Object)

class Cell (toGenericString)
private E Cell.value
public Cell(E)
public E Cell.getValue()
public static <T> Cell<T> Cell.copy(Cell<T>)
public void Cell.setValue(E)
```

constructors, and methods associated with the class, using the reflection library classes Field, Constructor, and Method. Two different methods are available for converting a field, constructor, or method to a string for printing: the old toString method and the new toGenericString method. The old method is maintained mainly for backward compatibility. A small sample class is shown in Example 7.3, and a sample run with this class is shown in Example 7.4.

The sample run shows that although the reified type information for objects and class tokens contains no information about generic types, the actual bytecode of the class does encode information about generic types as well as erased types. The information about generic types is essentially a comment. It is ignored when running the code, and it is preserved only for use in reflection.

Unfortunately, there is no toGenericString method for the class Class, even though this would be useful. Sun is considering adding such a method in future. In the meantime, all the necessary information is available, and we explain how to access it in the next section.

7.6 Reflecting Generic Types

The reflection library provides a Type interface to describe a generic type. There is one class that implements this interface and four other interfaces that extend it, corresponding to the five different kinds of types:

- The class Class, representing a primitive type or raw type

- The interface ParameterizedType, representing an application of a generic class or interface to parameter types, from which you can extract an array of the parameter types

- The interface TypeVariable, representing a type variable, from which you can extract the bounds on the type variable

- The interface GenericArrayType, representing an array, from which you can extract the array component type

- The interface WildcardType, representing a wildcard, from which you can extract a lower or upper bound on the wildcard

By performing a series of instance tests on each of these interfaces, you may determine which kind of type you have, and print or process the type; we will see an example of this shortly.

Methods are available to return the superclass and superinterfaces of a class as types, and to access the generic type of a field, the argument types of a constructor, and the argument and result types of a method.

You can also extract the type variables that stand for the formal parameters of a class or interface declaration, or of a generic method or constructor. The type for type variables takes a parameter, and is written TypeVariable<D>, where D represents the type of object that declared the type variable. Thus, the type variables of a class have type TypeVariable<Class<?>>, while the type variables of a generic method have type TypeVariable<Method>. Arguably, the type parameter is confusing and is not very helpful. Since it is responsible for the problem described in Section 6.6, Sun may remove it in the future.

Example 7.5 uses these methods to print out all of the header information associated with a class. Here are two examples of its use:

```
% java ReflectionDemo java.util.AbstractList
class java.util.AbstractList<E>
extends java.util.AbstractCollection<E>
implements java.util.List<E>

% java ReflectionDemo java.lang.Enum
class java.lang.Enum<E extends java.lang.Enum<E>>
implements java.lang.Comparable<E>,java.io.Serializable
```

The code in Example 7.5 is lengthy but straightforward. It contains methods to print every component of a class: its superclass, its interfaces, its fields, and its methods. The core of

Example 7.5. How to manipulate the type Type

```java
import java.util.*;
import java.lang.reflect.*;
import java.io.*;
class ReflectionDemo {
  private final static PrintStream out = System.out;
  public static void printSuperclass(Type sup) {
    if (sup != null && !sup.equals(Object.class)) {
      out.print("extends ");
      printType(sup);
      out.println();
    }
  }
  public static void printInterfaces(Type[] impls) {
    if (impls != null && impls.length > 0) {
      out.print("implements ");
      int i = 0;
      for (Type impl : impls) {
        if (i++ > 0) out.print(",");
        printType(impl);
      }
      out.println();
    }
  }
  public static void printTypeParameters(TypeVariable<?>[] vars) {
    if (vars != null && vars.length > 0) {
      out.print("<");
      int i = 0;
      for (TypeVariable<?> var : vars) {
        if (i++ > 0) out.print(",");
        out.print(var.getName());
        printBounds(var.getBounds());
      }
      out.print(">");
    }
  }
  public static void printBounds(Type[] bounds) {
    if (bounds != null && bounds.length > 0
      && !(bounds.length == 1 && bounds[0] == Object.class)) {
      out.print(" extends ");
      int i = 0;
      for (Type bound : bounds) {
        if (i++ > 0) out.print("&");
        printType(bound);
      }
    }
  }
}
```

Example 7.5. How to manipulate the type Type *(continued)*

```java
public static void printParams(Type[] types) {
  if (types != null && types.length > 0) {
    out.print("<");
    int i = 0;
    for (Type type : types) {
      if (i++ > 0) out.print(",");
      printType(type);
    }
    out.print(">");
  }
}
public static void printType(Type type) {
  if (type instanceof Class) {
    Class<?> c = (Class)type;
    out.print(c.getName());
  } else if (type instanceof ParameterizedType) {
    ParameterizedType p = (ParameterizedType)type;
    Class c = (Class)p.getRawType();
    Type o = p.getOwnerType();
    if (o != null) { printType(o); out.print("."); }
    out.print(c.getName());
    printParams(p.getActualTypeArguments());
  } else if (type instanceof TypeVariable<?>) {
    TypeVariable<?> v = (TypeVariable<?>)type;
    out.print(v.getName());
  } else if (type instanceof GenericArrayType) {
    GenericArrayType a = (GenericArrayType)type;
    printType(a.getGenericComponentType());
    out.print("[]");
  } else if (type instanceof WildcardType) {
    WildcardType w = (WildcardType)type;
    Type[] upper = w.getUpperBounds();
    Type[] lower = w.getLowerBounds();
    if (upper.length == 1 && lower.length == 0) {
      out.print("? extends ");
      printType(upper[0]);
    } else if (upper.length == 0 && lower.length == 1) {
      out.print("? super ");
      printType(lower[0]);
    } else throw new AssertionError();
  }
}
```

Example 7.5. How to manipulate the type Type *(continued)*

```
public static void printClass(Class c) {
  out.print("class ");
  out.print(c.getName());
  printTypeParameters(c.getTypeParameters());
  out.println();
  printSuperclass(c.getGenericSuperclass());
  printInterfaces(c.getGenericInterfaces());
}
public static void main(String[] args) throws ClassNotFoundException {
  for (String name : args) {
    Class<?> c = Class.forName(name);
    printClass(c);
  }
}
}
```

the code is the method printType, which uses a cascade of instance tests to classify a type according to the five cases above.

Much of this code would be unnecessary if the Type interface had a toGenericString method. Sun is considering this change.

CHAPTER 8

Effective Generics

This chapter contains advice on how to use generics effectively in practical coding. We consider checked collections, security issues, specialized classes, and binary compatibility. The title of this section is an homage to Joshua Bloch's book, *Effective Java* (Addison-Wesley).

8.1 Take Care when Calling Legacy Code

As we have seen, generic types are checked at compile time, not run time. Usually, this is just what we want, since checking at compile time reports errors earlier and incurs no run-time overhead. However, sometimes this may not be appropriate, either because we can't be sure that compile-time checks are adequate (say, because we are passing an instance of a parameterized type to a legacy client or to a client we don't trust), or because we need information about types at run time (say, because we want a reifiable type for use as an array component). A *checked* collection will often do the trick, and when that will not do, we can create a *specialized* class. We consider checked collections in this section, security issues in the next section, and specialized classes in the section after that.

Consider a legacy library that contains methods to add items to a given list and to return a new list containing given items:

```
class LegacyLibrary {
  public static void addItems(List list) {
    list.add(new Integer(1));  list.add("two");
  }
  public static List getItems() {
    List list = new ArrayList();
    list.add(new Integer(3));  list.add("four");
    return list;
  }
}
```

Now consider a client that uses this legacy library, having been told (incorrectly) that the items are always integers:

```
class NaiveClient {
  public static void processItems() {
    List<Integer> list = new ArrayList<Integer>();
    LegacyLibrary.addItems(list);
    List<Integer> list2 = LegacyLibrary.getItems(); // unchecked
    // sometime later ...
    int s = 0;
    for (int i : list) s += i; // class cast exception
    for (int i : list2) s += i; // class cast exception
  }
}
```

There is no warning when passing the integer list to the method addItems, because the parameterized type List<Integer> is considered a subtype of List. The conversion from List to List<Integer> of the list returned by getItems does issue an unchecked warning. At run-time, a class cast exception will be raised when attempting to extract data from these lists, since the cast to type Integer implicitly inserted by erasure will fail. (The failure of these casts does not constitute a violation of the cast-iron guarantee, because this guarantee doesn't hold in the presence of legacy code or unchecked warnings.) Because the exception is raised far from the place where the strings are added to the lists, the bug may be hard to pinpoint.

If the legacy library has been generified by applying the minimal changes or stubs techniques (see Sections 5.4.1 and 5.4.2), then these problems cannot arise as long as generic types have been assigned correctly.

A less-naïve client may design code that catches the error earlier and is easier to debug.

```
class WaryClient {
  public static void processItems() {
    List<Integer> list = new ArrayList<Integer>();
    List<Integer> view = Collections.checkedList(list, Integer.class);
    LegacyLibrary.addItems(view);  // class cast exception
    List<Integer> list2 = LegacyLibrary.getItems(); // unchecked
    for (int i : list2) {} // class cast exception
    // sometime later ...
    int s = 0;
    for (int i : list) s += i;
    for (int i : list2) s += i;
  }
}
```

The method checkedList in the convenience class Collections takes a list and a class token and returns a checked view of the list; whenever an attempt is made to add an element to the checked view, reflection is used to check that the element belongs to the specified class before adding it to the underlying list (see Section 17.3.3). Using a checked list view will cause a class cast exception to be raised inside the method addItems when it attempts to add a string to the list. Since the method getItems creates its own list, the client cannot use a wrapper in the same way. However, adding an empty loop at the point where the list is returned can guarantee that the error is caught close to the offending method call.

Checked lists provide useful guarantees only when the list elements are of a reifiable type. If you want to apply these techniques when the list is not of a reifiable type, you might want to consider applying the specialization technique of Section 8.3.

8.2 Use Checked Collections to Enforce Security

It is important to be aware that the guarantees offered by generic types apply only if there are no unchecked warnings. This means that generic types are useless for ensuring security in code written by others, since you have no way of knowing whether that code raised unchecked warnings when it was compiled.

Say we have a class that defines an order, with a subclass that defines an authenticated order:

```
class Order { ... }
class AuthenticatedOrder extends Order { ... }
```

Interfaces specify suppliers and processors of orders. Here the supplier is required to provide only authenticated orders, while the processor handles all kinds of orders:

```
interface OrderSupplier {
  public void addOrders(List<AuthenticatedOrder> orders);
}
interface OrderProcessor {
  public void processOrders(List<? extends Order> orders);
}
```

From the types involved, you might think that the following broker guarantees that only authenticated orders can pass from the supplier to the processor:

```
class NaiveBroker {
  public void connect(OrderSupplier supplier,
                      OrderProcessor processor)
  {
    List<AuthenticatedOrder> orders =
      new ArrayList<AuthenticatedOrder>();
    supplier.addOrders(orders);
    processor.processOrders(orders);
  }
}
```

But a devious supplier may, in fact, supply unauthenticated orders:

```
class DeviousSupplier implements OrderSupplier {
  public void addOrders(List<AuthenticatedOrder> orders) {
```

```
    List raw = orders;
    Order order = new Order();  // not authenticated
    raw.add(order);  // unchecked call
  }
}
```

Compiling the devious supplier will issue an unchecked warning, but the broker has no way of knowing this.

Incompetence can cause just as many problems as deviousness. Any code that issues unchecked warnings when compiled could cause similar problems, perhaps simply because the author made a mistake. In particular, legacy code may raise such problems, as described in the previous section.

The correct solution is for the broker to pass a checked list to the supplier:

```
class WaryBroker {
  public void connect(OrderSupplier supplier,
                      OrderProcessor processor)
  {
    List<AuthenticatedOrder> orders =
        new ArrayList<AuthenticatedOrder>();
    supplier.addOrders(
        Collections.checkedList(orders, AuthenticatedOrder.class));
    processor.processOrders(orders);
  }
}
```

Now a class cast exception will be raised if the supplier attempts to add anything to the list that is not an authenticated order.

Checked collections are not the only technique for enforcing security. If the interface that supplies orders returns a list instead of accepting a list, then the broker can use the empty loop technique of the previous section to ensure that lists contain only authorized orders before passing them on. One can also use specialization, as described in the next section, to create a special type of list that can contain only authorized orders.

8.3   Specialize to Create Reifiable Types

Parameterized types are not reifiable, but some operations, such as instance tests, casting, and array creation apply only to reifiable types. In such cases, one workaround is to create a specialized version of the parameterized type. Specialized versions can be created either by delegation (that is, wrappers) or by inheritance (that is, subclassing), and we discuss each in turn.

Example 8.1 shows how to specialize lists to strings; specializing to other types is similar. We begin by specializing the List interface to the desired type:

```
interface ListString extends List<String> {}
```

Example 8.1. Specialize to create reifiable types

```
interface ListString extends List<String> {}

class ListStrings {
  public static ListString wrap(final List<String> list) {
    class Random extends AbstractList<String>
      implements ListString, RandomAccess
    {
      public int size() { return list.size(); }
      public String get(int i) { return list.get(i); }
      public String set(int i, String s) { return list.set(i,s); }
      public String remove(int i) { return list.remove(i); }
      public void add(int i, String s) { list.add(i,s); }
    }
    class Sequential extends AbstractSequentialList<String>
      implements ListString
    {
      public int size() { return list.size(); }
      public ListIterator<String> listIterator(int index) {
        final ListIterator<String> it = list.listIterator(index);
        return new ListIterator<String>() {
          public void add(String s) { it.add(s); }
          public boolean hasNext() { return it.hasNext(); }
          public boolean hasPrevious() { return it.hasPrevious(); }
          public String next() { return it.next(); }
          public int nextIndex() { return it.nextIndex(); }
          public String previous() { return it.previous(); }
          public int previousIndex() { return it.previousIndex(); }
          public void remove() { it.remove(); }
          public void set(String s) { it.set(s); }
        };
      }
    }
    return list instanceof RandomAccess ? new Random() : new Sequential();
  }
}

class ArrayListString extends ArrayList<String> implements ListString {
  public ArrayListString() { super(); }
  public ArrayListString(Collection<? extends String> c) { super(c); }
  public ArrayListString(int capacity) { super(capacity); }
}
```

This declares ListString (an unparameterized type, hence reifiable) to be a subtype of List<String> (a parameterized type, hence not reifiable). Thus, every value of the first type also belongs to the second, but not conversely. The interface declares no new methods; it simply specializes the existing methods to the parameter type String.

Delegation To specialize by delegation, we define a static method wrap that takes an argument of type List<String> and returns a result of type ListString. The Java library places methods that act on the interface Collection in a class called Collections, so we place the method wrap in a class called ListStrings.

Here is an example of its use:

```
List<? extends List<?>> lists =
  Arrays.asList(
    ListStrings.wrap(Arrays.asList("one","two")),
    Arrays.asList(3,4),
    Arrays.asList("five","six"),
    ListStrings.wrap(Arrays.asList("seven","eight"))
  );
ListString[] array = new ListString[2];
int i = 0;
for (List<?> list : lists)
  if (list instanceof ListString)
    array[i++] = (ListString)list;
assert Arrays.toString(array).equals("[[one, two], [seven, eight]]");
```

This creates a list of lists, then scans it for those lists that implement ListString and places those into an array. Array creation, instance tests, and casts now pose no problems, as they act on the reifiable type ListString rather than the nonreifiable type List<String>. Observe that a List<String> that has not been wrapped will not be recognized as an instance of ListString; this is why the third list in the list of lists is not copied into the array.

The ListStrings class is straightforward to implement, although some care is required to preserve good performance. The Java Collections Framework specifies that whenever a list supports fast random access it should implement the marker interface RandomAccess, to allow generic algorithms to perform well when applied to either random or sequential access lists. It also provides two abstract classes, AbstractList and AbstractSequentialList, suitable for defining random and sequential access lists. For example, ArrayList implements RandomAccess and extends AbstractList, while LinkedList extends Abstract-SequentialList. Class AbstractList defines the methods of the List interface in terms of five abstract methods that provide random access and must be defined in a subclass (size, get, set, add, remove). Similarly, class AbstractSequentialList defines all methods of the List interface in terms of two abstract methods that provide sequential access and must be defined in a subclass (size, listIterator).

The wrap method checks whether the given list implements the interface RandomAccess. If so, it returns an instance of class Random that extends AbstractList and implements RandomAccess, and otherwise it returns an instance of class Sequential that extends

AbstractSequentialList. Class Random implements the five methods that must be provided by a subclass of AbstractList. Similarly, class Sequential implements the two methods that must be provided by a subclass of AbstractSequentialList, where the second of these returns a class that implements the nine methods of the ListIterator interface. Implementing the list iterator by delegation instead of simply returning the original list iterator improves the security properties of the wrapper, as discussed below. All of these methods are implemented straightforwardly by delegation.

The wrap method returns a view of the underlying list that will raise a class cast exception if any attempt is made to insert an element into the list that is not of type String. These checks are similar to those provided by the checkedList wrapper. However, for wrap the relevant casts are inserted by the compiler (one reason for implementing the nine methods of the listIterator interface by delegation is to ensure that these casts are inserted), while for checked lists the casts are performed by reflection. Generics usually render these checks redundant, but they can be helpful in the presence of legacy code or unchecked warnings, or when dealing with security issues such as those discussed in Section 8.2.

The code shown here was designed to balance power against brevity (it's only thiry-three lines), but other variations are possible. A less complete version might implement only random access if one could guarantee it was never applied to a sequential access list, or vice versa. A more efficient version might skip the use of AbstractList and Abstract-SequentialList, and instead directly delegate all 25 methods of the List interface together with the toString method (see the source code for Collections.checkedList for a model). You also might want to provide additional methods in the ListString interface, such as an unwrap method that returns the underlying List<String>, or a version of subList that returns a ListString rather than a List<String> by recursively applying wrap to the delegated call.

Inheritance To specialize by inheritance, we declare a specialized class that implements the specialized interface and inherits from a suitable implementation of lists. Example 8.1 shows an implementation that specializes ArrayList, which we repeat here:

```
class ArrayListString extends ArrayList<String> implements ListString {
  public ArrayListString() { super(); }
  public ArrayListString(Collection<? extends String> c) { super(c); }
  public ArrayListString(int capacity) { super(capacity); }
}
```

The code is quite compact. All methods are inherited from the superclass, so we only need to define specialized constructors. If the only constructor required was the default constructor, then the class body could be completely empty!

The previous example still works if we create the initial list using inheritance rather than delegation:

```
List<? extends List<?>> lists =
  Arrays.asList(
    new ArrayListString(Arrays.asList("one","two")),
```

```
    Arrays.asList(3,4),
    Arrays.asList("five","six"),
    new ArrayListString(Arrays.asList("seven","eight"))
  );
ListString[] array = new ListString[2];
int i = 0;
for (List<?> list : lists)
  if (list instanceof ListString)
    array[i++] = (ListString)list;
assert Arrays.toString(array).equals("[[one, two], [seven, eight]]");
```

As before, array creation, instance tests, and casts now pose no problem.

However, delegation and inheritance are not interchangeable. Specialization by delegation creates a view of an underlying list, while specialization by inheritance constructs a new list. Further, specialization by delegation has better security properties than specialization by inheritance. Here is an example:

```
List<String> original = new ArrayList<String>();
ListString delegated = ListStrings.wrap(original);
ListString inherited = new ArrayListString(original);
delegated.add("one");
inherited.add("two");
try {
  ((List)delegated).add(3);  // unchecked, class cast error
} catch (ClassCastException e) {}
((List)inherited).add(4);  // unchecked, no class cast error!
assert original.toString().equals("[one]");
assert delegated.toString().equals("[one]");
assert inherited.toString().equals("[two, 4]");
```

Here an original list serves as the basis for two specialized lists, one created by delegation and one by inheritance. Elements added to the delegated list appear in the original, but elements added to the inherited list do not. Type checking normally would prevent any attempt to add an element that is not a string to any object of type List<String>, specialized or not, but such attempts may occur in the presence of legacy code or unchecked warnings. Here we cast to a raw type and use an unchecked call to attempt to add an integer to the delegated and inherited lists. The attempt on the delegated list raises a class cast exception, while the attempt on the inherited list succeeds. To force the second attempt to fail, we should wrap the inherited list using checkedList, as described in Section 8.1.

Another difference is that inheritance can only be applied to a public implementation that can be subclassed (such as ArrayList or LinkedList), whereas delegation can create a view of any list (including lists returned by methods such as Arrays.asList or Collections.immutableList, or by the sublist method on lists).

The security properties of specialization by inheritance can be improved by declaring a specialized signature for any method that adds an element to the list or sets an element:

```
class ArrayListString extends ArrayList<String> implements ListString {
  public ArrayListString() { super(); }
  public ArrayListString(Collection<? extends String> c) { this.addAll(c); }
  public ArrayListString(int capacity) { super(capacity); }
  public boolean addAll(Collection<? extends String> c) {
    for (String s : c) {}  // check that c contains only strings
    return super.addAll(c);
  }
  public boolean add(String element) { return super.add(element); }
  public void add(int index, String element) { super.add(index, element); }
  public String set(int index, String element) {
    return super.set(index, element);
  }
}
```

Now, any attempt to add or set an element that is not a string will raise a class cast exception. However, this property depends on a subtle implementation detail, namely that any other methods that add or set an element (for instance, the add method in listIterator) are implemented in terms of the methods specialized above. In general, if security is desired, delegation is more robust.

Other Types Specialization at other types works similarly. For example, replacing String by Integer in Example 8.1 gives an interface ListInteger and classes List-Integers and ArrayListInteger. This even works for lists of lists. For example, replacing String by ListString in Example 8.1 gives an interface ListListString and classes ListListStrings and ArrayListListString.

However, specialization at wildcard types can be problematic. Say we wanted to specialize both of the types List<Number> and List<? extends Number>. We might expect to use the following declarations:

```
// illegal
interface ListNumber extends List<Number>, ListExtendsNumber {}
interface ListExtendsNumber extends List<? extends Number> {}
```

This falls foul of two problems: the first interface extends two different interfaces with the same erasure, which is not allowed (see Section 4.4), and the second interface has a supertype with a wildcard at the top level, which is also not allowed (see Section 2.8). The only workaround is to avoid specialization of types containing wildcards; fortunately, this should rarely be a problem.

8.4 Maintain Binary Compatibility

As we have stressed, generics are implemented via erasure in order to ease evolution. When evolving legacy code to generic code, we want to ensure that the newly-generified code will work with any existing code, including class files for which we do not have the source. When this is the case, we say that the legacy and generic versions are *binary compatible*.

Binary compatibility is guaranteed if the erasure of the signature of the generic code is identical to the signature of the legacy code and if both versions compile to the same bytecode. Usually, this is a natural consequence of generification, but in this section we look at some of the corner cases that can cause problems.

Some examples for this section were taken from internal Sun notes written by Mark Reinhold.

Adjusting the Erasure   One corner case arises in connection with the generification of the max method in the Collections class. We discussed this case in Sections 3.2 and 3.6, but it is worth a quick review.

Here is the legacy signature of this method:

```
// legacy version
public static Object max(Collection coll)
```

And here is the natural generic signature, using wildcards to obtain maximum flexibility (see Section 3.2):

```
// generic version -- breaks binary compatibility
public static <T extends Comparable<? super T>>
  T max(Collection<? extends T> coll)
```

But this signature has the wrong erasure—its return type is Comparable rather than Object. In order to get the right signature, we need to fiddle with the bounds on the type parameter, using multiple bounds (see Section 3.6). Here is the corrected version:

```
// generic version -- maintains binary compatibility
public static <T extends Object & Comparable<? super T>>
  T max(Collection<? extends T> coll)
```

When there are multiple bounds, the leftmost bound is taken for the erasure. So the erasure of T is now Object, giving the result type we require.

Some problems with generification arise because the original legacy code contains less-specific types than it might have. For example, the legacy version of max might have been given the return type Comparable, which is more specific than Object, and then there would have been no need to adjust the type using multiple bounds.

Bridges   Another important corner case arises in connection with bridges. Again, Comparable provides a good example.

Most legacy core classes that implement Comparable provide two overloads of the compareTo method: one with the argument type Object, which overrides the compareTo method in the interface; and one with a more-specific type. For example, here is the relevant part of the legacy version of Integer:

```
// legacy version
public class Integer implements Comparable {
  public int compareTo(Object o) { ... }
```

```
  public int compareTo(Integer i) { ... }
  ...
}
```

And here is the corresponding generic version:

```
// generic version -- maintains binary compatibility
public final class Integer implements Comparable<Integer> {
  public int compareTo(Integer i) { ... }
  ...
}
```

Both versions have the same bytecode, because the compiler generates a bridge method for compareTo with an argument of type Object (see Section 3.7).

However, some legacy code contains only the Object method. (Previous to generics, some programmers thought this was cleaner than defining two methods.) Here is the legacy version of javax.naming.Name.

```
// legacy version
public interface Name extends Comparable {
  public int compareTo(Object o);
  ...
}
```

In fact, names are compared only with other names, so we might hope for the following generic version:

```
// generic version -- breaks binary compatibility
public interface Name extends Comparable<Name> {
  public int compareTo(Name n);
  ...
}
```

However, choosing this generification breaks binary compatibility. Since the legacy class contains compareTo(Object) but not compareTo(Name), it is quite possible that users may have declared implementations of Name that provide the former but not the latter. Any such class would not work with the generic version of Name given above. The only solution is to choose a less-ambitious generification:

```
// generic version -- maintains binary compatibility
public interface Name extends Comparable<Object> {
  public int compareTo(Object o) { ... }
  ...
}
```

This has the same erasure as the legacy version and is guaranteed to be compatible with any subclass that the user may have defined.

In the preceding case, if the more-ambitious generification is chosen, then an error will be raised at run time, because the implementing class does not implement compareTo(Name).

But in some cases the difference can be insidious: rather than raising an error, a different value may be returned! For instance, Name may be implemented by a class SimpleName, where a simple name consists of a single string, base, and comparing two simple names compares the base names. Further, say that SimpleName has a subclass ExtendedName, where an extended name has a base string and an extension. Comparing an extended name with a simple name compares only the base names, while comparing an extended name with another extended name compares the bases and, if they are equal, then compares the extensions. Say that we generify Name and SimpleName so that they define compareTo(Name), but that we do not have the source for ExtendedName. Since it defines only compareTo(Object), client code that calls compareTo(Name) rather than compareTo(Object) will invoke the method on SimpleName (where it is defined) rather than ExtendedName (where it is not defined), so the base names will be compared but the extensions ignored. This is illustrated in Examples 8.2 and 8.3.

The lesson is that extra caution is in order whenever generifying a class, unless you are confident that you can compatibly generify all subclasses as well. Note that you have more leeway if generifying a class declared as final, since it cannot have subclasses.

Also note that if the original Name interface declared not only the general overload compareTo(Object), but also the more-specific overload compareTo(Name), then the legacy versions of both SimpleName and ExtendedName would be required to implement compareTo(Name) and the problem described here could not arise.

Covariant Overriding Another corner case arises in connection with covariant overriding (see Section 3.8). Recall that one method can override another if the arguments match exactly but the return type of the overriding method is a subtype of the return type of the other method.

An application of this is to the clone method:

```
class Object {
  public Object clone() { ... }
  ...
}
```

Here is the legacy version of the class HashSet:

```
// legacy version
class HashSet {
  public Object clone() { ... }
  ...
}
```

For the generic version, you might hope to exploit covariant overriding and choose a more-specific return type for clone:

```
// generic version -- breaks binary compatibility
class HashSet {
  public HashSet clone() { ... }
  ...
}
```

Example 8.2. Legacy code for simple and extended names

```java
interface Name extends Comparable {
  public int compareTo(Object o);
}

class SimpleName implements Name {
  private String base;
  public SimpleName(String base) {
    this.base = base;
  }
  public int compareTo(Object o) {
    return base.compareTo(((SimpleName)o).base);
  }
}

class ExtendedName extends SimpleName {
  private String ext;
  public ExtendedName(String base, String ext) {
    super(base); this.ext = ext;
  }
  public int compareTo(Object o) {
    int c = super.compareTo(o);
    if (c == 0 && o instanceof ExtendedName)
      return ext.compareTo(((ExtendedName)o).ext);
    else
      return c;
  }
}

class Client {
  public static void main(String[] args) {
    Name m = new ExtendedName("a","b");
    Name n = new ExtendedName("a","c");
    assert m.compareTo(n) < 0;
  }
}
```

Example 8.3. Generifying simple names and the client, but not extended names

```java
interface Name extends Comparable<Name> {
  public int compareTo(Name o);
}

class SimpleName implements Name {
  private String base;
  public SimpleName(String base) {
    this.base = base;
  }
  public int compareTo(Name o) {
    return base.compareTo(((SimpleName)o).base);
  }
}

// use legacy class file for ExtendedName

class Test {
  public static void main(String[] args) {
    Name m = new ExtendedName("a","b");
    Name n = new ExtendedName("a","c");
    assert m.compareTo(n) == 0;  // answer is now different!
  }
}
```

However, choosing this generification breaks binary compatibility. It is quite possible that users may have defined subclasses of HashSet that override clone. Any such subclass would not work with the generic version of HashSet given previously. The only solution is to choose a less-ambitious generification:

```java
// generic version -- maintains binary compatibility
class HashSet {
  public Object clone() { ... }
  ...
}
```

This is guaranteed to be compatible with any subclass that the user may have defined. Again, you have more freedom if you can also generify any subclasses, or if the class is final.

CHAPTER 9

Design Patterns

This chapter reviews five well-known design patterns—Visitor, Interpreter, Function, Strategy, and Subject-Observer—and shows how they can take advantage of generics. The Function pattern generalizes the idea behind the `Comparator` interface. The other four patterns are described in the seminal book *Design Patterns*, by Gamma, Helm, Johnson, and Vlissides (Addison-Wesley).

9.1 Visitor

Often, a data structure is defined by case analysis and recursion. For example, a binary tree of type `Tree<E>` is one of the following:

- A leaf, containing a single value of type `E`
- A branch, containing a left subtree and a right subtree, both of type `Tree<E>`

It is easy to think of many other examples: a shape may be either a triangle, a rectangle, a combination of two shapes, or the transposition of a shape; an XML node is either a text node, an attribute node, or an element node (which may contain other nodes); and so on.

To represent such a structure in an object-oriented language, the data structure is represented by an abstract class, and each case is represented by a subclass. The abstract class declares an abstract method for each possible operation on the data structure, and each subclass implements the method as appropriate for the corresponding case.

Example 9.1 illustrates this technique applied to trees. There is an abstract class, `Tree<E>`, with two abstract methods, `toString` and `sum`. (The former applies to any tree, while the latter applies only to a tree of numbers—for simplicity, this restriction is enforced by a cast at run time rather than a type at compile time, as discussed later.) There are two static factory methods, one to construct a leaf and one to construct a branch. Each of these contains a nested class that extends `Tree<E>` and implements each of the methods `toString` and `sum`.

This approach is adequate if you know in advance all of the operations required on the data structure, or can modify the classes that define the structure when the requirements change. However, sometimes this is not the case, particularly when different developers are

Example 9.1. A simple tree and client

```java
abstract class Tree<E> {
  abstract public String toString();
  abstract public Double sum();
  public static <E> Tree<E> leaf(final E e) {
    return new Tree<E>() {
      public String toString() {
        return e.toString();
      }
      public Double sum() {
        return ((Number)e).doubleValue();
      }
    };
  }
  public static <E> Tree<E> branch(final Tree<E> l, final Tree<E> r) {
    return new Tree<E>() {
      public String toString() {
        return "("+l.toString()+"^"+r.toString()+")";
      }
      public Double sum() {
        return l.sum() + r.sum();
      }
    };
  }
}
class TreeClient {
  public static void main(String[] args) {
    Tree<Integer> t =
      Tree.branch(Tree.branch(Tree.leaf(1),
                              Tree.leaf(2)),
                  Tree.leaf(3));
    assert t.toString().equals("((1^2)^3)");
    assert t.sum() == 6;
  }
}
```

responsible for the classes that define the structure and the classes that are clients of the structure.

The Visitor pattern makes it possible to provide new operations without modifying the classes that define the data structure. In this pattern, the abstract class that represents the structure declares an abstract `visit` method, which takes a *visitor* as an argument. The visitor implements an interface that specifies one method for each case in the specification of the structure. Each subclass implements the `visit` method by calling the method of the visitor for the corresponding case.

Example 9.2. A tree with visitors

```java
abstract class Tree<E> {
  public interface Visitor<E, R> {
    public R leaf(E elt);
    public R branch(R left, R right);
  }
  public abstract <R> R visit(Visitor<E, R> v);
  public static <T> Tree<T> leaf(final T e) {
    return new Tree<T>() {
      public <R> R visit(Visitor<T, R> v) {
        return v.leaf(e);
      }
    };
  }
  public static <T> Tree<T> branch(final Tree<T> l, final Tree<T> r) {
    return new Tree<T>() {
      public <R> R visit(Visitor<T, R> v) {
        return v.branch(l.visit(v), r.visit(v));
      }
    };
  }
}
```

Example 9.2 illustrates this pattern applied to trees. Now the abstract class Tree<E> has only one abstract method, visit, which accepts an argument of type Visitor<E, R>. The interface Visitor<E, R> specifies two methods, a leaf method that accepts a value of type E and returns a value of type R, and a branch method that accepts two values of type R and returns a value of type R. The subclass corresponding to a leaf implements visit by invoking the leaf method of the visitor on the element in the leaf, and the subclass corresponding to a branch implements visit by invoking the branch method of the visitor on the result of recursive calls of the visitor on the left and right subtrees.

Example 9.3 illustrates how to implement the toString and sum methods on trees within the client, rather than within the class that defines the data structure. Whereas before these were methods with the tree as the receiver, now they are static methods that take the tree as an argument.

There is a pleasing duality between the two approaches. For simple trees, each factory method (leaf and branch) groups together definitions for each operator method (toString and sum). For trees with visitors, each operator method (toString and sum) groups together definitions for each visitor method (leaf and branch).

With generics, each visitor has two type parameters, one for the element type of the tree and one for the return type of the visitor. Without generics, each visitor would have to return a result of type Object, and many additional casts would be required. Because of this, when generics are not present, often visitors are designed not to return a value; instead, the result

Example 9.3. A client with visitors

```
class TreeClient {
  public static <T> String toString(Tree<T> t) {
    return t.visit(new Tree.Visitor<T, String>() {
      public String leaf(T e) {
        return e.toString();
      }
      public String branch(String l, String r) {
        return "("+l+"^"+r+")";
      }
    });
  }
  public static <N extends Number> double sum(Tree<N> t) {
    return t.visit(new Tree.Visitor<N, Double>() {
      public Double leaf(N e) {
        return e.doubleValue();
      }
      public Double branch(Double l, Double r) {
        return l+r;
      }
    });
  }
  public static void main(String[] args) {
    Tree<Integer> t =
      Tree.branch(Tree.branch(Tree.leaf(1),
                              Tree.leaf(2)),
                  Tree.leaf(3));
    assert toString(t).equals("((1^2)^3)");
    assert sum(t) == 6;
  }
}
```

is accumulated in a variable local to the visitor, complicating the flow of data through the program.

It is interesting to note that the generic type of the sum method can be more precise with visitors. With simple trees, the sum method must have a type signature that indicates that it works on any element type; a cast is required to convert each leaf to type Number; and a class cast error is raised at run time if sum is invoked on a tree not containing numbers. With visitors, the sum method may have a type signature that indicates that it works only on elements that are numbers; no cast is required; and a type error is reported at compile time if sum is invoked on a tree not containing numbers.

In practice, you will often use a combination of the simple approach and the Visitor pattern. For instance, you might choose to define standard methods, such as toString, using the simple approach, while using Visitor for other methods, such as sum.

Example 9.4. An interpreter with generics

```
class Pair<A, B> {
  private final A left;
  private final B right;
  public Pair(A l, B r) { left=l; right=r; }
  public A left() { return left; }
  public B right() { return right; }
}
abstract class Exp<T> {
  abstract public T eval();
  static Exp<Integer> lit(final int i) {
    return new Exp<Integer>() { public Integer eval() { return i; } };
  }
  static Exp<Integer> plus(final Exp<Integer> e1, final Exp<Integer> e2) {
    return new Exp<Integer>() { public Integer eval() {
      return e1.eval()+e2.eval();
    } };
  }
  static <A, B> Exp<Pair<A, B>> pair(final Exp<A> e1, final Exp<B> e2) {
    return new Exp<Pair<A, B>>() { public Pair<A, B> eval() {
      return new Pair<A, B>(e1.eval(), e2.eval());
    } };
  }
  static <A, B> Exp<A> left(final Exp<Pair<A, B>> e) {
    return new Exp<A>() { public A eval() { return e.eval().left(); } };
  }
  static <A, B> Exp<B> right(final Exp<Pair<A, B>> e) {
    return new Exp<B>() { public B eval() { return e.eval().right(); } };
  }
  public static void main(String[] args) {
    Exp<Integer> e = left(pair(plus(lit(3),lit(4)),lit(5)));
    assert e.eval() == 7;
  }
}
```

9.2 Interpreter

One use of trees is to represent expressions in a programming language. As in the previous section, the expression type is represented by an abstract class, with each kind of expression represented by a subclass. There is an abstract method to evaluate an expression, and each subclass implements the method as appropriate for the corresponding kind of expression.

With generics, it is possible to parameterize the expression type by the type of the expression. For example, Exp<Integer> is an expression that returns an integer, while Exp<Pair<Integer, Integer>> is an expression that returns a pair of integers.

Example 9.4 demonstrates the Interpreter pattern with generics. It begins by defining a class Pair<A, B>, with a constructor and two methods to select the left and right components of a pair. It then declares an abstract class, Exp<A>, for an expression that returns a value of type A, with an abstract method eval that returns a value of type A. In our example, there are five kinds of expression:

- An integer literal, of type Exp<Integer>

- A sum expression, of type Exp<Integer>, which has two subexpressions, each of type Exp<Integer>

- An expression to construct a pair, of type Exp<Pair<A, B>>, which has two subexpressions of type Exp<A> and Exp<B>

- An expression to select the left component of a pair, of type Exp<A>, which has a subexpression of type Exp<Pair<A, B>>

- An expression to select the right component of a pair, of type Exp<B>, which has a subexpression of type Exp<Pair<A, B>>

There are five static methods corresponding to five kinds of expression, each returning an instance of an appropriate subclass of the expression class, with an appropriate definition of the eval method. Finally, the main method constructs and evaluates a sample expression.

Generics in Java were inspired by similar features in functional languages such as ML and Haskell. The generic Interpreter pattern is interesting because it shows a way in which generics in Java are more powerful than generics in these other languages. It is not possible to implement this pattern in the standard versions of ML and Haskell, although a recent version of Haskell includes an experimental feature, *generalized abstract data types*, designed specifically to support this pattern.

9.3 Function

The Function pattern converts an arbitrary method into an object. The relation between a function and the corresponding method is similar to the relation between Comparator and the compareTo method.

The generic version of the Function pattern demonstrates how to use a type variable in the throws clause of a method declaration. This may be useful when different instances of a class contain methods that may raise different checked exceptions.

Recall that the class Throwable has two major subclasses, Exception and Error, and that the first of these has another major subclass, RuntimeException. An exception is *checked* if it is a subclass of Exception but not a subclass of RuntimeException. The throws clause of a method may list any subclass of Throwable, but *must* list any checked exception that might be thrown by the method body, including any checked exceptions declared for the methods invoked within the body.

An example of the use of a type variable in a throws clause is shown in Example 9.5. The example defines a class, Function<A, B, X>, which represents a function. The class contains an abstract method, apply, that accepts an argument of type A, returns a result of type B, and may throw an exception of type X. The class also contains an applyAll method

---

Example 9.5. Type parameter in a throws *clause*

```java
import java.util.*;
import java.lang.reflect.*;
interface Function<A, B, X extends Throwable> {
  public B apply(A x) throws X;
}
class Functions {
  public <A, B, X extends Throwable>
  List<B> applyAll(List<A> list) throws X {
    List<B> result = new ArrayList<B>(list.size());
    for (A x : list) result.add(apply(x));
    return result;
  }
  public static void main(String[] args) {
    Function<String, Integer, Error> length =
      new Function<String, Integer, Error>() {
        public Integer apply(String s) {
          return s.length();
        }
      };
    Function<String, Class<?>, ClassNotFoundException> forName =
      new Function<String, Class<?>, ClassNotFoundException>() {
        public Class<?> apply(String s)
          throws ClassNotFoundException {
          return Class.forName(s);
        }
      };
    Function<String, Method, Exception> getRunMethod =
      new Function<String, Method, Exception>() {
        public Method apply(String s)
          throws ClassNotFoundException,NoSuchMethodException {
          return Class.forName(s).getMethod("run");
        }
      };
    List<String> strings = Arrays.asList(args);
    System.out.println(applyAll(length, strings));

    try { System.out.println(applyAll(forName, strings)); }
    catch (ClassNotFoundException e) { System.out.println(e); }

    try { System.out.println(applyAll(getRunMethod, strings)); }
    catch (ClassNotFoundException e) { System.out.println(e); }
    catch (NoSuchMethodException e) { System.out.println(e); }
    catch (RuntimeException e) { throw e; }
    catch (Exception e) { throw new AssertionError(); }
  }
}
```

that accepts an argument of type List<A>, returns a result of type List<B>, and again may throw an exception of type X; the method invokes the apply method on each element of the argument list to produce the result list.

The main method of the class defines three objects of this type. The first is length of type Function<String, Integer, Error>. It accepts a string and returns an integer, which is the length of the given string. Since it raises no checked exceptions, the third type is set to Error. (Setting it to RuntimeException would work as well.)

The second is forName of type Function<String, Class<?>,ClassNotFoundException>. It accepts a string and returns a class, namely the class named by the given string. The apply method may throw a ClassNotFoundException, so this is taken as the third type parameter.

The third is getRunMethod of type Function<String, Method, Exception>. It accepts a string and returns a method, namely the method named run in the class named by the given string. The body of the method might raise either a ClassNotFoundException or a NoSuchMethodException, so the third type parameter is taken to be Exception, the smallest class that contains both of these exceptions.

This last example shows the chief limitation of giving generic types to exceptions. Often there is no suitable class or interface that contains all exceptions the function may raise, and so you are forced to fall back on using Exception, which is too general to provide useful information.

The main method uses applyAll to apply each of the three functions to a list of strings. Each of the three invocations is wrapped in a try statement appropriate to the exceptions it may throw. The length function has no try statement, because it throws no checked exceptions. The forName function has a try statement with a catch clause for ClassNotFoundException, the one kind of exception it may throw. The getRunMethod function requires a try statement with catch clauses for ClassNotFoundException and NoSuchMethodException, the two kinds of exception it may throw. But the function is declared to throw type Exception, so we need two additional "catchall" clauses, one to rethrow any run-time exception that is raised, and one to assert that it is an error if any exception is raised that is not handled by the previous three clauses. For this particular example, re-raising runtime exceptions is not required, but it is good practice if there may be other code that handles such exceptions.

For example, here is a typical run of the code, printing the list of lengths, the list of classes, and the list of methods (the last list has been reformatted for readability, since it doesn't fit on one line):

```
% java Functions java.lang.Thread java.lang.Runnable
[16, 18]
[class java.lang.Thread, interface java.lang.Runnable]
[public void java.lang.Thread.run(),
 public abstract void java.lang.Runnable.run()]
```

And here is a run that raises `NoSuchMethodException`, since `java.util.List` has no run method:

```
% java Functions java.lang.Thread java.util.List
[16, 14]
[class java.lang.Thread, interface java.util.List]
java.lang.NoSuchMethodException: java.util.List.run()
```

And here is a run that raises `ClassNotFoundException`, since there is no class named `Fred`:

```
% java Functions java.lang.Thread Fred
[16, 4]
java.lang.ClassNotFoundException: Fred
java.lang.ClassNotFoundException: Fred
```

The exception is raised twice, once when applying `forName` and once when applying `getRunMethod`.

9.4 Strategy

The Strategy pattern is used to decouple a method from an object, allowing you to supply many possible instances of the method. Our discussion of the Strategy pattern illustrates a structuring technique found in many object-oriented programs, that of *parallel class hierarchies*. We will illustrate the Strategy pattern by considering how tax payers may apply different tax strategies. There will be a hierarchy for tax payers, and a related hierarchy for tax strategies. For example, there is a default strategy that applies to any tax payer. One subclass of tax payer is a trust, and one subclass of the default strategy is one that applies only to trusts.

Our discussion will also illustrate a technique often used with generic types—the use of type variables with *recursive bounds*. We have already seen this trick at work in the definition of the `Comparable` interface and the `Enum` class; here we will apply it to clarify the connection between tax payers and their associated tax strategies. We also explain the `getThis` trick, which allows us to assign a more precise type to `this` when type variables with recursive bounds appear.

First, we'll look at a basic version of the Strategy pattern, which shows how to use generics to design parallel class hierarchies. Next, we'll look at an advanced version where objects contain their own strategies, which uses type variables with recursive bounds and explains the `getThis` trick.

The example in this section was developed in discussion with Heinz M. Kabutz, and also appears in his online publication, *The Java Specialists' Newsletter*.

Parallel Class Hierarchies   A typical use of the Strategy pattern is for tax computation, as shown in Example 9.6. We have a class `TaxPayer` with subclasses `Person` and `Trust`. Every tax payer has an income, and, in addition, a trust may be nonprofit. For example, we

Example 9.6. A basic Strategy pattern with parallel class hierarchies

```java
abstract class TaxPayer {
  public long income;  // in cents
  public TaxPayer(long income) { this.income = income; }
  public long getIncome() { return income; }
}
class Person extends TaxPayer {
  public Person(long income) { super(income); }
}
class Trust extends TaxPayer {
  private boolean nonProfit;
  public Trust(long income, boolean nonProfit) {
    super(income); this.nonProfit = nonProfit;
  }
  public boolean isNonProfit() { return nonProfit; }
}

interface TaxStrategy<P extends TaxPayer> {
  public long computeTax(P p);
}
class DefaultTaxStrategy<P extends TaxPayer> implements TaxStrategy<P> {
  private static final double RATE = 0.40;
  public long computeTax(P payer) {
    return Math.round(payer.getIncome() * RATE);
  }
}
class DodgingTaxStrategy<P extends TaxPayer> implements TaxStrategy<P> {
  public long computeTax(P payer) { return 0; }
}
class TrustTaxStrategy extends DefaultTaxStrategy<Trust> {
  public long computeTax(Trust trust) {
    return trust.isNonProfit() ? 0 : super.computeTax(trust);
  }
}
```

may define a person with an income of $100,000.00 and two trusts with the same income, one nonprofit and one otherwise:

```java
Person person = new Person(10000000);
Trust nonProfit = new Trust(10000000, true);
Trust forProfit = new Trust(10000000, false);
```

In accordance with good practice, we represent all monetary values, such as incomes or taxes, by long integers standing for the value in cents (see "Item 31: Avoid float and double if exact answers are required," in *Effective Java* by Joshua Bloch, Addison-Wesley).

For each tax payer P there may be many possible strategies for computing tax. Each strategy implements the interface TaxStrategy<P>, which specifies a method computeTax that takes as argument a tax payer of type P and returns the tax paid. Class DefaultTaxStrategy computes the tax by multiplying the income by a fixed tax rate of 40 percent, while class DodgingTaxStrategy always computes a tax of zero:

```
TaxStrategy<Person> defaultStrategy = new DefaultStrategy<Person>();
TaxStrategy<Person> dodgingStrategy = new DodgingStrategy<Person>();
assert defaultStrategy.computeTax(person) == 4000000;
assert dodgingStrategy.computeTax(person) == 0;
```

Of course, our example is simplified for purposes of illustration—we do not recommend that you compute taxes using either of these strategies! But it should be clear how these techniques extend to more complex tax payers and tax strategies.

Finally, class TrustTaxStrategy computes a tax of zero if the trust is nonprofit and uses the default tax strategy otherwise:

```
TaxStrategy<Trust> trustStrategy = new TrustTaxStrategy();
assert trustStrategy.computeTax(nonProfit) == 0;
assert trustStrategy.computeTax(forProfit) == 4000000;
```

Generics allow us to specialize a given tax strategy to a given type of tax payer, and allow the compiler to detect when a tax strategy is applied to the wrong type of tax payer:

```
trustStrategy.computeTax(person); // compile-time error
```

Without generics, the computeTax method of TrustTaxStrategy would have to accept an argument of type TaxPayer and cast it to type Trust, and errors would throw an exception at run time rather than be caught at compile time.

This example illustrates a structuring technique found in many object-oriented programs—that of *parallel class hierarchies*. In this case, one class hierarchy consists of TaxPayer, Person, and Trust. A parallel class hierarchy consists of strategies corresponding to each of these: two strategies, DefaultTaxStrategy and DodgingTaxStrategy apply to any TaxPayer, no specialized strategies apply to Person, and there is one specialized strategy for Trust.

Usually, there is some connection between such parallel hierarchies. In this case, the computeTax method for a TaxStrategy that is parallel to a given TaxPayer expects an argument that is of the corresponding type; for instance, the computeTax method for TrustTaxStrategy expects an arguement of type Trust. With generics, we can capture this connection neatly in the types themselves. In this case, the computeTax method for TaxStrategy<P> expects an argument of type P, where P must be subclass of TaxPayer. Using the techniques we have described here, generics can often be used to capture similar relations in other parallel class hierarchies.

An Advanced Strategy Pattern with Recursive Generics In more advanced uses of the Strategy pattern, an object contains the strategy to be applied to it. Modelling this situation requires recursive generic types and exploits a trick to assign a generic type to this.

The revised Strategy pattern is shown in Example 9.7. In the advanced version, each tax payer object contains its own tax strategy, and the constructor for each kind of tax payer includes a tax strategy as an additional argument:

```
Person normal = new Person(10000000, new DefaultTaxStrategy<Person>());
Person dodger = new Person(10000000, new DodgingTaxStrategy<Person>());
Trust nonProfit = new Trust(10000000, true, new TrustTaxStrategy());
Trust forProfit = new Trust(10000000, false, new TrustTaxStrategy());
```

Now we may invoke a computeTax method of no arguments directly on the tax payer, which will in turn invoke the computeTax method of the tax strategy, passing it the tax payer:

```
assert normal.computeTax() == 4000000;
assert dodger.computeTax() == 0;
assert nonProfit.computeTax() == 0;
assert forProfit.computeTax() == 4000000;
```

This structure is often preferable, since one may associate a given tax strategy directly with a given tax payer.

Before, we used a class TaxPayer and an interface TaxStrategy<P>, where the type variable P stands for the subclass of TaxPayer to which the strategy applies. Now we must add the type parameter P to both, in order that the class TaxPayer<P> can have a field of type TaxStrategy<P>. The new declaration for the type variable P is necessarily recursive, as seen in the new header for the TaxPayer class:

```
class TaxPayer<P extends TaxPayer<P>>
```

We have seen similar recursive headers before:

```
interface Comparable<T extends Comparable<T>>
class Enum<E extends Enum<E>>
```

In all three cases, the class or interface is the base class of a type hierarchy, and the type parameter stands for a specific subclass of the base class. Thus, P in TaxPayer<P> stands for the specific kind of tax payer, such as Person or Trust; just as T in Comparable<T> stands for the specific class being compared, such as String; or E in Enum<E> stands for the specific enumerated type, such as Season.

The tax payer class contains a field for the tax strategy and a method that passes the tax payer to the tax strategy, as well as a recursive declaration for P just like the one used in TaxPayer. In outline, we might expect it to look like this:

```
// not well-typed!
class TaxPayer<P extends TaxPayer<P>> {
  private TaxStrategy<P> strategy;
```

```
  public long computeTax() { return strategy.computeTax(this); }
  ...
}
class Person extends TaxPayer<Person> { ... }
class Trust extends TaxPayer<Trust> { ... }
```

But the compiler rejects the above with a type error. The problem is that this has type TaxPayer<P>, whereas the argument to computeTax must have type P. Indeed, within each specific tax payer class, such as Person or Trust, it is the case that this does have type P; for example, Person extends TaxPayer<Person>, so P is the same as Person within this class. So, in fact, this will have the same type as P, but the type system does not know that!

We can fix this problem with a trick. In the base class TaxPayer<P> we define an abstract method getThis that is intended to return the same value as this but gives it the type P. The method is instantiated in each class that corresponds to a specific kind of tax payer, such as Person or Trust, where the type of this is indeed the same as the type P. In outline, the corrected code now looks like this:

```
// now correctly typed
abstract class TaxPayer<P extends TaxPayer<P>> {
  private TaxStrategy<P> strategy;
  protected abstract P getThis();
  public long computeTax() { return strategy.computeTax(getThis()); }
  ...
}
final class Person extends TaxPayer<Person> {
  protected Person getThis() { return this; }
  ...
}
final class Trust extends TaxPayer<Trust> {
  protected Trust getThis() { return this; }
  ...
}
```

The differences from the previous code are in bold. Occurences of this are replaced by calls to getThis; the method getThis is declared abstract in the base class and it is instantiated appropriately in each final subclass of the base class. The base class TaxPayer<P> must be declared abstract because it declares the type for getThis but doesn't declare the body. The body for getThis is declared in the final subclasses Person and Trust.

Since Trust is declared final, it cannot have subclasses. Say we wanted a subclass NonProfitTrust of Trust. Then not only would we have to remove the final declaration on the class Trust, we would also need to add a type parameter to it. Here is a sketch of the required code:

```
abstract class Trust<T extends Trust> extends TaxPayer<T> { ... }
final class NonProfitTrust extends Trust<NonProfitTrust> { ... }
final class ForProfitTrust extends Trust<ForProfitTrust> { ... }
```

Example 9.7. An advanced Strategy pattern with recursive bounds

```
abstract class TaxPayer<P extends TaxPayer<P>> {
  public long income;  // in cents
  private TaxStrategy<P> strategy;
  public TaxPayer(long income, TaxStrategy<P> strategy) {
    this.income = income; this.strategy = strategy;
  }
  protected abstract P getThis();
  public long getIncome() { return income; }
  public long computeTax() { return strategy.computeTax(getThis()); }
}
class Person extends TaxPayer<Person> {
  public Person(long income, TaxStrategy<Person> strategy) {
    super(income, strategy);
  }
  protected Person getThis() { return this; }
}
class Trust extends TaxPayer<Trust> {
  private boolean nonProfit;
  public Trust(long income, boolean nonProfit, TaxStrategy<Trust> strategy){
    super(income, strategy); this.nonProfit = nonProfit;
  }
  protected Trust getThis() { return this; }
  public boolean isNonProfit() { return nonProfit; }
}

interface TaxStrategy<P extends TaxPayer<P>> {
  public long computeTax(P p);
}
class DefaultTaxStrategy<P extends TaxPayer<P>> implements TaxStrategy<P> {
  private static final double RATE = 0.40;
  public long computeTax(P payer) {
    return Math.round(payer.getIncome() * RATE);
  }
}
class DodgingTaxStrategy<P extends TaxPayer<P>> implements TaxStrategy<P> {
  public long computeTax(P payer) { return 0; }
}
class TrustTaxStrategy extends DefaultTaxStrategy<Trust> {
  public long computeTax(Trust trust) {
    return trust.isNonprofit() ? 0 : super.computeTax(trust);
  }
}
```

Now an instance of NonProfitTrust takes a strategy that expects a NonProfitTrust as an argument, and ForProfitTrust behaves similarly. It is often convenient to set up a parameterized type hierarchy in this way, where classes with subclasses take a type parameter and are abstract and classes without subclasses do not take a type parameter and are final. A body for the getThis method is declared in each final subclass.

Summary   As we have seen, recursive type parameters often appear in Java:

```
class TaxPayer<P extends TaxPayer<P>>
Comparable<T extends Comparable<T>>
class Enum<E extends Enum<E>>
```

The getThis trick is useful in this situation whenever one wants to use this in the base type with the more specific type provided by the type parameter.

We will see another example of recursive type parameters in the next section, applied to two mutually recursive classes. However, although the getThis trick is often useful, we will not require it there.

9.5 Subject-Observer

We finish with a more extended example, illustrating the generic Subject-Observer pattern. Like the Strategy pattern, the Subject-Observer pattern uses parallel class hierarchies, but this time we require two type variables with mutually recursive bounds, one to stand for the specific kind of subject and one to stand for the specific kind of observer. This is our first example of type variables with mutually recursive bounds.

The Java library implements a nongeneric version of the Subject-Observer pattern in the package java.util with the class Observable and the interface Observer (the former corresponding to the subject), signatures for which are shown in Example 9.8.

The Observable class contains methods to register observers (addObserver), to indicate that the observable has changed (setChanged), and to notify all observers of any changes (notifyObservers), among others. The notifyObservers method may accept an arbitrary argument of type Object that is to be broadcast to all the observers. The Observer interface specifies the update method that is called by notifyObservers. This method takes two parameters: the first, of type Observable, is the subject that has changed; the second, of type Object, is the broadcast argument.

The appearance of Object in a method signature often indicates an opportunity to generify. So we should expect to generify the classes by adding a type parameter, A, corresponding to the argument type. Further, we can replace Observable and Observer themselves with the type parameters S and O (for Subject and Observer). Then within the update method of the observer, you may call on any method supported by the subject S without first requiring a cast.

Example 9.9 shows how to specify corresponding generic signatures for the Observable class and the Observer interface. Here are the relevant headers:

```
public class Observable<S extends Observable<S,O,A>,
                        O extends Observer<S,O,A>,
                        A>
public interface Observer<S extends Observable<S,O,A>,
                          O extends Observer<S,O,A>,
                          A>
```

Both declarations take the same three type parameters. The declarations are interesting in that they illustrate that the scope of type parameters can be mutually recursive: all three type parameters appear in the bounds of the first two. Previously, we saw other examples of simple recursion—for instance, in the declarations of Comparable and Enum, and in the previous section on the Strategy pattern. But this is the first time we have seen mutual recursion.

Examining the bodies of the declarations, you can see that O but not S appears in the body of the Observable class and that S but not O appears in the body of the Observer interface. So you might wonder: could the declarations be simplified by dropping the type parameter S from Observable and the type parameter O from Observer? But this won't work, since you need S to be in scope in Observable so that it can be passed as a parameter to Observer, and you needs O to be in scope in Observer so that it can be passed as a parameter to Observable.

The generic declarations use stubs, as explained in Section 5.4.2. We compile the client against the generic signatures of Observable and Observer, but run the code against the class files in the standard Java distribution. We use stubs because we don't want to make any changes to the source of the library, since it is maintained by Sun.

Example 9.8. Observable and Observer before generics

```
package java.util;
public class Observable {
  public void addObserver(Observer o) {...}
  protected void clearChanged() {...}
  public int countObservers() {...}
  public void deleteObserver(Observer o) {...}
  public boolean hasChanged() {...}
  public void notifyObservers() {...}
  public void notifyObservers(Object arg) {...}
  protected void setChanged() {...}
}

package java.util;
public interface Observer {
    public void update(Observable o, Object arg);
}
```

Example 9.9. Observable and Observer with generics

```
package java.util;
class StubException extends UnsupportedOperationException {}
public class Observable<S extends Observable<S,O,A>,
                        O extends Observer<S,O,A>,
                        A>
{
  public void addObserver(O o)     { throw new StubException(); }
  protected void clearChanged()    { throw new StubException(); }
  public int countObservers()      { throw new StubException(); }
  public void deleteObserver(O o)  { throw new StubException(); }
  public boolean hasChanged()      { throw new StubException(); }
  public void notifyObservers()    { throw new StubException(); }
  public void notifyObservers(A a) { throw new StubException(); }
  protected void setChanged()      { throw new StubException(); }
}

package java.util;
public interface Observer<S extends Observable<S,O,A>,
                          O extends Observer<S,O,A>,
                          A>
{
    public void update(S o, A a);
}
```

As a demonstration client for `Observable` and `Observer`, a currency converter is presented in Examples 9.10. A screenshot of the converter is shown in Figure 9.1. The converter allows you to enter conversion rates for each of three currencies (dollars, euros, and pounds), and to enter a value under any currency. Changing the entry for a rate causes the corresponding value to be recomputed; changing the entry for a value causes all the values to be recomputed.

The client instantiates the pattern by declaring `CModel` to be a subclass of `Observable`, and `CView` to be a subinterface of `Observer`. Furthermore, the argument type is instantiated to `Currency`, an enumerated type, which can be used to inform an observer which components of the subject have changed. Here are the relevant headers:

```
enum Currency { DOLLAR, EURO, POUND }
class CModel extends Observable<CModel, CView, Currency>
interface CView extends Observer<CModel, CView, Currency>
```

The classes `RateView` and `ValueView` implement `CView`, and the class `Converter` defines the top-level frame which controls the display.

The `CModel` class has a method to set and get the rate and value for a given currency. Rates are stored in a map that assigns a rate to each currency, and the value is stored (as a long,

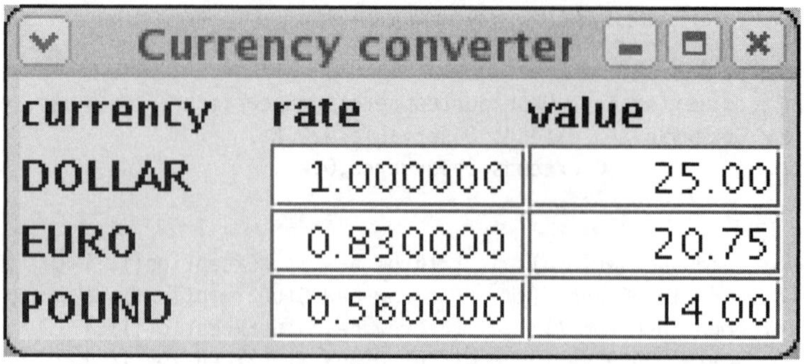

Figure 9.1: Currency converter

in cents, euro cents, or pence) together with its actual currency. To compute the value for a given currency, the value is divided by the rate for its actual currency and multiplied by the rate for the given currency.

The `CModel` class invokes the `update` method of `RateView` whenever a rate is changed, passing the corresponding currency as the argument (because only the rate and value for that currency need to be updated); and it invokes the `update` method of `ValueView` whenever a value is changed, passing null as the argument (because the values for all currencies need to be updated).

We compile and run the code as follows. First, we compile the generic versions of `Observable` and `Observer`:

```
% javac -d . java/util/Observable.java java/util/Observer.java
```

Since these are in the package `java.util`, they must be kept in the subdirectory `java/util` of the current directory. Second, we compile `Converter` and related classes in package `com.eg.converter`. By default, the Java compiler first searches the current directory for class files (even for the standard library). So the compiler uses the stub class files generated for `Observable` and `Observer`, which have the correct generic signature (but no runnable code):

```
% javac -d . com/eg/converter/Converter.java
```

Third, we run the class file for the converter. By default, the java runtime does *not* first search the current directory for class files in the packages `java` and `javax`—for reasons of security, these are always taken from the standard library. So the runtime uses the standard class files for `Observable` and `Observer`, which contain the legacy code we want to run (but do not have the correct generic signature):

```
% java com.eg.converter.Converter
```

Example 9.10. Currency converter

```
import java.util.*;
import javax.swing.*;
import javax.swing.event.*;
import java.awt.*;
import java.awt.event.*;

enum Currency { DOLLAR, EURO, POUND }

class CModel extends Observable<CModel,CView,Currency> {
  private final EnumMap<Currency,Double> rates;
  private long value = 0;  // cents, euro cents, or pence
  private Currency currency = Currency.DOLLAR;
  public CModel() {
    rates = new EnumMap<Currency,Double>(Currency.class);
  }
  public void initialize(double... initialRates) {
    for (int i=0; i<initialRates.length; i++)
      setRate(Currency.values()[i], initialRates[i]);
  }
  public void setRate(Currency currency, double rate) {
    rates.put(currency, rate);
    setChanged();
    notifyObservers(currency);
  }
  public void setValue(Currency currency, long value) {
    this.currency = currency;
    this.value = value;
    setChanged();
    notifyObservers(null);
  }
  public double getRate(Currency currency) {
    return rates.get(currency);
  }
  public long getValue(Currency currency) {
    if (currency == this.currency)
      return value;
    else
      return Math.round(value * getRate(currency) / getRate(this.currency));
  }
}
```

Example 9.10. Currency converter (continued)

```java
interface CView extends Observer<CModel,CView,Currency> {}

class RateView extends JTextField implements CView {
  private final CModel model;
  private final Currency currency;

  public RateView(final CModel model, final Currency currency) {
    this.model = model;
    this.currency = currency;
    addActionListener(new ActionListener() {
        public void actionPerformed(ActionEvent e) {
          try {
            double rate = Double.parseDouble(getText());
            model.setRate(currency, rate);
          } catch (NumberFormatException x) {}
        }
      });
    model.addObserver(this);
  }

  public void update(CModel model, Currency currency) {
    if (this.currency == currency) {
      double rate = model.getRate(currency);
      setText(String.format("%10.6f", rate));
    }
  }
}
```

Example 9.10. Currency converter (continued)

```java
class ValueView extends JTextField implements CView {
  private final CModel model;
  private final Currency currency;

  public ValueView(final CModel model, final Currency currency) {
    this.model = model;
    this.currency = currency;
    addActionListener(new ActionListener() {
        public void actionPerformed(ActionEvent e) {
          try {
            long value = Math.round(100.0*Double.parseDouble(getText()));
            model.setValue(currency, value);
          } catch (NumberFormatException x) {}
        }
      });
    model.addObserver(this);
  }

  public void update(CModel model, Currency currency) {
    if (currency == null || currency == this.currency) {
      long value = model.getValue(this.currency);
      setText(String.format("%15d.%02d", value/100, value%100));
    }
  }
}
```

Example 9.10. Currency converter (continued)

```java
class Converter extends JFrame {
  public Converter() {
    CModel model = new CModel();
    setTitle("Currency converter");
    setLayout(new GridLayout(Currency.values().length+1, 3));
    add(new JLabel("currency"));
    add(new JLabel("rate"));
    add(new JLabel("value"));
    for (Currency currency : Currency.values()) {
      add(new JLabel(currency.name()));
      add(new RateView(model, currency));
      add(new ValueView(model, currency));
    }
    model.initialize(1.0, 0.83, 0.56);
    setDefaultCloseOperation(JFrame.EXIT_ON_CLOSE);
    pack();
  }
  public static void main(String[] args) {
    new Converter().setVisible(true);
  }
}
```

So when we use stubs for standard library classes, we do not need to alter the classpath, as we did in Section 5.4.2, because the correct behavior is obtained by default. (If you do want to alter the standard library classes at runtime, you can use the -Xbootclasspath flag.)

This concludes our discussion of generics. You now have a thorough grounding that enables you to use generic libraries defined by others, to define your own libraries, to evolve legacy code to generic code, to understand restrictions on generics and avoid the pitfalls, to use checking and specialization where needed, and to exploit generics in design patterns.

One of the most important uses of generics is the Collection Framework, and in the next part of this book we will show you how to effectively use this framework and improve your productivity as a Java programmer.

PART II

Collections

The Java Collections Framework is a set of interfaces and classes in the packages `java.util` and `java.util.concurrent`. They provide client programs with various models of how to organize their objects, and various implementations of each model. These models are sometimes called *abstract data types*, and we need them because different programs need different ways of organizing their objects. In one situation, you might want to organize your program's objects in a sequential list because their ordering is important and there are duplicates. In another, a set might be the right data type because now ordering is unimportant and you want to discard the duplicates. These two data types (and others) are represented by different interfaces in the Collections Framework, and we will look at examples of their use in this chapter. But that's not all; none of these data types has a single "best" implementation—that is, one implementation that is better than all the others for all the operations. For example, a linked list may be better than an array implementation of lists for inserting and removing elements from the middle, but much worse for random access. So choosing the right implementation for your program involves knowing how it will be used as well as what is available.

This part of the book starts with an overview of the Framework and then looks in detail at each of the main interfaces and the standard implementations of them. Finally we will look at the special-purpose implementation and generic algorithms provided in the `Collections` class.

CHAPTER 10

The Main Interfaces of the Java Collections Framework

Figure 10.1 shows the main interfaces of the Java Collections Framework, together with one other—Iterable—which is outside the Framework but is an essential adjunct to it. Its purpose is as follows:

- Iterable defines the contract that a class has to fulfill for its instances to be usable with the *foreach* statement.

And the Framework interfaces have the following purposes:

- Collection contains the core functionality required of any collection other than a map. It has no direct concrete implementations; the concrete collection classes all implement one of its subinterfaces as well.

- Set is a collection, without duplicates, in which order is not significant. SortedSet automatically sorts its elements and returns them in order. NavigableSet extends this, adding methods to find the closest matches to a target element.

- Queue is a collection designed to accept elements at its *tail* for processing, yielding them up at its *head* in the order in which they are to be processed. Its subinterface Deque extends this by allowing elements to be added or removed at both head and tail. Queue and Deque have subinterfaces, BlockingQueue and BlockingDeque respectively, that support concurrent access and allow threads to be blocked, indefinitely or for a maximum time, until the requested operation can be carried out.

- List is a collection in which order is significant, accommodating duplicate elements.

- Map is a collection which uses key-value associations to store and retrieve elements. It is extended by ConcurrentMap, which provides support for concurrent access, by SortedMap, which guarantees to return its values in ascending key order, by Navigable-Map which extends SortedMap to find the closest matches to a target element, and by ConcurrentNavigableMap which extends ConcurrentMap and NavigableMap.

Chapters 12 through 16 will concentrate on each of the Collections Framework interfaces in turn. First, though, in Chapter 11, we need to cover some preliminary ideas which run through the entire Framework design.

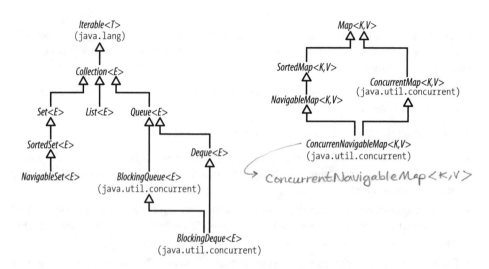

Figure 10.1: The main interfaces of the Java Collections Framework

CHAPTER 11

Preliminaries

In this chapter, we will take time to discuss the concepts underlying the framework, before we get into the detail of the collections themselves.

11.1   Iterable and Iterators

An iterator is an object that implements the interface Iterator:

```
public Iterator<E> {
  boolean hasNext();    // return true if the iteration has more elements
  E next();             // return the next element in the iteration
  void remove();        // remove the last element returned by the iterator
}
```

The purpose of iterators is to provide a uniform way of accessing collection elements sequentially, so whatever kind of collection you are dealing with, and however it is implemented, you always know how to process its elements in turn. This used to require some rather clumsy code; for example, in earlier versions of Java, you would write the following to print the string representation of a collection's contents:

```
// coll refers to an object which implements Collection
// ----- not the preferred idiom from Java 5 on -------
for (Iterator itr = coll.iterator() ; itr.hasNext() ; ) {
  System.out.println(itr.next());
}
```

The strange-looking for statement was the preferred idiom before Java 5 because, by restricting the scope of itr to the body of the loop, it eliminated accidental uses of it elsewhere. This code worked because any class implementing Collection has an iterator method which returns an iterator appropriate to objects of that class. It is no longer the approved idiom because Java 5 introduced something better: the *foreach* statement, which you met in Part I. Using *foreach*, we can write the preceding code more concisely:

```
for (Object o : coll) {
  System.out.println(o);
}
```

This code will work with anything that implements the interface Iterable—that is, anything that can produce an Iterator. This is the declaration of Iterable:

```
public Iterable<T> {
  Iterator<T> iterator();   // return an iterator over elements of type T
}
```

In Java 5 the Collection interface was made to extend Iterable, so any set, list, or queue can be the target of *foreach*, as can arrays. If you write your own implementation of Iterable, that too can be used with *foreach*. Example 11.1 shows just about the simplest possible example of how Iterable can be directly implemented. A Counter object is initialized with a count of Integer objects; its iterator returns these in ascending order in response to calls of next().

Now Counter objects can be the target of a *foreach* statement:

```
int total = 0;
for (int i : new Counter(3)) {
    total += i;
}
assert total == 6;
```

In practice, it is unusual to implement Iterable directly in this way, as *foreach* is most commonly used with arrays and the standard collections classes.

The iterators of the general-purpose collections in the Framework—ArrayList, HashMap, and so on—can puzzle novice users by throwing ConcurrentModificationException from single-threaded code. These iterators throw this exception whenever they detect that the collection from which they were derived has been structurally changed (broadly speaking, that elements have been added or removed). The motivation for this behavior is that the iterators are implemented as a view of their underlying collection so, if that collection is structurally changed, the iterator may well not be able to continue operating correctly when it reaches the changed part of the collection. Instead of allowing the manifestation of

Example 11.1. Directly implementing Iterable

```
class Counter implements Iterable<Integer> {
  private int count;
  public Counter(int count) { this.count = count; }
  public Iterator<Integer> iterator() {
    return new Iterator<Integer>() {
      private int i = 0;
      public boolean hasNext() { return i < count; }
      public Integer next() { i++; return i; }
      public void remove(){ throw new UnsupportedOperationException(); }
    };
  }
}
```

failure to be delayed, making diagnosis difficult, the general-purpose Collections Framework iterators are *fail-fast*. The methods of a fail-fast iterator check that the underlying collection has not been structurally changed (by another iterator, or by the methods of the collection itself) since the last iterator method call. If they detect a change, they throw `ConcurrentModificationException`. Although this restriction rules out some sound programs, it rules out many more unsound ones.

The concurrent collections have other strategies for handling concurrent modification, such as weakly consistent iterators. We discuss them in more detail in Section 11.5.

11.2 Implementations

We have looked briefly at the interfaces of the Collections Framework, which define the behavior that we can expect of each collection. But as we mentioned in the introduction to this chapter, there are several ways of implementing each of these interfaces. Why doesn't the Framework just use the best implementation for each interface? That would certainly make life simpler—too simple, in fact, to be anything like life really is. If an implementation is a greyhound for some operations, Murphy's Law tells us that it will be a tortoise for others. Because there is no "best" implementation of any of the interfaces, you have to make a tradeoff, judging which operations are used most frequently in your application and choosing the implementation that optimizes those operations.

The three main kinds of operations that most collection interfaces require are insertion and removal of elements by position, retrieval of elements by content, and iteration over the collection elements. The implementations provide many variations on these operations, but the main differences among them can be discussed in terms of how they carry out these three. In this section, we'll briefly survey the four main structures used as the basis of the implementations and later, as we need them, we will look at each in more detail. The four structures are:

Arrays These are the structures familiar from the Java language—and just about every other programming language since Fortran. Because arrays are implemented directly in hardware, they have the properties of random-access memory: very fast for accessing elements by position and for iterating over them, but slower for inserting and removing elements at arbitrary positions (because that may require adjusting the position of other elements). Arrays are used in the Collections Framework as the backing structure for `ArrayList`, `CopyOnWriteArrayList`, `EnumSet` and `EnumMap`, and for many of the `Queue` and `Deque` implementations. They also form an important part of the mechanism for implementing hash tables (discussed shortly).

Linked lists As the name implies, these consist of chains of linked cells. Each cell contains a reference to data and a reference to the next cell in the list (and, in some implementations, the previous cell). Linked lists perform quite differently from arrays: accessing elements by position is slow, because you have to follow the reference chain from the start of the list, but insertion and removal operations can be performed in constant time by rearranging the cell references. Linked lists are the primary backing structure used for the classes

ConcurrentLinkedQueue, LinkedBlockingQueue, and LinkedList, and the new skip list collections ConcurrentSkipListSet and ConcurrentSkipListMap. They are also used in implementing HashSet and LinkedHashSet.

Hash tables These provide a way of storing elements indexed on their content rather than on an integer-valued index, as with lists. In contrast to arrays and linked lists, hash tables provide no support for accessing elements by position, but access by content is usually very fast, as are insertion and removal. Hash tables are the backing structure for many Set and Map implementations, including HashSet and LinkedHashSet together with the corresponding maps HashMap and LinkedHashMap, as well as WeakHashMap, IdentityHashMap and ConcurrentHashMap.

Trees These also organize their elements by content, but with the important difference that they can store and retrieve them in sorted order. They are relatively fast for the operations of inserting and removing elements, accessing them by content and iterating over them. Trees are the backing structures for TreeSet and TreeMap. Priority heaps, used in the implementation of PriorityQueue and PriorityBlockingQueue, are tree-related structures.

11.3 Efficiency and the *O*-Notation

In the last section, we talked about different implementations being "good" for different operations. A good algorithm is economical in its use of two resources: time and space. Implementations of collections usually use space proportional to the size of the collection, but they can vary greatly in the time required for access and update, so that will be our primary concern. It's very hard to say precisely how quickly a program will execute, as that depends on many factors, including some that are outside the province of the programmer, such as the quality of the compiled code and the speed of the hardware. Even if we ignore these and limit ourselves to thinking only about how the execution time for an algorithm depends on its data, detailed analysis can be complex. A relatively simple example is provided in Donald Knuth's classic book *Sorting and Searching* (Addison-Wesley), where the worst-case execution time for a multiple list insertion sort program on Knuth's notional MIX machine is derived as

$$3.5N^2 + 24.5N + 4M + 2$$

where N is the number of elements being sorted and M is the number of lists.

As a shorthand way of describing algorithm efficiency, this isn't very convenient. Clearly we need a broader brush for general use. The one most commonly used is the *O-notation* (pronounced "big-oh notation"). The *O*-notation is a way of describing the performance of an algorithm in an abstract way, without the detail required to predict the precise performance of a particular program running on a particular machine. Our main reason for using it is that it gives us a way of describing how the execution time for an algorithm depends on the size of its data set, provided the data set is large enough. For example, in the previous expression the first two terms are comparable for low values of N; in fact, for $N < 8$, the second term is larger. But as N grows, the first term increasingly dominates

Table 11.1: Some common running times

Time	Common name	Effect on the running time if N is doubled	Example algorithms
$O(1)$	Constant	Unchanged	Insertion into a hash table (Section 13.1)
$O(\log N)$	Logarithmic	Increased by a constant amount	Insertion into a tree (Section 13.2.1)
$O(N)$	Linear	Doubled	Linear search
$O(N \log N)$		Doubled plus an amount proportional to N	Merge sort (Section 17.1.1)
$O(N^2)$	Quadratic	Increased fourfold	Bubble sort

the expression and, by the time it reaches 100, the first term is 15 times as large as the second one. Using a very broad brush, we say that the worst case for this algorithm takes time $O(N^2)$. We don't care too much about the coefficient because that doesn't make any difference to the single most important question we want to ask about any algorithm: what happens to the running time when the data size increases—say, when it doubles? For the worst-case insertion sort, the answer is that the running time goes up fourfold. That makes $O(N^2)$ pretty bad—worse than any we will meet in practical use in this book.

Table 11.1 shows some commonly found running times, together with examples of algorithms to which they apply. For example, many other running times are possible, including some that are much worse than those in the Figure. Many important problems can be solved only by algorithms that take $O(2^N)$—for these, when N doubles, the running time is squared! For all but the smallest data sets, such algorithms are infeasibly slow.

Sometimes we have to think about situations in which the cost of an operation varies with the state of the data structure. For example, adding an element to the end of an `ArrayList` can normally be done in constant time, unless the `ArrayList` has reached its capacity. In that case, a new and larger array must be allocated, and the contents of the old array transferred into it. The cost of this operation is linear in the number of elements in the array, but it happens relatively rarely. In situations like this, we calculate the *amortized cost* of the operation—that is, the total cost of performing it n times divided by n, taken to the limit as n becomes arbitrarily large. In the case of adding an element to an `ArrayList`, the total cost for N elements is $O(N)$, so the amortized cost is $O(1)$.

11.4 Contracts

In reading about software design, you are likely to come across the term *contract*, often without any accompanying explanation. In fact, software engineering gives this term a meaning that is very close to what people usually understand a contract to be. In everyday usage, a contract defines what two parties can expect of each other—their obligations to each other in some transaction. If a contract specifies the service that a supplier is offering to a client, the supplier's obligations are obvious. But the client, too, may have obligations—besides the obligation to pay—and failing to meet them will automatically release the supplier from her obligations as well. For example, airlines' conditions of carriage—for the class of tickets that we can afford, anyway—release them from the obligation to carry passengers who have failed to turn up on time. This allows the airlines to plan their service on the assumption that all the passengers they are carrying are punctual; they do not have to incur extra work to accommodate clients who have not fulfilled their side of the contract.

Contracts work just the same way in software. If the contract for a method states preconditions on its arguments (i.e., the obligations that a client must fulfill), the method is required to return its contracted results only when those preconditions are fulfilled. For example, binary search (see Section 17.1.4) is a fast algorithm to find a key within an ordered list, and it fails if you apply it to an unordered list. So the contract for `Collections.binarySearch` can say, "if the list is unsorted, the results are undefined", and the implementer of binary search is free to write code which, given an unordered list, returns random results, throws an exception, or even enters an infinite loop. In practice, this situation is relatively rare in the contracts of the core API because, instead of restricting input validity, they mostly allow for error states in the preconditions and specify the exceptions that the method must throw if it gets bad input. This design may be appropriate for general libraries such as the Collections Framework, which will be very heavily used in widely varying situations and by programmers of widely varying ability. You should probably avoid it for less-general libraries, because it restricts the flexibility of the supplier unnecessarily. In principle, all that a client should need to know is how to keep to its side of the contract; if it fails to do that, all bets are off and there should be no need to say exactly what the supplier will do.

It's good practice in Java to code to an interface rather than to a particular implementation, so as to provide maximum flexibility in choosing implementations. For that to work, what does it imply about the behavior of implementations? If your client code uses methods of the `List` interface, for example, and at run time the object doing the work is actually an `ArrayList`, you need to know that the assumptions you have made about how `List`s behave are true for `ArrayList`s also. So a class implementing an interface has to fulfill all the obligations laid down by the terms of the interface contract. Of course, a weaker form of these obligations is already imposed by the compiler; a class claiming to implement an interface must provide concrete method definitions matching the declarations in the interface. Contracts take this further by specifying the behavior of these methods as well.

The Collections Framework separates interface and implementation obligations in an unusual way. Some API methods return collections with restricted functionality—for example, the set of keys that you can obtain from a `Map` can have elements removed but not added (see Chapter 16). Others can have elements neither added nor removed (e.g., the list view returned by `Arrays.asList`), or may be completely read-only, for example collections that have been wrapped in an unmodifiable wrapper (see Section 17.3.2). To accommodate this variety of behaviors in the Framework without an explosion in the number of interfaces, the designers labeled the modification methods in the `Collection` interface (and in the

Iterator and ListIterator interfaces) as *optional operations*. If a client tries to modify a collection using an optional operation that the collection does not implement, the method must throw UnsupportedOperationException. The advantage to this approach is that the structure of the Framework interfaces is very simple, a great virtue in a library that every Java programmer must learn. The drawback is that a client programmer can no longer rely on the contract for the interface, but has to know which implementation is being used and to consult the contract for that as well. That's so serious that you will probably never be justified in subverting interfaces in this way in your own designs.

The contract for a class spells out what a client can rely on in using it, often including performance guarantees. To fully understand the performance characteristics of a class, however, you may need to know some detail about the algorithms it uses. In this part of the book, while we concentrate mainly on contracts and how, as a client programmer, you can make use of them, we also give some further implementation detail from the platform classes where it might be of interest. This can be useful in deciding between implementations, but remember that it is not stable; while contracts are binding, one of the main advantages of using them is that they allow implementations to change as better algorithms are discovered or as hardware improvements change their relative merits. And of course, if you are using another implementation, such as GNU Classpath, algorithm details not governed by the contract may be entirely different.

11.5   Collections and Thread Safety

When a Java program is running, it is executing one or more execution streams, or *threads*. A thread is like a lightweight process, so a program simultaneously executing several threads can be thought of as a computer running several programs simultaneously, but with one important difference: different threads can simultaneously access the same memory locations and other system resources. On machines with multiple processors, truly concurrent thread execution can be achieved by assigning a processor to each thread. If, however, there are more threads than processors—the usual case—multithreading is implemented by *time slicing*, in which a processor executes some instructions from each thread in turn before switching to the next one.

There are two good reasons for using multithread programming. An obvious one, in the case of multicore and multiprocessor machines, is to share the work and get it done quicker. (This reason is becoming ever more compelling as hardware designers turn increasingly to parallelism as the way of improving overall performance.) A second one is that two operations may take varying, perhaps unknown, amounts of time, and you do not want the response to one operation to await the completion of the other. This is particularly true for the a graphical user interface (GUI), where the response to the user clicking a button should be immediate, and should not be delayed if, say, the program happens to be running a compute-intensive part of the application at the time.

Although concurrency may be essential to achieving good performance, it comes at a price. Different threads simultaneously accessing the same memory location can produce unexpected results, unless you take care to constrain their access. Consider Example 11.2,

Example 11.2. A non-thread-safe stack implementation

```
interface Stack {
  public void push(int elt);
  public int pop();
  public boolean isEmpty();
}

class ArrayStack implements Stack{
  private final int MAX_ELEMENTS = 10;
  private int[] stack;
  private int index;
  public ArrayStack() {
    stack = new int[MAX_ELEMENTS];
    index = -1;
  }
  public void push(int elt) {
    if (index != stack.length - 1) {
      index++;                                         //1
      stack[index] = elt;                              //2
    } else {
      throw new IllegalStateException("stack overflow");
    }
  }
  public int pop() {
    if (index != -1) {
      return stack[index];
      index--;
    } else {
      throw new IllegalStateException("stack underflow");
    }
  }
  public boolean isEmpty() { return index == -1; }
}
```

in which the class ArrayStack uses an array and an index to implement the interface Stack, which models a stack of int (despite the similarity of names, this example is different from Example 5.1). For ArrayStack to work correctly, the variable index should always point at the top element of the stack, no matter how many elements are added to or removed from the stack. This is an *invariant* of the class. Now think about what can happen if two threads simultaneously attempt to push an element on to the stack. As part of the push method, each will execute the lines //1 and //2, which are correct in a single-threaded environment but in a multi-threaded environment may break the invariant. For example, if thread A executes line //1, thread B executes line //1 and then line //2, and finally thread A executes line //2, only the value added by thread B will now be on the stack, and it will have overwritten the value added by thread A. The stack pointer, though, will have been incremented by two, so the value in the top position of the stack is whatever happened to be there before. This is called a *race condition*, and it will leave the program in an inconsistent state, likely to fail because other parts of it will depend on the invariant being true.

The increasing importance of concurrent programming during the lifetime of Java has led to a corresponding emphasis in the collections library on flexible and efficient concurrency policies. As a user of the Java collections, you need a basic understanding of the concurrency policies of the different collections in order to know how to choose between them and how to use them appropriately. In this section, we'll briefly outline the different ways in which the Framework collections handle concurrency, and the implications for the programmer. For a full treatment of the general theory of concurrent programming, see *Concurrent Programming in Java* by Doug Lea (Addison-Wesley), and for detail about concurrency in Java, and the collections implementations, see *Java Concurrency in Practice* by Brian Goetz et. al. (Addison-Wesley).

11.5.1 Synchronization and the Legacy Collections

Code like that in `ArrayStack` is not *thread-safe*—it works when executed by a single thread, but may break in a multi-threaded environment. Since the incorrect behavior we observed involved two threads simultaneously executing the `push` method, we could change the program to make that impossible. Using `synchronized` to modify the declaration of the `push` method will guarantee that once a thread has started to execute it, all other threads are excluded from that method until the execution is done:

```
public synchronized void push(int elt) { ... }
```

This is called *synchronizing* on a *critical section* of code, in this case the whole of the `push` method. Before a thread can execute synchronized code, it has to get the *lock* on some object—by default, as in this case, the current object. While a lock is held by one thread, another thread that tries to enter any critical section synchronized on that lock will *block*— that is, will be suspended—until it can get the lock. This synchronized version of `push` is thread-safe; in a multi-threaded environment, each thread behaves consistently with its behavior in a single-threaded environment. To safeguard the invariant and make `ArrayStack` as a whole thread-safe, the methods `pop` and `isEmpty` must also be synchronized on the same object. The method `isEmpty` doesn't write to shared data, so synchronizing it isn't required to prevent a race condition, but for a different reason. Each thread may use a separate memory cache, which means that writes by one thread may not be seen by another unless either they both take place within blocks synchronized on the same lock, or unless the variable is marked with the `volatile` keyword.

Full method synchronization was, in fact, the policy of the collection classes provided in JDK1.0: `Vector`, `Hashtable`, and their subclasses; all methods that access their instance data are synchronized. These are now regarded as legacy classes to be avoided because of the high price this policy imposes on all clients of these classes, whether they require thread safety or not. Synchronization can be very expensive: forcing threads to queue up to enter the critical section one at a time slows down the overall execution of the program, and the overhead of administering locks can be very high, especially if they are often contended.

11.5.2 JDK 1.2: Synchronized Collections and Fail-Fast Iterators

The performance cost of internal synchronization in the JDK1.0 collections led the designers to avoid it when the Collections Framework was first introduced in JDK 1.2. Instead, the platform implementations of the interfaces List, Set, and Map widened the programmer's choice of concurrency policies. To provide maximum performance for single-threaded execution, the new collections provided no concurrency control at all. (More recently, the same policy change has been made for the synchronized class StringBuffer, which was complemented in Java 5 by its unsynchronized equivalent, StringBuilder.)

Along with this change came a new concurrency policy for collection iterators. In multi-threaded environments, a thread which has obtained an iterator will usually continue to use it while other threads modify the original collection. So iterator behavior has to be considered as an integral part of a collection®s concurrency policy. The policy of the iterators for the Java 2 collections is to *fail fast*, as described in Section 11.1: every time they access the backing collection, they check it for structural modification (which, in general, means that elements have been added or removed from the collection). If they detect structural modification, they fail immediately, throwing ConcurrentModificationException rather than continuing to attempt to iterate over the modified collection with unpredictable results. Note that this fail-fast behavior is provided to help find and diagnose bugs; it is not guaranteed as part of the collection contract.

The appearance of Java collections without compulsory synchronization was a welcome development. However, thread-safe collections were still required in many situations, so the Framework provided an option to use the new collections with the old concurrency policy, by means of synchronized wrappers (see Chapter 17). These are created by calling one of the factory methods in the Collections class, supplying an unsynchronized collection which it will encapsulate. For example, to make a synchronized List, you could supply an instance of ArrayList to be wrapped. The wrapper implements the interface by delegating method calls to the collection you supplied, but the calls are synchronized on the wrapper object itself. Example 11.3 shows a synchronized wrapper for the interface Stack of Example 11.2. To get a thread-safe Stack, you would write:

```
Stack threadSafe = new SynchronizedArrayStack(new ArrayStack());
```

This is the preferred idiom for using synchronized wrappers; the only reference to the wrapped object is held by the wrapper, so all calls on the wrapped object will be synchronized on the same lock—that belonging to the wrapper object itself. It's important to have the synchronized wrappers available, but you won't use them more than you have to, because they suffer the same performance disadvantages as the legacy collections.

Example 11.3. A synchronized wrapper for `ArrayStack`

```
public class SynchronizedArrayStack implements Stack {
  private final Stack stack;
  public SynchronizedArrayStack(Stack stack) {
    this.stack = stack;
  }
  public synchronized void push(int elt) { stack.push(elt); }
  public synchronized int pop() { return stack.pop(); }
  public synchronized boolean isEmpty() { return stack.isEmpty(); }
}
```

Using Synchronized Collections Safely Even a class like `SynchronizedArrayStack`, which has fully synchronized methods and is itself thread-safe, must still be used with care in a concurrent environment. For example, this client code is not thread-safe:

```
Stack stack = new SynchronizedArrayStack(new ArrayStack());
...
// don't do this in a multi-threaded environment
if (!stack.isEmpty()) {
  stack.pop();                 // can throw IllegalStateException
}
```

The exception would be raised if the last element on the stack were removed by another thread in the time between the evaluation of `isEmpty` and the execution of `pop`. This is an example of a common concurrent program bug, sometimes called *test-then-act*, in which program behavior is guided by information that in some circumstances will be out of date. To avoid it, the test and action must be executed atomically. For synchronized collections (as for the legacy collections), this must be enforced with *client-side locking*:

```
synchronized(stack) {
  if (!stack.isEmpty()) {
    stack.pop();
  }
}
```

For this technique to work reliably, the lock that the client uses to guard the atomic action should be the same one that is used by the methods of the synchronized wrapper. In this example, as in the synchronized collections, the methods of the wrapper are synchronized on the wrapper object itself. (An alternative is to confine references to the collection within a single client, which enforces its own synchronization discipline. But this strategy has limited applicability.)

Client-side locking ensures thread-safety, but at a cost: since other threads cannot use any of the collection's methods while the action is being performed, guarding a long-lasting action (say, iterating over an entire array) will have an impact on throughput. This impact can be very large if the synchronized methods are heavily used; unless your application needs a feature of the synchronized collections, such as exclusive locking, the Java 5 concurrent collections are almost always a better option.

11.5.3 Concurrent Collections: Java 5 and Beyond

Java 5 introduced thread-safe concurrent collections as part of a much larger set of concurrency utilities, including primitives—atomic variables and locks—which give the Java programmer access to relatively recent hardware innovations for managing concurrent threads, notably *compare-and-swap* operations, explained below. The concurrent collections remove the necessity for client-side locking as described in the previous section—in fact, external synchronization is not even possible with these collections, as there is no one object which when locked will block all methods. Where operations need to be atomic—for example, inserting an element into a Map only if it is currently absent—the concurrent collections provide a method specified to perform atomically—in this case, ConcurrentMap.putIfAbsent.

If you need thread safety, the concurrent collections generally provide much better performance than synchronized collections. This is primarily because their throughput is not reduced by the need to serialize access, as is the case with the synchronized collections. Synchronized collections also suffer the overhead of managing locks, which can be high if there is much contention. These differences can lead to efficiency differences of two orders of magnitude for concurrent access by more than a few threads.

Mechanisms The concurrent collections achieve thread-safety by several different mechanisms. The first of these—the only one that does not use the new primitives—is *copy-on-write*. Classes that use copy-on-write store their values in an internal array, which is effectively immutable; any change to the value of the collection results in a new array being created to represent the new values. Synchronization is used by these classes, though only briefly, during the creation of a new array; because read operations do not need to be synchronized, copy-on-write collections perform well in the situations for which they are designed—those in which reads greatly predominate over writes. Copy-on-write is used by the collection classes CopyOnWriteArrayList and CopyOnWriteArraySet.

A second group of thread-safe collections relies on compare-and-swap (CAS), a fundamental improvement on traditional synchronization. To see how it works, consider a computation in which the value of a single variable is used as input to a long-running calculation whose eventual result is used to update the variable. Traditional synchronization makes the whole computation atomic, excluding any other thread from concurrently accessing the variable. This reduces opportunities for parallel execution and hurts throughput. An algorithm based on CAS behaves differently: it makes a local copy of the variable and performs the calculation without getting exclusive access. Only when it is ready to update the variable does it call CAS, which in one atomic operation compares the variable's value with its value at the start and, if they are the same, updates it with the new value. If they are not the same, the variable must have been modified by another thread; in this situation, the CAS thread can try the whole computation again using the new value, or give up, or—in some algorithms—

continue, because the interference will have actually done its work for it! Collections using CAS include `ConcurrentLinkedQueue` and `ConcurrentSkipListMap`.

The third group uses implementations of `java.util.concurrent.locks.Lock`, an interface introduced in Java 5 as a more flexible alternative to classical synchronization. A `Lock` has the same basic behavior as classical synchronization, but a thread can also acquire it under special conditions: only if the lock is not currently held, or with a timeout, or if the thread is not interrupted. Unlike synchronized code, in which an object lock is held while a code block or a method is executed, a `Lock` is held until its `unlock` method is called. Some of the collection classes in this group make use of these facilities to divide the collection into parts that can be separately locked, giving improved concurrency. For example, `LinkedBlockingQueue` has separate locks for the head and tail ends of the queue, so that elements can be added and removed in parallel. Other collections using these locks include `ConcurrentHashMap` and most of the implementations of `BlockingQueue`.

Iterators The mechanisms described above lead to iterator policies more suitable for concurrent use than fail-fast, which implicitly regards concurrent modification as a problem to be eliminated. Copy-on-write collections have *snapshot iterators*. These collections are backed by arrays which, once created, are never changed; if a value in the collection needs to be changed, a new array is created. So an iterator can read the values in one of these arrays (but never modify them) without danger of them being changed by another thread. Snapshot iterators do not throw `ConcurrentModificationException`.

Collections which rely on CAS have *weakly consistent* iterators, which reflect some but not necessarily all of the changes that have been made to their backing collection since they were created. For example, if elements in the collection have been modified or removed before the iterator reaches them, it definitely will reflect these changes, but no such guarantee is made for insertions. Weakly consistent iterators also do not throw `ConcurrentModificationException`.

The third group described above also mostly have weakly consistent iterators. Two concurrent queues, `DelayQueue` and `PriorityLockingQueue`, have fail-fast iterators, because the priority heaps on which they are based can reorder many elements during insertion. In effect, this means that you cannot iterate over one of these queues unless it is quiescent, at a time when no elements are being added or inserted; at other times you should copy its elements into an array using `toArray` and iterate over that instead.

CHAPTER 12

The Collection Interface

The interface `Collection` (see Figure 12.1) defines the core functionality that we expect of any collection other than a map. It provides methods in four groups.

Adding Elements

```
boolean add(E e)                       // add the element e
boolean addAll(Collection<? extends E> c)  // add the contents of c
```

The boolean result returned by these methods indicates whether the collection was changed by the call. It can be false for collections, such as sets, which will be unchanged if they are asked to add an element that is already present. But the method contracts specify that the elements being added must be present after execution so, if the collection refuses an element for any other reason (for example, some collections don't permit `null` elements), these methods must throw an exception.

Collection<E>
+add(o : E) : boolean
+addAll(c : Collection<? extends E>) : boolean
+remove(o : Object) : boolean
+clear() : void
+removeAll(c : Collection<?>) : boolean
+retainAll(c : Collection<?>) : boolean
+contains(o : Object) : boolean
+containsAll(c : Collection<?>) : boolean
+isEmpty() : boolean
+size() : int
+iterator() : Iterator<E>
+toArray() : Object[]
+<T>toArray(T[] a) : T[]

Figure 12.1: Collection

The signatures of these methods show that, as you might expect, you can add elements or element collections only of the parametric type.

Removing Elements

```
boolean remove(Object o)              // remove the element o
void clear()                          // remove all elements
boolean removeAll(Collection<?> c)    // remove the elements in c
boolean retainAll(Collection<?> c)    // remove the elements *not* in c
```

If the element o is null, remove removes a null from the collection if one is present. Otherwise, if an element e is present for which o.equals(e), it removes it. If not, it leaves the collection unchanged. Where a method in this group returns a boolean, the value is true if the collection changed as a result of applying the operation.

In contrast to the methods for adding elements, these methods—and those of the next group—will accept elements or element collections of any type. We will explain this in a moment, when we look at examples of the use of these methods.

Querying the Contents of a Collection

```
boolean contains(Object o)              // true if o is present
boolean containsAll(Collection<?> c)    // true if all elements of c
                                        // are present in the collection
boolean isEmpty()                       // true if no elements are present
int size()                              // return the element count (or
                                        // Integer.MAX_VALUE if that is less)
```

The decision to make size return Integer.MAX_VALUE for extremely large collections was probably taken on the assumption that such collections—with more than two billion elements—will rarely arise. Even so, an alternative design which raises an exception instead of returning an arbitrary value would have the merit of ensuring that the contract for size could clearly state that if it does succeed in returning a value, that value will be correct.

Making a Collection's Contents Available for Further Processing

```
Iterator<E> iterator()       // return an Iterator over the elements
Object[] toArray()           // copy contents to an Object[]
<T> T[] toArray(T[] t)       // copy contents to a T[] (for any T)
```

The last two methods in this group convert collections into arrays. The first method will create a new array of Object, and the second takes an array of T and returns an array of the same type containing the elements of the collection.

These methods are important because, although arrays should now be regarded as a legacy data type (see Section 6.9), many APIs, especially older ones that predate the Java Collections Framework, have methods that accept or return arrays.

As discussed in Section 6.4, the argument of the second method is required in order to provide at run time the reifiable type of the array, though it can have another purpose as well: if there is room, the elements of the collection are placed in it—otherwise, a new array of that type is created. The first case can be useful if you want to allow the `toArray` method to reuse an array that you supply; this can be more efficient, particularly if the method is being called repeatedly. The second case is more convenient—a common and straightforward idiom is to supply an array of zero length:

```
Collection<String> cs = ...
String[] sa = cs.toArray(new String[0]);
```

A more efficient alternative, if a class uses this idiom more than once, is to declare a single empty array of the required type, that can then be used as many times as required:

```
private static final String[] EMPTY_STRING_ARRAY = new String[0];
Collection<String> cs = ...
String[] sa = cs.toArray(EMPTY_STRING_ARRAY);
```

Why is *any* type allowed for T in the declaration of `toArray`? One reason is to give the flexibility to allocate a more specific array type if the collection happens to contain elements of that type:

```
List<Object> l = Array.asList("zero","one");
String[] a = l.toArray(new String[0]);
```

Here, a list of objects happens to contain only strings, so it can be converted into a string array, in an operation analogous to the `promote` method described in Section 6.2.

If the list contains an object that is not a string, the error is caught at run time rather than compile time:

```
List<Object> l = Array.asList("zero","one",2);
String[] a = l.toArray(new String[0]);  // run-time error
```

Here, the call raises `ArrayStoreException`, the exception that occurs if you try to assign to an array with an incompatible reified type.

In general, one may want to copy a collection of a given type into an array of a more specific type (for instance, copying a list of objects into an array of strings, as we showed earlier), or of a more general type (for instance, copying a list of strings into an array of objects). One would never want to copy a collection of a given type into an array of a completely unrelated type (for instance, copying a list of integers into an array of strings is always wrong). However, there is no way to specify this constraint in Java, so such errors are caught at run time rather than compile time.

One drawback of this design is that it does not work with arrays of primitive type:

```
List<Integer> l = Array.asList(0,1,2);
int[] a = l.toArray(new int[0]);  // compile-time error
```

This is illegal because the type parameter T in the method call must, as always, be a reference type. The call would work if we replaced both occurrences of `int` with `Integer`, but often this will not do because, for performance or compatibility reasons, we require an array of primitive type. In such cases, there is nothing for it but to copy the array explicitly:

```
List<Integer> l = Array.asList(0,1,2);
int[] a = new int[l.size()];
for (int i=0; i<l.size(); i++) a[i] = l.get(i);
```

The Collections Framework does not include convenience methods to convert collections to arrays of primitive type. Fortunately, this requires only a few lines of code.

12.1 Using the Methods of Collection

To illustrate the use of the collection classes, let's construct a tiny example. Your authors are forever trying to get organized; let's imagine that our latest effort involves writing our own to-do manager. We begin by defining a class to represent tasks, and subclasses to represent different kinds of tasks, such as writing some code or making a phone call.

Here is the definition of tasks that we shall use:

```
public abstract class Task implements Comparable<Task> {
  protected Task() {}
  public boolean equals(Object o) {
    if (o instanceof Task) {
      return toString().equals(o.toString());
    } else return false;
  }
  public int compareTo(Task t) {
    return toString().compareTo(t.toString());
  }
  public int hashCode() {
    return toString().hashCode();
  }
  public abstract String toString();
}
```

We only require four operations on tasks: equals, compareTo, hashCode and toString. Equality will be used to test whether a collection contains a given task, comparison will be used to by ordered collections (such as OrderedSet and OrderedMap) and the hash code will be used by collections based on hash tables (such as HashSet and HashMap), and the string representation of a task will be used whenever we show the contents of a collection. The first three methods are defined in terms of the toString method, which is declared abstract, so it must be defined in each subclass of Task. We consider two tasks equal if they are represented by the same string, and the natural ordering on tasks is the same as the ordering on their strings. This guarantees that the natural ordering on tasks is consistent with equality, as discussed in Section 3.1—that is, compareTo returns 0 exactly when equals returns true.

We define subclasses for two kinds of tasks, writing some code and making a phone call:

```
public final class CodingTask extends Task {
  private final String spec;
  public CodingTask(String spec) {
    this.spec = spec;
  }
  public String getSpec() { return spec; }
  public String toString() { return "code " + spec; }
}


public final class PhoneTask extends Task {
  private final String name;
  private final String number;
  public PhoneTask(String name, String number) {
    this.name = name;
    this.number = number;
  }
  public String getName() { return name; }
  public String getNumber() { return number; }
  public String toString() { return "phone " + name; }
}
```

A coding task is specified by a string, and a phone task is specified by the name and number of the person to be called. In each case we provide a constructor for the class, methods to access its fields, and a way to convert it to a string. In accordance with good practice, we have made both kinds of task immutable by declaring the fields to be final, and we have declared both subclasses to be final so that no one can later define mutable subclasses (see "Item 13: Favor immutability", in *Effective Java* by Joshua Bloch, Addison-Wesley).

The toString method prefaces every coding task with the string "code" and every phone task with the string "phone". Since the first precedes the second in alphabetic order, and since tasks are ordered according to the results returned by toString, it follows that coding tasks come before phone tasks in the natural ordering on tasks. This suits our needs—we are geeks, after all!

For compactness, the toString method on phone tasks only returns the name of the person to call and not the phone number. We assume we never create two phone tasks with the same name and different numbers; if we did, it would be wrong to test equality using the result returned by toString.

We also define an empty task:

```
public class EmptyTask extends Task {
  public EmptyTask() {}
  public String toString() { return ""; }
}
```

Example 12.1. Example tasks and task collections for the task manager

```
PhoneTask mikePhone = new PhoneTask("Mike", "987 6543");
PhoneTask paulPhone = new PhoneTask("Paul", "123 4567");
CodingTask databaseCode = new CodingTask("db");
CodingTask interfaceCode = new CodingTask("gui");
CodingTask logicCode = new CodingTask("logic");

Collection<PhoneTask> phoneTasks = new ArrayList<PhoneTask>();
Collection<CodingTask> codingTasks = new ArrayList<CodingTask>();
Collection<Task> mondayTasks = new ArrayList<Task>();
Collection<Task> tuesdayTasks = new ArrayList<Task>();

Collections.addAll(phoneTasks, mikePhone, paulPhone);
Collections.addAll(codingTasks, databaseCode, interfaceCode, logicCode);
Collections.addAll(mondayTasks, logicCode, mikePhone);
Collections.addAll(tuesdayTasks, databaseCode, interfaceCode, paulPhone);

assert phoneTasks.toString().equals("[phone Mike, phone Paul]");
assert codingTasks.toString().equals("[code db, code gui, code logic]");
assert mondayTasks.toString().equals("[code logic, phone Mike]");
assert tuesdayTasks.toString().equals("[code db, code gui, phone Paul]");
```

Since the empty string precedes all others in the natural ordering on strings, the empty task comes before all others in the natural ordering on tasks. This task will be useful when we construct range views of sorted sets (see Section 13.2).

Example 12.1 shows how we can define a series of tasks to be carried out (even if, in a real system, they would be more likely to be retrieved from a database). We've chosen `ArrayList` as the implementation of `Collection` to use in this example, but we're not going to take advantage of any of the special properties of lists; we're treating `ArrayList` as an implementation of `Collection` and nothing more. As part of the retrieval process, we have organized the tasks into various categories represented by lists, using the method`Collections.addAll` introduced in Section 1.4.

Now we can use the methods of `Collection` to work with these categories. The examples we present here use the methods in the order in which they were presented earlier.

Adding Elements We can add new tasks to the schedule:

```
mondayTasks.add(new PhoneTask("Ruth", "567 1234"));
assert mondayTasks.toString().equals(
  "[code logic, phone Mike, phone Ruth]");
```

or we can combine schedules together:

```
Collection<Task> allTasks = new ArrayList<Task>(mondayTasks);
allTasks.addAll(tuesdayTasks);
```

```
assert allTasks.toString().equals(
  "[code logic, phone Mike, phone Ruth, code db, code gui, phone Paul]");
```

Removing Elements   When a task is completed, we can remove it from a schedule:

```
boolean wasPresent = mondayTasks.remove(mikePhone);
assert wasPresent;
assert mondayTasks.toString().equals("[code logic, phone Ruth]");
```

and we can clear a schedule out altogether because all of its tasks have been done (yeah, right):

```
mondayTasks.clear();
assert mondayTasks.toString().equals("[]");
```

The removal methods also allow us to combine entire collections in various ways. For example, to see which tasks other than phone calls are scheduled for Tuesday, we can write:

```
Collection<Task> tuesdayNonphoneTasks = new ArrayList<Task>(tuesdayTasks);
tuesdayNonphoneTasks.removeAll(phoneTasks);
assert tuesdayNonphoneTasks.toString().equals("[code db, code gui]");
```

or to see which phone calls are scheduled for that day:

```
Collection<Task> phoneTuesdayTasks = new ArrayList<Task>(tuesdayTasks);
phoneTuesdayTasks.retainAll(phoneTasks);
assert phoneTuesdayTasks.toString().equals("[phone Paul]");
```

This last example can be approached differently to achieve the same result:

```
Collection<PhoneTask> tuesdayPhoneTasks =
  new ArrayList<PhoneTask>(phoneTasks);
tuesdayPhoneTasks.retainAll(tuesdayTasks);
assert tuesdayPhoneTasks.toString().equals("[phone Paul]");
```

Note that phoneTuesdayTasks has the type List<Task>, while tuesdayPhoneTasks has the more precise type List<PhoneTask>.

This example provides an explanation of the signatures of methods in this group and the next. We have already discussed (Section 2.6) why they take arguments of type Object or Collection<?> when the methods for adding to the collection restrict their arguments to its parametric type. Taking the example of retainAll, its contract requires the removal of those elements of this collection which do not occur in the argument collection. That gives no justification for restricting what the argument collection may contain; in the preceding example it can contain instances of any kind of Task, not just PhoneTask. And it is too narrow even to restrict the argument to collections of supertypes of the parametric type; we want the least restrictive type possible, which is Collection<?>. Similar reasoning applies to remove, removeAll, contains, and containsAll.

Querying the Contents of a Collection These methods allow us to check, for example, that the operations above have worked correctly. We are going to use assert here to make the system check our belief that we have programmed the previous operations correctly. For example the first statement will throw an AssertionError if tuesdayPhoneTasks does not contain paulPhone:

```
assert tuesdayPhoneTasks.contains(paulPhone);
assert tuesdayTasks.containsAll(tuesdayPhoneTasks);
assert mondayTasks.isEmpty();
assert mondayTasks.size() == 0;
```

Making the Collection Contents Available for Further Processing The methods in this group provide an iterator over the collection or convert it to an array.

Section 11.1 showed how the simplest—and most common—explicit use of iterators has been replaced in Java 5 by the *foreach* statement, which uses them implicitly. But there are uses of iteration with which *foreach* can't help; you must use an explicit iterator if you want to change the structure of a collection without encountering ConcurrentModification-Exception, or if you want to process two lists in parallel. For example, suppose that we decide that we don't have time for phone tasks on Tuesday. It may perhaps be tempting to use *foreach* to filter them from our task list, but that won't work for the reasons described in Section 11.1:

```
// throws ConcurrentModificationException
for (Task t : tuesdayTasks) {
  if (t instanceof PhoneTask) {
    tuesdayTasks.remove(t);
  }
}
```

Using an iterator explicitly is no improvement if you still use the Collection methods that modify the structure:

```
// throws ConcurrentModificationException
for (Iterator<Task> it = tuesdayTasks.iterator() ; it.hasNext() ; ) {
  Task t = it.next();
  if (t instanceof PhoneTask) {
    tuesdayTasks.remove(t);
  }
}
```

But using the iterator's structure-changing methods gives the result we want:

```
for (Iterator<Task> it = tuesdayTasks.iterator() ; it.hasNext() ; ) {
  Task t = it.next();
  if (t instanceof PhoneTask) {
    it.remove();
  }
}
```

Example 12.2. Merging collections using natural ordering

```java
public class MergeCollections {
  static <T extends Comparable<? super T>>
    List<T> merge(Collection<? extends T> c1, Collection<? extends T> c2)
  {
    List<T> mergedList = new ArrayList<T>();
    Iterator<? extends T> itr1 = c1.iterator();
    Iterator<? extends T> itr2 = c2.iterator();
    T c1Element = getNextElement(itr1);
    T c2Element = getNextElement(itr2);
    // each iteration will take a task from one of the iterators;
    // continue until neither iterator has any further tasks
    while (c1Element != null || c2Element != null) {
      // use the current c1 element if either the current c2
      // element is null, or both are non-null and the c1 element
      // precedes the c2 element in the natural order
      boolean useC1Element = c2Element == null ||
              c1Element != null && c1Element.compareTo(c2Element) < 0;
      if (useC1Element) {
        mergedList.add(c1Element);
        c1Element = getNextElement(itr1);
      } else {
        mergedList.add(c2Element);
        c2Element = getNextElement(itr2);
      }
    }
    return mergedList;
  }
  static <E> E getNextElement(Iterator<E> itr) {
    if (itr.hasNext()){
      E nextElement = itr.next();
      if (nextElement == null) throw new NullPointerException();
      return nextElement;
    } else {
      return null;
    }
  }
}
```

For another example, suppose we are fastidious people that like to keep all our lists of tasks in ascending order, and we want to merge two lists of tasks into a single list, while maintaining the order. Example 12.2 shows how we can merge two collections into a third, provided that the iterators of each return their elements ascending in natural order. This method relies on the fact that the collections to be merged contain no null elements; if one is encountered, the method throws a NullPointerException. As it happens, the collections mondayTasks and `tuesdayTasks` in Example 12.1 are both in ascending order, and we can merge them as follows:

```
Collection<Task> mergedTasks =
  MergeCollections.merge(mondayTasks, tuesdayTasks);
assert mergedTasks.toString().equals(
  "[code db, code gui, code logic, phone Mike, phone Paul]");
```

12.2 Implementing Collection

There are no concrete implementations of `Collection`. The class `AbstractCollection`, which partially implements it, is one of a series of skeletal implementations—including `AbstractSet`, `AbstractList`, and so on—which provide functionality common to the different concrete implementations of each interface. These skeletal implementations are available to help the designer of new implementations of the Framework interfaces. For example, `Collection` could serve as the interface for *bags* (unordered lists), and a programmer implementing bags could extend `AbstractCollection` and find most of the implementation work already done.

12.3 Collection Constructors

We will go on to look at these three main kinds of collection in the next three chapters, but we should first explain two common forms of constructor which are shared by most collection implementations. Taking `HashSet` as an example, these are:

```
public HashSet()
public HashSet(Collection<? extends E> c)
```

The first of these creates an empty set, and the second a set that will contain the elements of any collection of the parametric type—or one of its subtypes, of course. Using this constructor has the same effect as creating an empty set with the default constructor, and then adding the contents of a collection using `addAll`. This is sometimes called a "copy constructor", but that term should really be reserved for constructors which make a copy of an object of the same *class*, whereas constructors of the second form can take any object which implements the *interface* `Collection<? extends E>`. Joshua Bloch has suggested the term "conversion constructor".

Not all collection classes have constructors of both forms—`ArrayBlockingQueue`, for example, cannot be created without fixing its capacity, and `SynchronousQueue` cannot hold any elements at all, so no constructor of the second form is appropriate. In addition, many collection classes have other constructors besides these two, but which ones they have depends not on the interface they implement but on the underlying implementation; these additional constructors are used to configure the implementation.

CHAPTER 13

Sets

A *set* is a collection of items that cannot contain duplicates; adding an item if it is already present in the set has no effect. The Set interface has the same methods as those of Collection, but it is defined separately in order to allow the contract of add (and addAll, which is defined in terms of add) to be changed in this way. Returning to the task manager example in the previous chapter, suppose that on Monday you have free time to carry out your telephone tasks. You can make the appropriate collection by adding all your telephone tasks to your Monday tasks. Let mondayTasks and phoneTasks be as declared in Example 12.1. Using a set (again choosing a conveniently common implementation of Set), you can write:

```
Set<Task> phoneAndMondayTasks = new TreeSet<Task>(mondayTasks);
phoneAndMondayTasks.addAll(phoneTasks);
assert phoneAndMondayTasks.toString().equals(
  "[code logic, phone Mike, phone Paul]");
```

This works because of the way that duplicate elements are handled. The task mikePhone, which is in both mondayTasks and phoneTasks, appears as intended, only once, in phoneAndMondayTasks—you definitely don't want to have to do all such tasks twice over!

13.1 Implementing Set

When we used the methods of Collection in the examples of Chapter 12, we emphasized that they would work with any implementation of Collection. What if we had decided that we would use one of the Set implementations from the Collections Framework? We would have had to choose between the various concrete implementations that the Framework provides, which differ both in how fast they perform the basic operations of add, contains, and iteration, and in the order in which their iterators return their elements. In this section and the next we will look at these differences, then at the end of the Chapter we will summarize the comparative performance of the different implementations.

There are six concrete implementations of Set in the Collections Framework. Figure 13.1 shows their relationship to Set and its subinterfaces SortedSet and NavigableSet. In this section, we will look at HashSet, LinkedHashSet, CopyOnWriteArraySet and EnumSet.

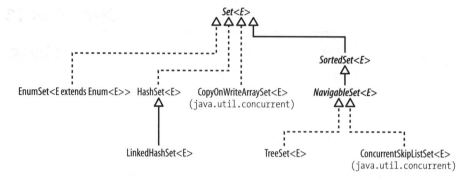

Figure 13.1: Implementations of the Set interface

We will discuss `SortedSet` and `NavigableSet`, together with their implementations, `TreeSet` and `ConcurrentSkipListSet`, in Section 13.2.

13.1.1 HashSet

This class is the most commonly used implementation of `Set`. As the name implies, it is implemented by a *hash table*, an array in which elements are stored at a position derived from their contents. Since hash tables store and retrieve elements by their content, they are well suited to implementing the operations of `Set` (the Collections Framework also uses them for various implementations of `Map`). For example, to implement `contains(Object o)` you would look for the element `o` and return `true` if it were found.

An element's position in a hash table is calculated by a *hash function* of its contents. Hash functions are designed to give, as far as possible, an even spread of results (*hash codes*) over the element values that might be stored. For example, here is code like that used in the `String` class to calculate a hash code:

```
int hash = 0;
for (char ch : str.toCharArray()) {
  hash = hash * 31 + ch;
}
```

Traditionally, hash tables obtain an index from the hash code by taking the remainder after division by the table length. The Collections Framework classes actually use bit masking rather than division. Since that means it is the pattern of bits at the low end of the hash code that is significant, prime numbers (such as 31, here) are used in calculating the hash code because multiplying by primes will not tend to shift information away from the low end—as would multiplying by a power of 2, for example.

A moment's thought will show that, unless your table has more locations than there are values that might be stored in it, sometimes two distinct values must hash to the same location in the hash table. For instance, no `int`-indexed table can be large enough to store all string values without collisions. We can minimize the problem with a good hash function—

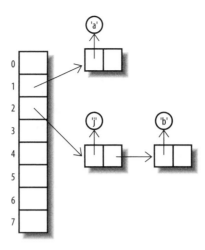

Figure 13.2: A hash table with chained overflow

one which spreads the elements out equally in the table—but, when collisions do occur, we have to have a way of keeping the colliding elements at the same table location or *bucket*. This is often done by storing them in a linked list, as shown in Figure 13.2. We will look at linked lists in more detail as part of the implementations of ConcurrentSkipListSet (see Section 13.2.2) but, for now, it's enough to see that elements stored at the same bucket can still be accessed, at the cost of following a chain of cell references. Figure 13.2 shows the situation resulting from running this code on Sun's implementation of Java 5:

```
Set<Character> s1 = new HashSet<Character>(8);
s1.add('a');
s1.add('b');
s1.add('j');
```

The index values of the table elements have been calculated by using the bottom three bits (for a table of length 8) of the hash code of each element. In this implementation, a Character's hash code is just the Unicode value of the character it contains. (In practice, of course, a hash table would be much bigger than this. Also, this diagram is simplified from the real situation; because HashSet is actually implemented by a specialized HashMap, each of the cells in the chain contains not one but two references, to a key and a value (see Chapter 16). Only the key is shown in this diagram because, when a hash table is being used to represent a set, all values are the same—only the presence of the key is significant.)

As long as there are no collisions, the cost of inserting or retrieving an element is constant. As the hash table fills, collisions become more likely; assuming a good hash function, the probability of a collision in a lightly loaded table is proportional to its *load*, defined as the number of elements in the table divided by its capacity (the number of buckets). If a collision does take place, a linked list has to be created and subsequently traversed, adding an extra cost to insertion proportional to the number of elements in the list. If the size of the hash table is fixed, performance will worsen as more elements are added and the load increases. To prevent this from happening, the table size is increased by *rehashing*—copying to a new and larger table—when the load reaches a specified threshold (its *load factor*).

Iterating over a hash table requires each bucket to be examined to see whether it is occupied and therefore costs a time proportional to the capacity of the hash table plus the number of elements it contains. Since the iterator examines each bucket in turn, the order in which elements are returned depends on their hash codes, so there is no guarantee as to the order in which the elements will be returned. The hash table shown in Figure 13.2 yields its elements in order of descending table index and forward traversal of the linked lists. Printing it produces the following output:

```
[j, b, a]
```

Later in this section we will look at `LinkedHashSet`, a variant of this implementation with an iterator that does return elements in their insertion order.

The chief attraction of a hash table implementation for sets is the (ideally) constant-time performance for the basic operations of `add`, `remove`, `contains`, and `size`. Its main disadvantage is its iteration performance; since iterating through the table involves examining every bucket, its cost is proportional to the table size regardless of the size of the set it contains.

`HashSet` has the standard constructors that we introduced in Section 12.3, together with two additional constructors:

```
HashSet(int initialCapacity)
HashSet(int initialCapacity, float loadFactor)
```

Both of these constructors create an empty set but allow some control over the size of the underlying table, creating one with a length of the next-largest power of 2 after the supplied capacity. Most of the hash table–based implementations in the Collections Framework have similar constructors, although Joshua Bloch, the original designer of the Framework, has told us that new classes will no longer usually have configuration parameters like the load factor; they are not generally useful, and they limit the possibilities of improving implementations at a later date.

`HashSet` is unsynchronized and not thread-safe; its iterators are fail-fast.

13.1.2 LinkedHashSet

This class inherits from `HashSet`, still implementing `Set` and refining the contract of its superclass in only one respect: it guarantees that its iterators will return their elements in the order in which they were first added. It does this by maintaining a linked list of the set elements, as shown by the curved arrows in Figure 13.3. The situation in the figure would result from this code:

```
Set<Character> s2 = new LinkedHashSet<Character>(8);
Collections.addAll(s2, 'a', 'b', 'j');
```

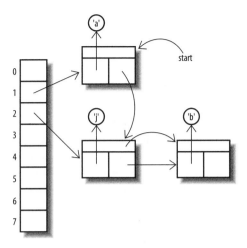

Figure 13.3: A linked hash table

```
// iterators of a LinkedHashSet return their elements in proper order:
assert s2.toString().equals("[a, b, j]");
```

The linked structure also has a useful consequence in terms of improved performance for iteration: next performs in constant time, as the linked list can be used to visit each element in turn. This is in contrast to HashSet, for which every bucket in the hash table must be visited whether it is occupied or not, but the overhead involved in maintaining the linked list means that you would choose LinkedHashSet in preference to HashSet only if the order or the efficiency of iteration were important for your application.

The constructors for LinkedHashSet provide the same facilities as those of HashSet for configuring the underlying hash table. Like HashSet, it is unsynchronized and not thread-safe; its iterators are fail-fast.

13.1.3 CopyOnWriteArraySet

In functional terms, CopyOnWriteArraySet is another straightforward implementation of the Set contract, but with quite different performance characteristics from HashSet. This class is implemented as a thin wrapper around an instance of CopyOnWriteArrayList, which in turn is backed by an array. This array is treated as immutable; a change to the contents of the set results in an entirely new array being created. So add has complexity $O(n)$, as does contains, which has to be implemented by a linear search. Clearly you wouldn't use CopyOnWriteArraySet in a context where you were expecting many searches or insertions. But the array implementation means that iteration costs $O(1)$ per element—faster than HashSet—and it has one advantage which is really compelling in some applications: it provides thread safety (see Section 11.5) without adding to the cost of read operations. This is in contrast to those collections which use locking to achieve thread safety for all operations (for example, the synchronized collections of Section 17.3.1). Such collections are a bottleneck in multi-threaded use because a thread must get exclusive access to the collection object before it can use it in any way. By contrast, read operations on copy-on-write collections are implemented on the backing array, which is never modified after its creation, so they can be used by any thread without danger of interference from a concurrent write operation.

When would you want to use a set with these characteristics? In fairly specialized cases; one that is quite common is in the implementation of the Subject-Observer design pattern (see Section 9.5), which requires events to be notified to a set of observers. This set must not be modified during the process of notification; with locking set implementations, read and write operations share the overhead necessary to ensure this, whereas with CopyOnWriteArraySet the overhead is carried entirely by write operations. This makes sense for Subject-Observer; in typical uses of this pattern, event notifications occur much more frequently than changes to the listener set.

Iterators for CopyOnWriteArraySet can be used only to read the set. When they are created, they are attached to the instance of the backing array being used by the set at that moment. Since no instance of this array should ever be modified, the iterators' remove method is not implemented. These are snapshot iterators (see Section 11.5); they reflect the state of the set at the time it was created, and can subsequently be traversed without any danger of interference from threads modifying the set from which they were derived.

Since there are no configuration parameters for CopyOnWriteArraySet, the constructors are just the standard ones discussed in Section 12.3.

13.1.4 EnumSet

This class exists to take advantage of the efficient implementations that are possible when the number of possible elements is fixed and a unique index can be assigned to each. These two conditions hold for a set of elements of the same Enum; the number of keys is fixed by the constants of the enumerated type, and the ordinal method returns values that are guaranteed to be unique to each constant. In addition, the values that ordinal returns form a compact range, starting from zero—ideal, in fact, for use as array indices or, in the standard implementation, indices of a bit vector. So add, remove, and contains are implemented as bit manipulations, with constant-time performance. Bit manipulation on a single word is extremely fast, and a long value can be used to represent EnumSets over enum types with up to 64 values. Larger enums can be treated in a similar way, with some overhead, using more than one word for the representation.

EnumSet is an abstract class that implements these different representations by means of different package-private subclasses. It hides the concrete implementation from the programmer, instead exposing factory methods that call the constructor for the appropriate subclass. The following group of factory methods provide ways of creating EnumSets with different initial contents: empty, specified elements only, or all elements of the enum.

```
<E extends Enum<E>> EnumSet<E> of(E first, E... rest)
        // create a set initially containing the specified elements
<E extends Enum<E>> EnumSet<E> range(E from, E to)
        // create a set initially containing all of the elements in
        // the range defined by the two specified endpoints
<E extends Enum<E>> EnumSet<E> allOf(Class<E> elementType)
        // create a set initially containing all elements in elementType
<E extends Enum<E>> EnumSet<E> noneOf(Class<E> elementType)
        // create a set of elementType, initially empty
```

An EnumSet contains the reified type of its elements, which is used at run time for checking the validity of new entries. This type is supplied by the above factory methods in two different ways. The methods of and range receive at least one enum argument, which can be queried for its declaring class (that is, the Enum that it belongs to). For allOf and noneOf, which have no enum arguments, a class token is supplied instead.

Common cases for EnumSet creation are optimized by the second group of methods, which allow you to efficiently create sets with one, two, three, four, or five elements of an enumerated type.

```
<E extends Enum<E>> EnumSet<E> of(E e)
<E extends Enum<E>> EnumSet<E> of(E e1, E e2)
<E extends Enum<E>> EnumSet<E> of(E e1, E e2, E e3)
<E extends Enum<E>> EnumSet<E> of(E e1, E e2, E e3, E e4)
<E extends Enum<E>> EnumSet<E> of(E e1, E e2, E e3, E e4, E e5)
```

The third set of methods allows the creation of an EnumSet from an existing collection:

```
<E extends Enum<E>> EnumSet<E> copyOf(EnumSet<E> s)
        // create an EnumSet with the same element type as s, and
        // with the same elements
<E extends Enum<E>> EnumSet<E> copyOf(Collection<E> c)
        // create an EnumSet from the elements of c, which must contain
        // at least one element
<E extends Enum<E>> EnumSet<E> complementOf(EnumSet<E> s)
        // create an EnumSet with the same element type as s,
        // containing the elements not in s
```

The collection supplied as the argument to the second version of copyOf must be nonempty so that the element type can be determined.

In use, EnumSet obeys the contract for Set, with the added specification that its iterators will return their elements in their natural order (the order in which their enum constants are declared). It is not thread-safe, but unlike the unsynchronized general-purpose collections, its iterators are not fail-fast. They may be either snapshot or weakly consistent; to be conservative, the contract guarantees only that they will be weakly consistent (see Section 11.5).

SortedSet<E>
+first() : <E>
+last() : <E>
+comparator() : Comparator<? super E>
+subSet(fromElement : <E>, toElement : <E>) : SortedSet<E>
+headSet(toElement : <E>) : SortedSet<E>
+tailSet(fromElement : <E>) : SortedSet<E>

Figure 13.4: SortedSet

13.2 SortedSet and NavigableSet

Set has one subinterface, SortedSet (Figure 13.4), which adds to the Set contract a
guarantee that its iterator will traverse the set in ascending element order. SortedSet
was itself extended in Java 6 by the interface NavigableSet (see Figure 13.5), which
adds methods to find the closest matches to a target element. The only implementation of
SortedSet before Java 6 was TreeSet, which has been retrofitted with the methods required
to implement the new interface. Since there is no platform implementation of SortedSet
in Java 6 that does not also implement NavigableSet, it makes sense to discuss them in
the same section. For new client code developed for the Java 6 platform, there is no need
to use the SortedSet interface at all, but for the benefit of readers still constrained to use
Java 5 we shall present the methods of the two interfaces separately in this section.

In Chapter 3 we saw that element ordering can either be defined by the element class itself,
if that implements Comparable, or it can be imposed by an external Comparator, supplied
by a constructor such as this one, for TreeSet:

```
TreeSet(Comparator<? super E> comparator)
```

Task does implement Comparable (its natural ordering is the natural ordering of its string
representation), so we don't need to supply a separate comparator. Now merging two ordered
lists, which was quite tricky using parallel iterators, is trivial if we get a SortedSet to do
the work. Using the task collections of Example 12.1, it requires two lines of code:

```
Set<Task> naturallyOrderedTasks = new TreeSet<Task>(mondayTasks);
naturallyOrderedTasks.addAll(tuesdayTasks);
assert naturallyOrderedTasks.toString().equals (
  "[code db, code gui, code logic, phone Mike, phone Paul]");
```

This simplicity comes at a price, though; merging two sorted lists of size n is $O(n)$, but
adding n elements to a TreeSet of size n is $O(n \log n)$.

We could use SortedSet to add some function to the to-do manager. Until now, the methods
of Collection and Set have given us no help in ordering our tasks—surely one of the
central requirements of a to-do manager. Example 13.1 defines a class PriorityTask which

Example 13.1. The class `PriorityTask`

```java
public enum Priority { HIGH, MEDIUM, LOW }
public final class PriorityTask implements Comparable<PriorityTask> {
  private final Task task;
  private final Priority priority;
  PriorityTask(Task task, Priority priority) {
    this.task = task;
    this.priority = priority;
  }
  public Task getTask() { return task; }
  public Priority getPriority() { return priority; }
  public int compareTo(PriorityTask pt) {
    int c = priority.compareTo(pt.priority);
    return c != 0 ? c : task.compareTo(pt.task);
  }
  public boolean equals(Object o) {
    if (o instanceof PriorityTask) {
      PriorityTask pt = (PriorityTask)o;
      return task.equals(pt.task) && priority.equals(pt.priority);
    } else return false;
  }
  public int hashCode() { return task.hashCode(); }
  public String toString() { return task + ": " + priority; }
}
```

attaches a priority to a task. There are three priorities, `HIGH`, `MEDIUM`, and `LOW`, declared so that `HIGH` priority comes first in the natural ordering. To compare two `PriorityTasks`, we first compare their priorities; if the priorities are unequal, the higher priority tasks comes first, and if the priorities are equal, we use the natural ordering on the underlying tasks. To test whether two `PriorityTasks` are equal, we check whether they have the same priority and the same task. These definitions ensure that the natural ordering is consistent with equals (see Section 3.1). As when we defined tasks in Section 12.1, we have followed good practice by making `PriorityTask` immutable.

The following code shows `SortedSet` working with a set of `PriorityTasks` (in fact, we have declared a `NavigableSet` so that we can use the same set in later examples. But for the moment, we will just use the methods of `SortedSet`):

```java
NavigableSet<PriorityTask> priorityTasks = new TreeSet<PriorityTask>();
priorityTasks.add(new PriorityTask(mikePhone, Priority.MEDIUM));
priorityTasks.add(new PriorityTask(paulPhone, Priority.HIGH));
priorityTasks.add(new PriorityTask(databaseCode, Priority.MEDIUM));
priorityTasks.add(new PriorityTask(interfaceCode, Priority.LOW));

assert(priorityTasks.toString()).equals(
  "[phone Paul: HIGH, code db: MEDIUM, phone Mike: MEDIUM, code gui: LOW]");
```

Could you not simply compare the priorities of the tasks, without using the string representation as a secondary key? A partial ordering like that would be useful if you want to preserve some aspects of the original ordering; for example, you might wish to sort tasks by priority but, within each priority, preserve the order in which they were added to the set. But the contract for SortedSet (and, as we shall see later, SortedMap) states that it will use the compare method of its Comparator—or, if it does not have one, the compareTo method of its elements—instead of the elements' equals method to determine when elements are distinct. This means that if a number of elements compare as the same, the set will treat them as duplicates, and all but one will be discarded.

The methods defined by the SortedSet interface fall into three groups:

Getting the First and Last Elements

```
E first()    // return the first element in the set
E last()     // return the last element in the set
```

If the set is empty, these operations throw NoSuchElementException.

Retrieving the Comparator

```
Comparator<? super E> comparator()
```

This method returns the set's comparator if it has been given one at construction time. The type Comparator<? super E> is used because a SortedSet parameterized on E can rely for ordering on a Comparator defined on any supertype of E. For example, recalling Section 3.3, a Comparator<Fruit> could be used with a SortedSet<Apple>.

Getting Range Views

```
SortedSet<E> subSet(E fromElement, E toElement)
SortedSet<E> headSet(E toElement)
SortedSet<E> tailSet(E fromElement)
```

The method subSet returns a set containing every element of the original set that is greater than or equal to fromElement and less than toElement. Similarly, the method headSet returns every element that is less than toElement, and tailSet returns every element that is greater than or equal to fromElement. Note that the arguments to these operations do not themselves have to be members of the set. The sets returned are *half-open intervals*: they are inclusive of the fromElement—provided it actually is a set member, of course—and exclusive of the toElement.

In our example, these methods could be useful in providing different views of the elements in priorityTasks. For instance, we can use headSet to obtain a view of the high- and medium-priority tasks. To do this, we need a special task that comes before all others in the task ordering; fortunately, we defined a class EmptyTask for just this purpose in Section 12.1. Using this, it is easy to extract all tasks that come before any low-priority task:

```
PriorityTask firstLowPriorityTask =
  new PriorityTask(new EmptyTask(), Priority.LOW);
```

```
SortedSet<PriorityTask> highAndMediumPriorityTasks =
  priorityTasks.headSet(firstLowPriorityTask);
assert highAndMediumPriorityTasks.toString().equals(
  "[phone Paul: HIGH, code db: MEDIUM, phone Mike: MEDIUM]");
```

In fact, because we know that tasks with empty details will never normally occur, we can also use one as the first endpoint in a half-open interval:

```
PriorityTask firstMediumPriorityTask =
  new PriorityTask(new EmptyTask(), Priority.MEDIUM);
SortedSet<PriorityTask> mediumPriorityTasks =
  priorityTasks.subSet(
    firstMediumPriorityTask, firstLowPriorityTask);
assert mediumPriorityTasks.toString().equals(
  "[code db: MEDIUM, phone Mike: MEDIUM]");
```

Not all orderings can be treated so conveniently; suppose, for example, that we want to work with the set of all the medium-priority tasks up to and including the mikePhone task. To define that set as a half-open interval, users of SortedSet would need to construct the task that immediately follows the mikePhone task in the PriorityTask ordering, and for that you would need to know that the string that succeeds "Mike" in the natural ordering is "Mike\0" (that is, "Mike" with a null character appended). Fortunately, users of NavigableSet have a much more intuitive way of defining this set, as we shall see in a moment.

Notice that the sets returned by these operations are not independent sets but new views of the original SortedSet. So we can add elements to the original set and see the changes reflected in the view:

```
PriorityTask logicCodeMedium =
  new PriorityTask(logicCode, Priority.MEDIUM);
priorityTasks.add(logicCodeMedium);
assert mediumPriorityTasks.toString().equals(
  "[code db: MEDIUM, code logic: MEDIUM, phone Mike: MEDIUM]");
```

The reverse applies also; changes in the view are reflected in the original set:

```
mediumPriorityTasks.remove(logicCodeMedium);
assert priorityTasks.toString().equals(
  "[phone Paul: HIGH, code db: MEDIUM, phone Mike: MEDIUM, code gui: LOW]");
```

To understand how this works, think of all the possible values in an ordering as lying on a line, like the number line used in arithmetic. A range is defined as a fixed segment of that line, regardless of which values are actually in the original set. So a subset, defined on a SortedSet and a range, will allow you to work with whichever elements of the SortedSet currently lie within the range.

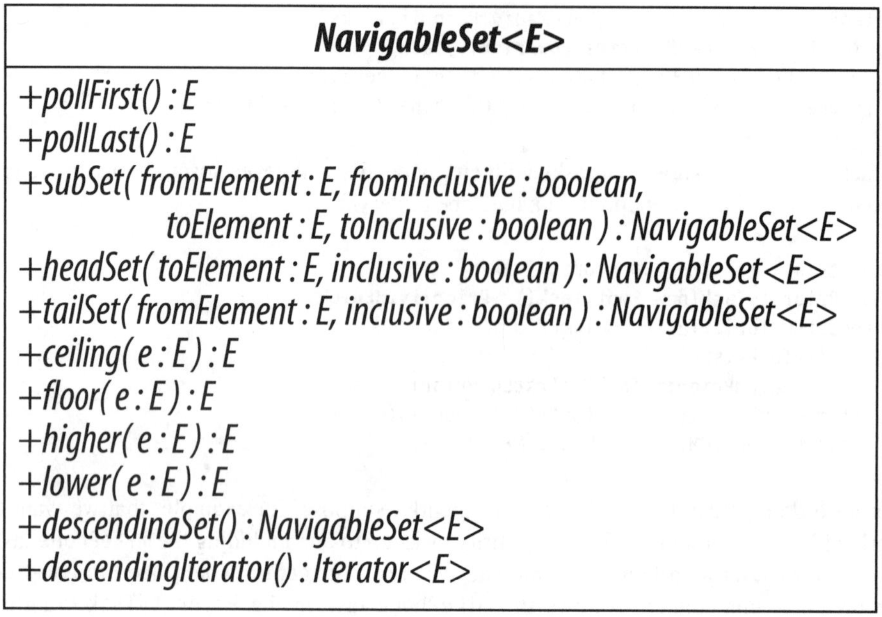

NavigableSet<E>
+pollFirst() : E
+pollLast() : E
+subSet(fromElement : E, fromInclusive : boolean,
toElement : E, toInclusive : boolean) : NavigableSet<E>
+headSet(toElement : E, inclusive : boolean) : NavigableSet<E>
+tailSet(fromElement : E, inclusive : boolean) : NavigableSet<E>
+ceiling(e : E) : E
+floor(e : E) : E
+higher(e : E) : E
+lower(e : E) : E
+descendingSet() : NavigableSet<E>
+descendingIterator() : Iterator<E>

Figure 13.5: NavigableSet

NavigableSet

NavigableSet (see Figure 13.5) was introduced in Java 6 to supplement deficiencies in SortedSet. As we mentioned at the beginning of this section, new client code should use it in preference to SortedSet. It adds methods in four groups.

Getting the First and Last Elements

```
E pollFirst()    // retrieve and remove the first (lowest) element,
                 // or return null if this set is empty
E pollLast()     // retrieve and remove the last (highest) element,
                 // or return null if this set is empty
```

These are analogous to the methods of the same name in Deque (see Section 14.4), and help to support the use of NavigableSet in applications which require queue functionality. For example, in the version of the to-do manager in this section, we could get the highest-priority task off the list, ready to be carried out, by means of this:

```
PriorityTask nextTask = priorityTasks.pollFirst();
assert nextTask.toString().equals("phone Paul: HIGH");
```

Notice that although Deque also contains methods peekFirst and peekLast—which allow clients to retrieve an element without removing it—NavigableSet has no need of them, because their functions are already supplied by the methods `first` and `last` inherited from `SortedSet`.

Getting Range Views

```
NavigableSet<E> subSet(E fromElement, boolean fromInclusive,
                                E toElement, boolean toInclusive)
NavigableSet<E> headSet(E toElement, boolean inclusive)
NavigableSet<E> tailSet(E fromElement, boolean inclusive)
```

This group is an improvement on the methods of the same name in `SortedSet`, which return subsets that are always inclusive of the lower bound and exclusive of the higher one. The `NavigableSet` methods, by contrast, allow you to specify for each bound whether it should be inclusive or exclusive. This makes it much easier to define range views over some sets. We considered earlier the set containing all the medium-priority tasks up to and including the (medium-prioritized) `mikePhone` task. To obtain that set using `SortedSet`, we would have to define it as a half-open interval, using a little-known technicality of string ordering. But `NavigableSet` allows us to define it as a closed interval simply by specifying that the higher bound should be inclusive:

```
PriorityTask mikePhoneMedium = new PriorityTask(mikePhone, Priority.MEDIUM);
NavigableSet closedInterval = priorityTasks.subSet(
  firstMediumPriorityTask, true, mikePhoneMedium, true);
assert(closedInterval.toString()).equals(
  "[code db: MEDIUM, phone Mike: MEDIUM]");
```

Getting Closest Matches

```
E ceiling(E e)   // return the least element in this set greater than
                 // or equal to e, or null if there is no such element
E floor(E e)     // return the greatest element in this set less than
                 // or equal to e, or null if there is no such element
E higher(E e)    // return the least element in this set strictly
                 // greater than e, or null if there is no such element
E lower(E e)     // return the greatest element in this set strictly
                 // less than e, or null if there is no such element
```

These methods are useful for short-distance navigation. For example, suppose that we want to find, in a sorted set of strings, the last three strings in the subset that is bounded above by "x-ray", including that string itself if it is present in the set. `NavigableSet` methods make this easy:

```
NavigableSet<String> stringSet = new TreeSet<String>();
Collections.addAll(stringSet, "abc", "cde", "x-ray" ,"zed");
String last = stringSet.floor("x-ray");
assert last.equals("x-ray");
String secondToLast =
  last == null ? null : stringSet.lower(last);
```

```
String thirdToLast =
  secondToLast == null ? null : stringSet.lower(secondToLast);
assert thirdToLast.equals("abc");
```

Notice that in line with a general trend in the design of the Collections Framework, NavigableSet returns null values to signify the absence of elements where, for example, the first and last methods of SortedSet would throw NoSuchElementException. For this reason, you should avoid null elements in NavigableSets, and in fact the newer implementation, ConcurrentSkipListSet, does not permit them (though TreeSet must continue to do so, for backward compatibility).

Navigating the Set in Reverse Order

```
NavigableSet<E> descendingSet()    // return a reverse-order view of
                                   // the elements in this set
Iterator<E> descendingIterator()   // return a reverse-order iterator
```

Methods of this group make traversing a NavigableSet equally easy in the descending (that is, reverse) ordering. As a simple illustration, let's generalise the example above using the nearest-match methods. Suppose that, instead of finding just the last three strings in the sorted set bounded above by "x-ray", we want to iterate over all the strings in that set, in descending order:

```
NavigableSet<String> headSet = stringSet.headSet(last, true);
NavigableSet<String> reverseHeadSet = headSet.descendingSet();
assert reverseHeadSet.toString().equals("[x-ray, cde, abc]");
String conc = " ";
for (String s : reverseHeadSet) {
  conc += s + " ";
}
assert conc.equals(" x-ray cde abc ");
```

If the iterative processing involves structural changes to the set, and the implementation being used is TreeSet (which has fail-fast iterators), we will have to use an explicit iterator to avoid ConcurrentModificationException:

```
for (Iterator<String> itr = headSet.descendingIterator(); itr.hasNext(); ) {
  itr.next(); itr.remove();
}
assert headSet.isempty();
```

13.2.1 TreeSet

This is the first tree implementation that we have seen, so we should take a little time now to consider how trees perform in comparison to the other implementation types used by the Collections Framework.

Trees are the data structure you would choose for an application that needs fast insertion and retrieval of individual elements but which also requires that they be held in sorted order.

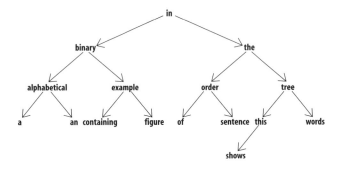

Figure 13.6: An ordered, balanced binary tree

For example, suppose you want to match all the words from a set against a given prefix, a common requirement in visual applications where a drop-down should ideally show all the possible elements that match against the prefix that the user has typed. A hash table can't return its elements in sorted order and a list can't retrieve its elements quickly by their content, but a tree can do both.

In computing, a tree is a branching structure that represents hierarchy. Computing trees borrow a lot of their terminology from genealogical trees, though there are some differences; the most important is that, in computing trees, each node has only one parent (except the root, which has none). An important class of tree often used in computing is a *binary* tree— one in which each node can have at most two children. Figure 13.6 shows an example of a binary tree containing the words of this sentence in alphabetical order.

The most important property of this tree can be seen if you look at any nonleaf node—say, the one containing the word *the*: all the nodes below that on the left contain words that precede *the* alphabetically, and all those on the right, words that follow it. To locate a word, you would start at the root and descend level by level, doing an alphabetic comparison at each level, so the cost of retrieving or inserting an element is proportional to the depth of the tree.

How deep, then, is a tree that contains n elements? The complete binary tree with two levels has three elements (that's $2^2 - 1$), and the one with three levels has seven elements ($2^3 - 1$). In general, a binary tree with n complete levels will have $2^n - 1$ elements. Hence the depth of a tree with n elements will be bounded by $\log n$ (since $2^{\log n} = n$). Just as n grows much more slowly than 2^n, $\log n$ grows much more slowly than n. So contains on a large tree is much faster than on a list containing the same elements. It's still not as good as on a hash table—whose operations can ideally work in constant time—but a tree has the big advantage over a hash table that its iterator can return its elements in sorted order.

Not all binary trees will have this nice performance, though. Figure 13.6 shows a *balanced* binary tree—one in which each node has an equal number of descendants (or as near as possible) on each side. An unbalanced tree can give much worse performance—in the worst case, as bad as a linked list (see Figure 13.7). TreeSet uses a data type called a *red-black*

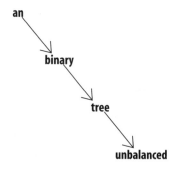

Figure 13.7: An unbalanced binary tree

tree, which has the advantage that if it becomes unbalanced through insertion or removal of an element, it can always be rebalanced in $O(\log n)$ time.

The constructors for `TreeSet` include, besides the standard ones, one which allows you to supply a `Comparator` (see Section 3.4) and one which allows you to create one from another `SortedSet`:

```
TreeSet(Comparator<? super E> c)
                // construct an empty set which will be sorted using the
                // specified comparator
TreeSet(SortedSet<E> s)
                // construct a new set containing the elements of the
                // supplied set, sorted according to the same ordering
```

The second of these is rather too close in its declaration to the standard "conversion constructor" (see Section 12.3):

```
TreeSet(Collection<? extends E> c)
```

As Joshua Bloch explains in Item 26 of *Effective Java* (Addison-Wesley), calling one of two constructor or method overloads which take parameters of related type can give confusing results. This is because, in Java, calls to overloaded constructors and methods are resolved at compile time on the basis of the static type of the argument, so applying a cast to an argument can make a big difference to the result of the call, as the following code shows:

```
// construct and populate a verb$NavigableSet$ whose iterator returns its
// elements in the reverse of natural order:
NavigableSet<String> base = new TreeSet<String>(Collections.reverseOrder());
Collections.addAll(base, "b", "a", "c");

// call the two different constructors for verb$TreeSet$, supplying the
// set just constructed, but with different static types:
NavigableSet<String> sortedSet1 = new TreeSet<String>((Set<String>)base);
NavigableSet<String> sortedSet2 = new TreeSet<String>(base);
```

```
// and the two sets have different iteration orders:
List<String> forward = new ArrayList<String>();
forward.addAll(sortedSet1);
List<String> backward = new ArrayList<String>();
backward.addAll(sortedSet2);
assert !forward.equals(backward);
Collections.reverse(forward);
assert forward.equals(backward);
```

This problem afflicts the constructors for all the sorted collections in the Framework (TreeSet, TreeMap, ConcurrentSkipListSet, and ConcurrentSkipListMap). To avoid it in your own class designs, choose parameter types for different overloads so that an argument of a type appropriate to one overload cannot be cast to the type appropriate to a different one. If that is not possible, the two overloads should be designed to behave identically with the same argument, regardless of its static type. For example, a PriorityQueue (Section 14.2.1) constructed from a collection uses the ordering of the original, whether the static type with which the constructor is supplied is one of the Comparator-containing types PriorityQueue or SortedSet, or just a plain Collection. To achieve this, the conversion constructor uses the Comparator of the supplied collection, only falling back on natural ordering if it does not have one.

TreeSet is unsynchronized and not thread-safe; its iterators are fail-fast.

13.2.2 ConcurrentSkipListSet

ConcurrentSkipListSet was introduced in Java 6 as the first concurrent set implementation. It is backed by a *skip list*, a modern alternative to the binary trees of the previous section. A skip list for a set is a series of *linked lists*, each of which is a chain of cells consisting of two fields: one to hold a value, and one to hold a reference to the next cell. Elements are inserted into and removed from a linked list in constant time by pointer rearrangement, as shown in Figure 13.8, parts (a) and (b) respectively.

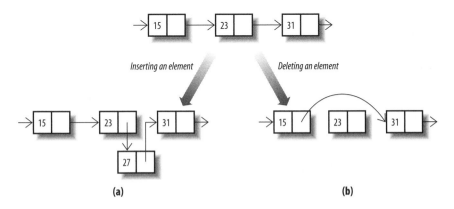

Figure 13.8: Modifying a linked list

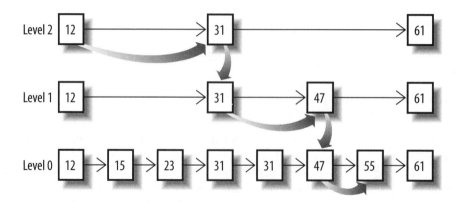

Figure 13.9: Searching a skip list

Figure 13.9 shows a skip list consisting of three linked lists, labelled levels 0, 1 and 2. The first linked list of the collection (level 0 in the figure) contains the elements of the set, sorted according to their natural order or by the comparator of the set. Each list above level 0 contains a subset of the list below, chosen randomly according to a fixed probability. For this example, let's suppose that the probability is 0.5; on average, each list will contain half the elements of the list below it. Navigating between links takes a fixed time, so the quickest way to find an element is to start at the beginning (the left-hand end) of the top list and to go as far as possible on each list before dropping to the one below it.

The curved arrows of Figure 13.9 shows the progress of a search for the element 55. The search starts with the element 12 at the top left of level 2, steps to the element 31 on that level, then finds that the next element is 61, higher than the search value. So it drops one level, and then repeats the process; element 47 is still smaller than 55, but 61 is again too large, so it once more drops a level and finds the search value in one further step.

Inserting an element into a skip list always involves at least inserting it at level 0. When that has been done, should it also be inserted at level 1? If level 1 contains, on average, half of the elements at level 0, then we should toss a coin (that is, randomly choose with probability 0.5) to decide whether it should be inserted at level 1 as well. If the coin toss does result in it being inserted at level 1, then the process is repeated for level 2, and so on. To remove an element from the skip list, it is removed from each level in which it occurs.

If the coin tossing goes badly, we could end up with every list above level 0 empty—or full, which would be just as bad. These outcomes have very low probability, however, and analysis shows that, in fact, the probability is very high that skip lists will give performance comparable to binary trees: search, insertion and removal all take $O(\log n)$. Their compelling advantage for concurrent use is that they have efficient lock-free insertion and deletion algorithms, whereas there are none known for binary trees.

The iterators of ConcurrentSkipListSet are weakly consistent.

Table 13.1: Comparative performance of different Set implementations

	add	contains	next	notes
HashSet	$O(1)$	$O(1)$	$O(h/n)$	h is the table capacity
LinkedHashSet	$O(1)$	$O(1)$	$O(1)$	
CopyOnWriteArraySet	$O(n)$	$O(n)$	$O(1)$	
EnumSet	$O(1)$	$O(1)$	$O(1)$	
TreeSet	$O(\log n)$	$O(\log n)$	$O(\log n)$	
ConcurrentSkipListSet	$O(\log n)$	$O(\log n)$	$O(1)$	

13.3 Comparing Set Implementations

Table 13.1 shows the comparative performance of the different Set implementations. When you are choosing an implementation, of course, efficiency is only one of the factors you should take into account. Some of these implementations are specialized for specific situations; for example, EnumSet should always (and only) be used to represent sets of enum. Similarly, CopyOnWriteArraySet should only be used where set size will remain relatively small, read operations greatly outnumber writes, thread safety is required, and read-only iterators are acceptable.

That leaves the general-purpose implementations: HashSet, LinkedHashSet, TreeSet, and ConcurrentSkipListSet. The first three are not thread-safe, so can only be used in multi-threaded code either in conjunction with client-side locking, or wrapped in Collection.synchronizedSet (see Section 17.3.1). For single-threaded applications where there is no requirement for the set to be sorted, your choice is between HashSet and LinkedHashSet. If your application will be frequently iterating over the set, or if you require access ordering, LinkedHashSet is the implementation of choice.

Finally, if you require the set to sort its elements, the choice is between TreeSet and ConcurrentSkipListSet. In a multi-threaded environment, ConcurrentSkipListSet is the only sensible choice. Even in single-threaded code ConcurrentSkipListSet may not show a significantly worse performance for small set sizes. For larger sets, however, or for applications in which there are frequent element deletions, TreeSet will perform better if your application doesn't require thread safety.

CHAPTER 14

Queues

A *queue* is a collection designed to hold elements for processing, yielding them up in the order in which they are to be processed. The corresponding Collections Framework interface Queue (see Figure 14.1) has a number of different implementations embodying different rules about what this order should be. Many of the implementations use the rule that tasks are to be processed in the order in which they were submitted (*First In First Out*, or *FIFO*), but other rules are possible—for example, the Collections Framework includes queue classes whose processing order is based on task priority. The Queue interface was introduced in Java 5, motivated in part by the need for queues in the concurrency utilities included in that release. A glance at the hierarchy of implementations shown in Figure 14.2 shows that, in fact, nearly all of the Queue implementations in the Collections Framework are in the package java.util.concurrent.

One classic requirement for queues in concurrent systems comes when a number of tasks have to be executed by a number of threads working in parallel. An everyday example of this situation is that of a single queue of airline passengers being handled by a line of check-in operators. Each operator works on processing a single passenger (or a group of passengers) while the remaining passengers wait in the queue. As they arrive, passengers join the *tail* of the queue, wait until they reach its *head*, and are then assigned to the next operator who becomes free. A good deal of fine detail is involved in implementing a queue such as this; operators have to be prevented from simultaneously attempting to process the same passenger, empty queues have to be handled correctly, and in computer systems there

Queue<E>
+*offer(e : E) :boolean*
+*element() :E*
+*removed() : E*
+*peek() :E*
+*poll() : E*

Figure 14.1: Queue

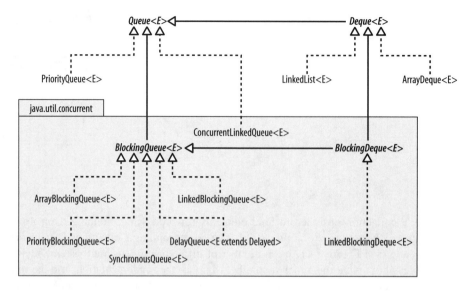

Figure 14.2: Implementations of Queue in the Collections Framework

has to be a way of defining queues with a maximum size, or *bound*. (This last requirement may not often be imposed in airline terminals, but it can be very useful in systems in which there is a maximum waiting time for a task to be executed.) The Queue implementations in java.util.concurrent look after these implementation details for you.

In addition to the operations inherited from Collection, the Queue interface includes operations to add an element to the tail of the queue, to inspect the element at its head, or to remove the element at its head. Each of these three operations comes in two varieties, one which returns a value to indicate failure and one which throws an exception.

Adding an Element to a Queue The exception-throwing variant of this operation is the add method inherited from Collection. Although add does return a boolean signifying its success in inserting an element, that value can't be used to report that a bounded queue is full; the contract for add specifies that it may return false only if the collection refused the element because it was already present—otherwise, it must throw an exception.

The value-returning variant is offer:

```
boolean offer(E e)  // insert the given element if possible
```

The value returned by offer indicates whether the element was successfully inserted or not. Note that offer does throw an exception if the element is illegal in some way (for example, the value null for a queue that doesn't permit nulls). Normally, if offer returns false, it has been called on a bounded queue that has reached capacity.

Retrieving an Element from a Queue The methods in this group are peek and element for inspecting the head element, and poll and remove for removing it from the queue and returning its value.

The methods that throw an exception for an empty queue are:

```
E element()  // retrieve but do not remove the head element
E remove()   // retrieve and remove the head element
```

Notice that this is a different method from the Collection method remove(Object). The methods that return null for an empty queue are:

```
E peek()     // retrieve but do not remove the head element
E poll()     // retrieve and remove the head element
```

Because these methods return null to signify that the queue is empty, you should avoid using null as a queue element. In general, the use of null as a queue element is discouraged by the Queue interface, and the only standard implementation that allows it is the legacy implementation LinkedList.

14.1 Using the Methods of Queue

Let's look at examples of the use of these methods. Queues should provide a good way of implementing a task manager, since their main purpose is to yield up elements, such as tasks, for processing. For the moment we shall use ArrayDeque as the fastest and most straightforward implementation of Queue (and also of Deque, of course). But, as before, we shall confine ourselves to the methods of the interface—though you should note that, in choosing a queue implementation, you are also choosing an ordering. With ArrayDeque, you get FIFO ordering—well, our attempts to get organized using fancy scheduling methods never seem to work very well; perhaps it's time to try something simpler.

ArrayDeque is unbounded, so we could use either add or offer to set up the queue with new tasks.

```
Queue<Task> taskQueue = new ArrayDeque<Task>();
taskQueue.offer(mikePhone);
taskQueue.offer(paulPhone);
```

Any time we feel ready to do a task, we can take the one that has reached the head of the queue:

```
Task nextTask = taskQueue.poll();
if (nextTask != null) {
  // process nextTask
}
```

The choice between using poll and remove depends on whether we want to regard queue emptiness as an exceptional condition. Realistically—given the nature of the application—that might be a sensible assumption, so this is an alternative:

```
try {
  Task nextTask = taskQueue.remove();
  // process nextTask
} catch (NoSuchElementException e) {
  // but we *never* run out of tasks!
}
```

This scheme needs some refinement to allow for the nature of different kinds of tasks. Phone tasks fit into relatively short time slots, whereas we don't like to start coding unless there is reasonably substantial time to get into the task. So if time is limited—say, until the next meeting—we might like to check that the next task is of the right kind before we take it off the queue:

```
Task nextTask = taskQueue.peek();
if (nextTask instanceof PhoneTask) {
  taskQueue.remove();
  // process nextTask
}
```

These inspection and removal methods are a major benefit of the `Queue` interface; `Collection` has nothing like them (though `NavigableSet` now does). The price we pay for this benefit is that the methods of `Queue` are useful to us only if the head element is actually one that we want. True, the class `PriorityQueue` allows us to provide a comparator that will order the queue elements so that the one we want is at the head, but that may not be a particularly good way of expressing the algorithm for choosing the next task (for example, if you need to know something about *all* the outstanding tasks before you can choose the next one). So in this situation, if our to-do manager is entirely queue-based, we may end up going for coffee until the meeting starts. As an alternative, we could consider using the `List` interface, which provides more flexible means of accessing its elements but has the drawback that its implementations provide much less support for multi-thread use.

This may sound too pessimistic; after all, `Queue` is a subinterface of `Collection`, so it inherits methods that support traversal, like `iterator`. In fact, although these methods are implemented, their use is not recommended in normal situations. In the design of the queue classes, efficiency in traversal has been traded against fast implementation of the methods of `Queue`; in addition, queue iterators do not guarantee to return their elements in proper sequence and, for some concurrent queues, will actually fail in normal conditions (see Section14.3.2).

In the next section we shall look at the direct implementations of `Queue`—`PriorityQueue` and `ConcurrentLinkedList`—and, in Section 14.3, at `BlockingQueue` and its implementations. The classes in these two sections differ widely in their behavior. Most of them are thread-safe; most provide *blocking* facilities (that is, operations that wait for conditions to be right for them to execute); some support priority ordering; one—`DelayQueue`—holds elements until their delay has expired, and another—`SynchronousQueue`—is purely a synchronization facility. In choosing between Queue implementations, you would be influenced more by these functional differences than by their performances.

14.2 Implementing Queue

14.2.1 PriorityQueue

PriorityQueue is one of the two nonlegacy Queue implementations not designed primarily for concurrent use (the other one is ArrayDeque). It is not thread-safe, nor does it provide blocking behavior. It gives up its elements for processing according to an ordering like that used by NavigableSet—either the natural order of its elements if they implement Comparable, or the ordering imposed by a Comparator supplied when the PriorityQueue is constructed. So PriorityQueue would be an alternative design choice (obviously, given its name) for the priority-based to-do manager that we outlined in Section 13.2 using NavigableSet. Your application will dictate which alternative to choose: if it needs to examine and manipulate the set of waiting tasks, use NavigableSet. If its main requirement is efficient access to the next task to be performed, use PriorityQueue.

Choosing PriorityQueue allows us to reconsider the ordering: since it accommodates duplicates, it does not share the requirement of NavigableSet for an ordering consistent with equals. To emphasize the point, we will define a new ordering for our to-do manager that depends only on priorities. Contrary to what you might expect, PriorityQueue gives no guarantee of how it presents multiple elements with the same value. So if, in our example, several tasks are tied for the highest priority in the queue, it will choose one of them arbitrarily as the head element.

The constructors for PriorityQueue are:

```
PriorityQueue()        // natural ordering, default initial capacity (11)
PriorityQueue(Collection<? extends E> c)
                       // natural ordering of elements taken from c, unless
                       // c is a PriorityQueue or SortedSet, in which case
                       // copy c's ordering
PriorityQueue(int initialCapacity)
                       // natural ordering, specified initial capacity
PriorityQueue(int initialCapacity, Comparator<? super E> comparator)
                       // Comparator ordering, specified initial capacity
PriorityQueue(PriorityQueue<? extends E> c)
                       // ordering and elements copied from c
PriorityQueue(SortedSet<? extends E> c)
                       // ordering and elements copied from c
```

Notice how the second of these constructors avoids the problem of the overloaded TreeSet constructor that we discussed in Section 13.2.1. We can use PriorityQueue for a simple implementation of our to-do manager with the PriorityTask class defined in Section 13.2, and a new Comparator depending only on the task's priority:

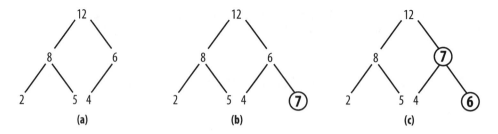

Figure 14.3: Adding an element to a PriorityQueue

```
final int INITIAL_CAPACITY = 10;
Comparator<PriorityTask> priorityComp = new Comparator<PriorityTask>() {
  public int compare(PriorityTask o1, PriorityTask o2) {
    return o1.getPriority().compareTo(o2.getPriority());
  }
};
Queue<PriorityTask> priorityQueue =
  new PriorityQueue<PriorityTask>(INITIAL_CAPACITY, priorityComp);
priorityQueue.add(new PriorityTask(mikePhone, Priority.MEDIUM));
priorityQueue.add(new PriorityTask(paulPhone, Priority.HIGH));
...
PriorityTask nextTask = priorityQueue.poll();
```

Priority queues are usually efficiently implemented by *priority heaps*. A priority heap is a binary tree somewhat like those we saw implementing TreeSet in Section 13.2.1, but with two differences: first, the only ordering constraint is that each node in the tree should be larger than either of its children, and second, that the tree should be complete at every level except possibly the lowest; if the lowest level is incomplete, the nodes it contains must be grouped together at the left. Figure 14.3(a) shows a small priority heap, with each node shown only by the field containing its priority. To add a new element to a priority heap, it is first attached at the leftmost vacant position, as shown by the circled node in Figure 14.3(b). Then it is repeatedly exchanged with its parent until it reaches a parent that has higher priority. In the figure, this required only a single exchange of the new element with its parent, giving Figure 14.3(c). (Nodes shown circled in Figures 14.3 and 14.4 have just changed position.)

Getting the highest-priority element from a priority heap is trivial: it is the root of the tree. But, when that has been removed, the two separate trees that result must be reorganized into a priority heap again. This is done by first placing the rightmost element from the bottom row into the root position. Then—in the reverse of the procedure for adding an element—it is repeatedly exchanged with the larger of its children until it has a higher priority than either. Figure 14.4 shows the process—again requiring only a single exchange—starting from the heap in Figure 14.3(c) after the head has been removed.

Apart from constant overheads, both addition and removal of elements require a number of operations proportional to the height of the tree. So PriorityQueue provides $O(\log n)$

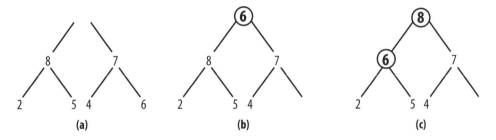

Figure 14.4: Removing the head of a PriorityQueue

time for `offer`, `poll`, `remove()`, and `add`. The methods `remove(Object)` and `contains` may require the entire tree to be traversed, so they require $O(n)$ time. The methods `peek` and `element`, which just retrieve the root of the tree without removing it, take constant time, as does `size`, which uses an object field that is continually updated.

`PriorityQueue` is not suitable for concurrent use. Its iterators are fail-fast, and it doesn't offer support for client-side locking. A thread-safe version, `PriorityBlockingQueue` (see Section 14.3.2), is provided instead.

14.2.2 ConcurrentLinkedQueue

The other nonblocking `Queue` implementation is `ConcurrentLinkedQueue`, an unbounded, thread-safe, FIFO-ordered queue. It uses a linked structure, similar to those we saw in Section 13.2.2 as the basis for skip lists, and in Section 13.1.1 for hash table overflow chaining. We noticed there that one of the main attractions of linked structures is that the insertion and removal operations implemented by pointer rearrangements perform in constant time. This makes them especially useful as queue implementations, where these operations are always required on cells at the ends of the structure—that is, cells that do not need to be located using the slow sequential search of linked structures.

`ConcurrentLinkedQueue` uses a CAS-based *wait-free* algorithm—that is, one that guarantees that any thread can always complete its current operation, regardless of the state of other threads accessing the queue. It executes queue insertion and removal operations in constant time, but requires linear time to execute `size`. This is because the algorithm, which relies on co-operation between threads for insertion and removal, does not keep track of the queue size and has to iterate over the queue to calculate it when it is required.

`ConcurrentLinkedQueue` has the two standard constructors discussed in Section 12.3. Its iterators are weakly consistent.

14.3 BlockingQueue

Java 5 added a number of classes to the Collections Framework for use in concurrent applications. Most of these are implementations of the `Queue` subinterface `BlockingQueue` (see Figure 14.5), designed primarily to be used in producer-consumer queues.

```
┌─────────────────────────────────────────────────────────┐
│               BlockingQueue<E>                          │
├─────────────────────────────────────────────────────────┤
│ +offer( e : E, timeout: long, unit : TimeUnit ) : boolean │
│ +put( e : E ) : void                                     │
│ +poll( timeout : long, unit : TimeUnit ) : E             │
│ +take() : E                                              │
│ +drainTo( c : Collection<? super E> ) : int              │
│ +drainTo( c : Collection<? super E>, maxElements ) : int │
│ +remainingCapacity() : int                               │
└─────────────────────────────────────────────────────────┘
```

Figure 14.5: BlockingQueue

One common example of the use of producer-consumer queues is in systems that perform print spooling; client processes add print jobs to the spool queue, to be processed by one or more print service processes, each of which repeatedly "consumes" the task at the head of the queue.

The key facilities that `BlockingQueue` provides to such systems are, as its name implies, enqueuing and dequeueing methods that do not return until they have executed successfully. So, for example, a print server does not need to constantly poll the queue to discover whether any print jobs are waiting; it need only call the `poll` method, supplying a timeout, and the system will suspend it until either a queue element becomes available or the timeout expires. `BlockingQueue` defines seven new methods, in three groups:

Adding an Element

```
boolean offer(E e, long timeout, TimeUnit unit)
                // insert e, waiting up to the timeout
void put(E e)   // add e, waiting as long as necessary
```

The nonblocking overload of `offer` defined in `Queue` will return `false` if it cannot immediately insert the element. This new overload waits for a time specified using `java.util.concurrent.TimeUnit`, an Enum which allows timeouts to be defined in units such as milliseconds or seconds.

Taking these methods together with those inherited from `Queue`, there are four ways in which the methods for adding elements to a `BlockingQueue` can behave: `offer` returns `false` if it does not succeed immediately, blocking `offer` returns `false` if it does not succeed within its timeout, `add` throws an exception if it does not succeed immediately, and `put` blocks until it succeeds.

Removing an Element

```
E poll(long timeout, TimeUnit unit)
                // retrieve and remove the head, waiting up to the timeout
E take()        // retrieve and remove the head of this queue, waiting
                // as long as necessary
```

Again taking these methods together with those inherited from Queue, there are four ways in which the methods for removing elements from a BlockingQueue can behave: poll returns null if it does not succeed immediately, blocking poll returns null if it does not succeed within its timeout, remove throws an exception if it does not succeed immediately, and take blocks until it succeeds.

Retrieving or Querying the Contents of the Queue

```
int drainTo(Collection<? super E> c)
                // clear the queue into c
int drainTo(Collection<? super E> c, int maxElements)
                // clear at most the specified number of elements into c
int remainingCapacity()
                // return the number of elements that would be accepted
                // without blocking, or Integer.MAX_VALUE if unbounded
```

The drainTo methods perform atomically and efficiently, so the second overload is useful in situations in which you know that you have processing capability available immediately for a certain number of elements, and the first is useful—for example—when all producer threads have stopped working. Their return value is the number of elements transferred. RemainingCapacity reports the spare capacity of the queue, although as with any such value in multi-threaded contexts, the result of a call should not be used as part of a test-then-act sequence; between the test (the call of remainingCapacity) and the action (adding an element to the queue) of one thread, another thread might have intervened to add or remove elements.

BlockingQueue guarantees that the queue operations of its implementations will be thread-safe and atomic. But this guarantee doesn't extend to the bulk operations inherited from Collection—addAll, containsAll, retainAll and removeAll—unless the individual implementation provides it. So it is possible, for example, for addAll to fail, throwing an exception, after adding only some of the elements in a collection.

14.3.1 Using the Methods of BlockingQueue

A to-do manager that works for just one person at a time is very limited; we really need a cooperative solution—one that will allow us to share both the production and the processing of tasks. Example 14.1 shows StoppableTaskQueue, a simple version of a concurrent task manager based on PriorityBlockingQueue, that will allow its users—us—to independently add tasks to the task queue as we discover the need for them, and to take them off for processing as we find the time. The class StoppableTaskQueue has three methods: addTask, getTask, and shutDown. A StoppableTaskQueue is either working or stopped. The method addTask returns a boolean value indicating whether it successfully added a task; this value will be true unless the StoppableTaskQueue is stopped. The method getTask returns the head task from the queue. If no task is available, it does not block but returns null. The method shutDown stops the StoppableTaskQueue, waits until all pending addTask operations are completed, then drains the StoppableTaskQueue and returns its contents.

Example 14.1. A concurrent queue-based task manager

```java
public class StoppableTaskQueue {
  private final int MAXIMUM_PENDING_OFFERS = Integer.MAX_VALUE;
  private final BlockingQueue<PriorityTask> taskQueue =
        new PriorityBlockingQueue<PriorityTask>();
  private boolean isStopped = false;
  private Semaphore semaphore = new Semaphore(MAXIMUM_PENDING_OFFERS);

  // return true if the task was successfully placed on the queue, false
  // if the queue has been shut down.
  public boolean addTask(PriorityTask task) {
    synchronized (this) {
      if (isStopped) return false;
      if (! semaphore.tryAcquire()) throw new Error("too many threads");
    }
    try {
      return taskQueue.offer(task);
    } finally {
      semaphore.release();
    }
  }

  // return the head task from the queue, or null if no task is available
  public PriorityTask getTask() {
    return taskQueue.poll();
  }

  // stop the queue, wait for producers to finish, then return the contents
  public Collection<PriorityTask> shutDown() {
    synchronized(this) { isStopped = true; }
    semaphore.acquireUninterruptibly(MAXIMUM_PENDING_OFFERS);
    Set<PriorityTask> returnCollection = new HashSet<PriorityTask>();
    taskQueue.drainTo(returnCollection);
    return returnCollection;
  }
}
```

In this example, as in most uses of the `java.util.concurrent` collections, the collection itself takes care of the problems arising from the interaction of different threads in adding or removing items from the queue. Most of the code of Example 14.1 is instead solving the problem of providing an orderly shutdown mechanism. The reason for this emphasis is that when we go on to use the class `StoppableTaskQueue` as a component in a larger system, we will need to be able to stop daily task queues without losing task information. Achieving graceful shutdown can often be a problem in concurrent systems: for more detail, see Chapter 7 of *Java Concurrency in Practice* by Brian Goetz et. al. (Addison-Wesley).

The larger system will model each day's scheduled tasks over the next year, allowing consumers to process tasks from each day's queue. An implicit assumption of the example of this section is that if there are no remaining tasks scheduled for this day, a consumer will not wait for one to become available, but will immediately go on to look for a task in the next day's queue. (In the real world, we would go home at this point, or more likely go out to celebrate.) This assumption simplifies the example, as we don't need to invoke any of the blocking methods of `PriorityBlockingQueue`, though we will use one method, `drainTo`, from the `BlockingQueue` interface.

There are a number of ways of shutting down a producer-consumer queue such as this; in the one we've chosen for this example, the manager exposes a `shutdown` method that can be called by a "supervisor" thread in order to stop producers writing to the queue, to drain it, and to return the result. The `shutdown` method sets a boolean `stopped`, which task-producing threads will read before trying to put a task on to the queue. Task-consuming threads simply `poll` the queue, returning `null` if no tasks are available. The problem with this simple idea is that a producer thread might read the `stopped` flag, find it false, but then be suspended for some time before it places its value on the queue. We have to prevent this by ensuring that the `shutdown` method, having stopped the queue, will wait until all the pending values have been inserted before draining it.

Example 14.1 achieves this using a *semaphore*—a thread-safe object that maintains a fixed number of *permits*. Semaphores are usually used to regulate access to a finite set of resources—a pool of database connections, for example. The permits the semaphore has available at any time represent the resources not currently in use. A thread requiring a resource acquires a permit from the semaphore, and releases it when it releases the resource. If all the resources are in use, the semaphore will have no permits available; at that point, a thread attempting to acquire a permit will block until some other thread returns one.

The semaphore in this example is used differently. We don't want to restrict producer threads from writing to the queue—it's an unbounded concurrent queue, after all, quite capable of handling concurrent access without help from us. We just want to keep a count of the writes currently in progress. So we create the semaphore with the largest possible number of permits, which in practice will never all be required. The producer method `addTask` checks to see if the queue has been stopped—in which case its contract says it should return `null`— and, if not, it acquires a permit using the semaphore method `tryAcquire`, which does not block (unlike the more commonly used blocking method `acquire`, `tryAcquire` returns `null` immediately if no permits are available). This test-then-act sequence is made atomic to ensure that at any point visible to another thread the program maintains its invariant: the number of unwritten values is no greater than the number of permits available.

The `shutdown` method sets the `stopped` flag in a synchronized block (remember that the only way of ensuring that variable writes made by one thread are visible to reads by another is for both writes and reads to take place within blocks synchronized on the same lock). Now the `addTask` method cannot acquire any more permits, and `shutdown` just has to wait until all the permits previously acquired have been returned. To do that, it calls `acquire`, specifying that it needs *all* the permits; that call will block until they are all released by the producer threads. At that point, the invariant guarantees that there are no tasks still to be written to the queue, and shutdown can be completed.

14.3.2 Implementing BlockingQueue

The Collections Framework provides five implementations of `BlockingQueue`.

LinkedBlockingQueue

This class is a thread-safe, FIFO-ordered queue, based on a linked node structure. It is the implementation of choice whenever you need an unbounded blocking queue. Even for bounded use, it may still be better than `ArrayBlockingQueue` (linked queues typically have higher throughput than array-based queues but less predictable performance in most concurrent applications).

The two standard collection constructors create a thread-safe blocking queue with a capacity of `Integer.MAX_VALUE`. You can specify a lower capacity using a third constructor:

```
LinkedBlockingQueue(int capacity)
```

The ordering imposed by `LinkedBlockingQueue` is FIFO. Queue insertion and removal are executed in constant time; operations such as `contains` which require traversal of the array require linear time. The iterators are weakly consistent.

ArrayBlockingQueue

This implementation is based on a *circular array*—a linear structure in which the first and last elements are logically adjacent. Figure 14.6(a) shows the idea. The position labeled "head" indicates the head of the queue; each time the head element is removed from the queue, the head index is advanced. Similarly, each new element is added at the tail position, resulting in that index being advanced. When either index needs to be advanced past the last element of the array, it gets the value 0. If the two indices have the same value, the queue is either full or empty, so an implementation must separately keep track of the count of elements in the queue.

A circular array in which the head and tail can be continuously advanced in this way this is better as a queue implementation than a noncircular one (e.g., the standard implementation of `ArrayList`, which we cover in Section 15.2) in which removing the head element requires changing the position of all the remaining elements so that the new head is at position 0. Notice, though, that only the elements at the ends of the queue can be inserted and removed in constant time. If an element is to be removed from near the middle, which can be done for queues via the method `Iterator.remove`, then all the elements from one end must be moved along to maintain a compact representation. Figure 14.6(b) shows the element at index 6 being removed from the queue. As a result, insertion and removal of elements in the middle of the queue has time complexity $O(n)$.

Constructors for array-backed collection classes generally have a single configuration parameter, the initial length of the array. For fixed-size classes like `ArrayBlockingQueue`, this

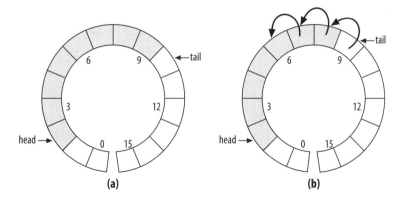

Figure 14.6: A circular array

parameter is necessary in order to define the capacity of the collection. (For variable-size classes like ArrayList, a default initial capacity can be used, so constructors are provided that don't require the capacity.) For ArrayBlockingQueue, the three constructors are:

```
ArrayBlockingQueue(int capacity)
ArrayBlockingQueue(int capacity, boolean fair)
ArrayBlockingQueue(int capacity, boolean fair, Collection<? extends E> c)
```

The Collection parameter to the last of these allows an ArrayBlockingQueue to be initialized with the contents of the specified collection, added in the traversal order of the collection's iterator. For this constructor, the specified capacity must be at least as great as that of the supplied collection, or be at least 1 if the supplied collection is empty. Besides configuring the backing array, the last two constructors also require a boolean argument to control how the queue will handle multiple blocked requests. These will occur when multiple threads attempt to remove items from an empty queue or enqueue items on to a full one. When the queue becomes able to service one of these requests, which one should it choose? The alternatives are to require a guarantee that the queue will choose the one that has been waiting longest—that is, to implement a *fair* scheduling policy—or to allow the implementation to choose one. Fair scheduling sounds like the better alternative, since it avoids the possibility that an unlucky thread might be delayed indefinitely but, in practice, the benefits it provides are rarely important enough to justify incurring the large overhead that it imposes on a queue's operation. If fair scheduling is not specified, ArrayBlockingQueue will normally approximate fair operation, but with no guarantees.

The ordering imposed by ArrayBlockingQueue is FIFO. Queue insertion and removal are executed in constant time; operations such as contains which require traversal of the array require linear time. The iterators are weakly consistent.

PriorityBlockingQueue

This implementation is a thread-safe, blocking version of PriorityQueue (see Section 14.2), with similar ordering and performance characteristics. Its iterators are fail-fast, so in normal use they will throw `ConcurrentModificationException`; only if the queue is quiescent will they succeed. To iterate safely over a `PriorityBlockingQueue`, transfer the elements to an array and iterate over that instead.

DelayQueue

This is a specialized priority queue, in which the ordering is based on the *delay time* for each element—the time remaining before the element will be ready to be taken from the queue. If all elements have a positive delay time—that is, none of their associated delay times has expired—an attempt to `poll` the queue will return `null` (although `peek` will still allow you to see the first unexpired element). If one or more elements has an expired delay time, the one with the longest-expired delay time will be at the head of the queue. The elements of a `DelayQueue` belong to a class that implements `java.util.concurrent.Delayed`:

```
interface Delayed extends Comparable<Delayed> {
    long getDelay(TimeUnit unit);
}
```

The `getDelay` method of a `Delayed` object returns the remaining delay associated with that object. The `compareTo` method (see Section 3.1) of `Comparable` must be defined to give results that are consistent with the delays of the objects being compared. This means that it will rarely be compatible with `equals`, so `Delayed` objects are not suitable for use with implementations of `SortedSet` and `SortedMap`.

For example, in our to-do manager we are likely to need reminder tasks, to ensure that we follow up e-mail and phone messages that have gone unanswered. We could define a new class `DelayedTask` as in Example 14.2, and use it to implement a reminder queue.

```
BlockingQueue<DelayedTask> reminderQueue = new DelayQueue<DelayedTask>();
reminderQueue.offer(new DelayedTask (databaseCode, 1));
reminderQueue.offer(new DelayedTask (interfaceCode, 2));
...
// now get the first reminder task that is ready to be processed
DelayedTask t1 = reminderQueue.poll();
if (t1 == null) {
  // no reminders ready yet
} else {
  // process t1
}
```

Most queue operations respect delay values and will treat a queue with no unexpired elements as if it were empty. The exceptions are `peek` and `remove`, which, perhaps surprisingly, will allow you to examine the head element of a `DelayQueue` whether or not it is expired. Like them and unlike the other methods of `Queue`, collection operations on a `DelayQueue` do not respect delay values. For example, here are two ways of copying the elements of `reminderQueue` into a set:

```
Set<DelayedTask> delayedTaskSet1 = new HashSet<DelayedTask>();
delayedTaskSet1.addAll(reminderQueue);
```

```
Set<DelayedTask> delayedTaskSet2 = new HashSet<DelayedTask>();
reminderQueue.drainTo(delayedTaskSet2);
```

The set delayedTaskSet1 will contain all the reminders in the queue, whereas the set delayedTaskSet2 will contain only those ready to be used.

DelayQueue shares the performance characteristics of the PriorityQueue on which it is based and, like it, has fail-fast iterators. The comments on PriorityBlockingQueue iterators apply to these too.

SynchronousQueue

At first sight, you might think there is little point to a queue with no internal capacity, which is a short description of SynchronousQueue. But, in fact, it can be very useful; a thread that wants to add an element to a SynchronousQueue must wait until another thread is ready to simultaneously take it off, and the same is true—in reverse—for a thread that wants to take an element off the queue. So SynchronousQueue has the function that its name suggests, that of a *rendezvous*—a mechanism for synchronizing two threads. (Don't confuse the concept of synchronizing threads in this way—allowing them to cooperate by exchanging data— with Java's keyword synchronized, which prevents simultaneous execution of code by different threads.) There are two constructors for SynchronousQueue:

```
SynchronousQueue()
SynchronousQueue(boolean fair)
```

Example 14.2. The class DelayedTask

```
public class DelayedTask implements Delayed {
  public final static long MILLISECONDS_IN_DAY = 60 * 60 * 24 * 1000;
  private long endTime;     // in milliseconds after January 1, 1970
  private Task task;
  DelayedTask(Task t, int daysDelay) {
    endTime = System.currentTimeMillis() + daysDelay * MILLISECONDS_IN_DAY;
    task = t;
  }
  public long getDelay(TimeUnit unit) {
    long remainingTime = endTime - System.currentTimeMillis();
    return unit.convert(remainingTime, TimeUnit.MILLISECONDS);
  }
  public int compareTo(Delayed t) {
    long thisDelay = getDelay(TimeUnit.MILLISECONDS);
    long otherDelay = t.getDelay(TimeUnit.MILLISECONDS);
    return (thisDelay < otherDelay) ? -1 : (thisDelay > otherDelay) ? 1 : 0;
  }
  Task getTask() { return task; }
}
```

A common application for SynchronousQueue is in work-sharing systems where the design ensures that there are enough consumer threads to ensure that producer threads can hand tasks over without having to wait. In this situation, it allows safe transfer of task data between threads without incurring the BlockingQueue overhead of enqueuing, then dequeuing, each task being transferred.

As far as the Collection methods are concerned, a SynchronousQueue behaves like an empty Collection; Queue and BlockingQueue methods behave as you would expect for a queue with zero capacity, which is therefore always empty. The iterator method returns an empty iterator, in which hasNext always returns false.

14.4 Deque

A *deque* (pronounced "deck") is a double-ended queue. Unlike a queue, in which elements can be inserted only at the tail and inspected or removed only at the head, a deque can accept elements for insertion and present them for inspection or removal at either end. Also unlike Queue, Deque's contract specifies the ordering it will use in presenting its elements: it is a linear structure in which elements added at the tail are yielded up in the same order at the head. Used as a queue, then, a Deque is always a FIFO structure; the contract does not allow for, say, priority deques. If elements are removed from the same end (either head or tail) at which they were added, a Deque acts as a stack or *LIFO* (*Last In First Out*) structure.

Deque and its subinterface BlockingDeque were introduced in Java 6. The fast Deque implementation ArrayDeque uses a circular array (see Section 14.3.2), and is now the implementation of choice for stacks and queues. Concurrent deques have a special role to play in parallelization, discussed in Section 14.4.2.

The Deque interface (see Figure 14.7) extends Queue with methods symmetric with respect to head and tail. For clarity of naming, the Queue methods that implicitly refer to one end of the queue acquire a synonym that makes their behavior explicit for Deque. For example, the methods peek and offer, inherited from Queue, are equivalent to peekFirst and offerLast. (First and last refer to the head and tail of the deque; the JavaDoc for Deque also uses "front" and "end".)

Collection-like Methods

```
void addFirst(E e)      // insert e at the head if there is enough space
void addLast(E e)       // insert e at the tail if there is enough space
void push(E e)          // insert e at the head if there is enough space
boolean removeFirstOccurrence(Object o);
                        // remove the first occurrence of o
boolean removeLastOccurrence(Object o);
                        // remove the last occurrence of o
Iterator<E> descendingIterator()
                        // get an iterator, returning deque elements in
                        // reverse order
```

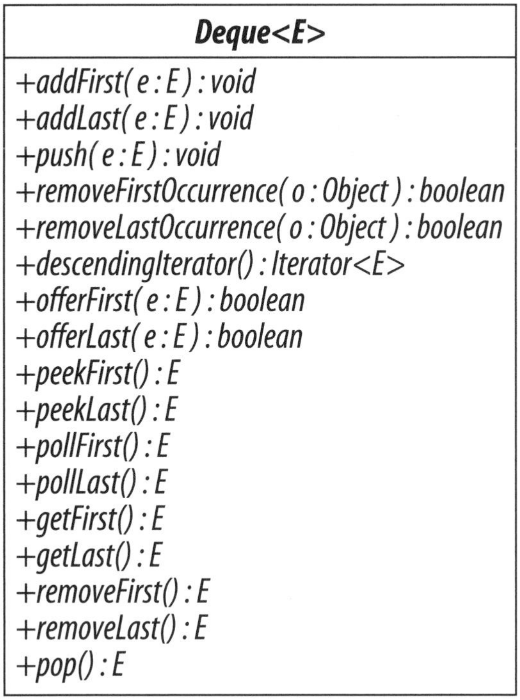

```
                    Deque<E>

+addFirst( e : E ) : void
+addLast( e : E ) : void
+push( e : E ) : void
+removeFirstOccurrence( o : Object ) : boolean
+removeLastOccurrence( o : Object ) : boolean
+descendingIterator() : Iterator<E>
+offerFirst( e : E ) : boolean
+offerLast( e : E ) : boolean
+peekFirst() : E
+peekLast() : E
+pollFirst() : E
+pollLast() : E
+getFirst() : E
+getLast() : E
+removeFirst() : E
+removeLast() : E
+pop() : E
```

Figure 14.7: Deque

The contracts for the methods addFirst and addLast are similar to the contract for the add method of Collection, but specify in addition where the element to be added should be placed, and that the exception to be thrown if it cannot be added is IllegalState-Exception. As with bounded queues, users of bounded deques should avoid these methods in favor of offerFirst and offerLast, which can report "normal" failure by means of a returned boolean value.

The method name push is a synonym of addFirst, provided for the use of Deque as a stack. The methods removeFirstOccurrence and removeLastOccurrence are analogues of Collection.remove, but specify in addition exactly which occurrence of the element should be removed. The return value signifies whether an element was removed as a result of the call.

Queue-like Methods

```
boolean offerFirst(E e) // insert e at the head if the deque has space
boolean offerLast(E e)  // insert e at the tail if the deque has space
```

The method offerLast is a renaming of the equivalent method offer on the Queue interface.

The methods that return `null` for an empty deque are:

```
E peekFirst()        // retrieve but do not remove the first element
E peekLast()         // retrieve but do not remove the last element
E pollFirst()        // retrieve and remove the first element
E pollLast()         // retrieve and remove the last element
```

The methods `peekFirst` and `pollFirst` are renamings of the equivalent methods `peek` and `poll` on the `Queue` interface.

The methods that throw an exception for an empty deque are:

```
E getFirst()         // retrieve but do not remove the first element
E getLast()          // retrieve but do not remove the last element
E removeFirst()      // retrieve and remove the first element
E removeLast()       // retrieve and remove the last element
E pop()              // retrieve and remove the first element
```

The methods `getFirst` and `removeFirst` are renamings of the equivalent methods `element` and `remove` on the `Queue` interface. The method name `pop` is a synonym for `removeFirst`, again provided for stack use.

14.4.1   Implementing Deque

ArrayDeque

Along with the interface Deque, Java 6 also introduced a very efficient implementation, `ArrayDeque`, based on a circular array like that of `ArrayBlockingQueue` (see Section 14.3.2). It fills a gap among Queue classes; previously, if you wanted a FIFO queue to use in a single-threaded environment, you would have had to use the class `LinkedList` (which we cover next, but which should be avoided as a general-purpose Queue implementation), or else pay an unnecessary overhead for thread safety with one of the concurrent classes `ArrayBlockingQueue` or `LinkedBlockingQueue`. `ArrayDeque` is now the general-purpose implementation of choice, for both deques and FIFO queues. It has the performance characteristics of a circular array: adding or removing elements at the head or tail takes constant time. The iterators are fail-fast.

LinkedList

Among Deque implementations `LinkedList` is an oddity; for example, it is alone in permitting `null` elements, which are discouraged by the `Queue` interface because of the common use of `null` as a special value. It has been in the Collections Framework from the start, originally as one of the standard implementations of `List` (see Section 15.2), and was retrofitted with the methods of Queue for Java 5, and those of Deque for Java 6. It is based on a linked list structure similar to those we saw in Section 13.2.2 as the basis for skip lists, but with an extra field in each cell, pointing to the previous entry (see Figure 14.8). These pointers allow the list to be traversed backwards—for example, for reverse iteration, or to remove an element from the end of the list.

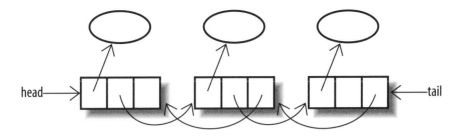

Figure 14.8: A doubly linked list

As an implementation of Deque, LinkedList is unlikely to be very popular. Its main advantage, that of constant-time insertion and removal, is rivalled in Java 6—for queues and deques—by the otherwise superior ArrayDeque. Previously you would have used it in situations where thread safety isn't an issue and you don't require blocking behavior. Now, the only likely reason for using LinkedList as a queue or deque implementation would be that you also needed random access to the elements. With LinkedList, even that comes at a high price; because random access has to be implemented by linear search, it has time complexity of $O(n)$.

The constructors for LinkedList are just the standard ones of Section 12.3. Its iterators are fail-fast.

14.4.2 BlockingDeque

Figure 14.9 shows the methods that BlockingDeque adds to BlockingQueue (see Figure 14.5). Each of the two blocking insertion methods and two removal methods of BlockingQueue is given a synonym to make explicit which end of the deque it modifies, together with a matching method to provide the same action at the other end. So offer, for example, acquires a synonym offerLast and a matching method offerFirst. As a result, the same four basic behaviors that were defined for BlockingQueue—returning a special value on failure, returning a special value on failure after a timeout, throwing an exception on failure, and blocking until success—can be applied for element insertion or removal at either end of the deque.

Good load balancing algorithms will be increasingly important as multicore and multiprocessor architectures become standard. Concurrent deques are the basis of one of the best load balancing methods, *work stealing*. To understand work stealing, imagine a load-balancing algorithm that distributes tasks in some way—round-robin, say—to a series of queues, each of which has a dedicated consumer thread that repeatedly takes a task from the head of its queue, processes it, and returns for another. Although this scheme does provide speedup through parallelism, it has a major drawback: we can imagine two adjacent queues, one with a backlog of long tasks and a consumer thread struggling to keep up with them, and next to it an empty queue with an idle consumer waiting for work. It would clearly improve throughput if we allowed the idle thread to take a task from the head of another queue. Work

```
┌─────────────────────────────────────────────────────────┐
│              BlockingDeque<E>                           │
├─────────────────────────────────────────────────────────┤
│ +offerFirst( e : E, timeout : long, unit : TimeUnit ) : boolean │
│ +offerLast( e : E, timeout : long, unit : TimeUnit ) : boolean  │
│ +putFirst( e : E ) : E                                  │
│ +putLast( e : E ) : E                                   │
│ +pollFirst( timeout : long, unit : TimeUnit ) : E       │
│ +pollLast( timeout : long, unit : TimeUnit ) : E        │
│ +takeFirst() : E                                        │
│ +takeLast() : E                                         │
└─────────────────────────────────────────────────────────┘
```

Figure 14.9: BlockingDeque

stealing improves still further on this idea; observing that for the idle thread to steal work from the head of another queue risks contention for the head element, it changes the queues for deques and instructs idle threads to take a task from the *tail* of another thread's deque. This turns out to be a highly efficient mechanism, and is becoming widely used.

Implementing BlockingDeque

The interface BlockingDeque has a single implementation, LinkedBlockingDeque. LinkedBlockingDeque is based on a doubly linked list structure like that of LinkedList. It can optionally be bounded so, besides the two standard constructors, it provides a third which can be used to specify its capacity:

```
LinkedBlockingDeque(int capacity)
```

It has similar performance characteristics to LinkedBlockingQueue—queue insertion and removal take constant time and operations such as contains, which require traversal of the queue, require linear time. The iterators are weakly consistent.

14.5   Comparing Queue Implementations

Table 14.1 shows the sequential performance, disregarding locking and CAS overheads, for some sample operations of the Deque and Queue implementations we have discussed. These results should be interesting to you in terms of understanding the behavior of your chosen implementation but, as we mentioned at the start of the chapter, they are unlikely to be the deciding factor. Your choice is more likely to be dictated by the functional and concurrency requirements of your application.

In choosing a Queue, the first question to ask is whether the implementation you choose needs to support concurrent access; if not, your choice is straightforward. For FIFO ordering, choose ArrayDeque; for priority ordering, PriorityQueue.

If your application does demand thread safety, you next need to consider ordering. If you need priority or delay ordering, the choice obviously must be PriorityBlockingQueue or DelayQueue, respectively. If, on the other hand, FIFO ordering is acceptable, the third

Table 14.1: Comparative performance of different Queue and Deque implementations

	offer	peek	poll	size
PriorityQueue	$O(\log n)$	$O(1)$	$O(\log n)$	$O(1)$
ConcurrentLinkedQueue	$O(1)$	$O(1)$	$O(1)$	$O(n)$
ArrayBlockingQueue	$O(1)$	$O(1)$	$O(1)$	$O(1)$
LinkedBlockingQueue	$O(1)$	$O(1)$	$O(1)$	$O(1)$
PriorityBlockingQueue	$O(\log n)$	$O(1)$	$O(\log n)$	$O(1)$
DelayQueue	$O(\log n)$	$O(1)$	$O(\log n)$	$O(1)$
LinkedList	$O(1)$	$O(1)$	$O(1)$	$O(1)$
ArrayDeque	$O(1)$	$O(1)$	$O(1)$	$O(1)$
LinkedBlockingDeque	$O(1)$	$O(1)$	$O(1)$	$O(1)$

question is whether you need blocking methods, as you usually will for producer-consumer problems (either because the consumers must handle an empty queue by waiting, or because you want to constrain demand on them by bounding the queue, and then producers must sometimes wait). If you don't need blocking methods or a bound on the queue size, choose the efficient and wait-free ConcurrentLinkedQueue.

If you do need a blocking queue, because your application requires support for producer-consumer cooperation, pause to think whether you really need to buffer data, or whether all you need is to safely hand off data between the threads. If you can do without buffering (usually because you are confident that there will be enough consumers to prevent data from piling up), then SynchronousQueue is an efficient alternative to the remaining FIFO blocking implementations, LinkedBlockingQueue and ArrayBlockingQueue.

Otherwise, we are finally left with the choice between these two. If you cannot fix a realistic upper bound for the queue size, then you must choose LinkedBlockingQueue, as ArrayBlockingQueue is always bounded. For bounded use, you will choose between the two on the basis of performance. Their performance characteristics in Figure 14.1 are the same, but these are only the formulae for sequential access; how they perform in concurrent use is a different question. As we mentioned above, LinkedBlockingQueue performs better on the whole than ArrayBlockingQueue if more than three or four threads are being serviced. This fits with the fact that the head and tail of a LinkedBlockingQueue are locked independently, allowing simultaneous updates of both ends. On the other hand, an ArrayBlockingQueue does not have to allocate new objects with each insertion. If queue performance is critical to the success of your application, you should measure both implementations with the benchmark that means the most to you: your application itself.

CHAPTER 15

Lists

Lists are probably the most widely used Java collections in practice. A *list* is a collection which—unlike a set—can contain duplicates, and which—unlike a queue—gives the user full visibility and control over the ordering of its elements. The corresponding Collections Framework interface is List (see Figure 15.1).

In addition to the operations inherited from Collection, the List interface includes operations for the following:

Positional Access   Methods that access elements based on their numerical position in the list:

```
void add(int index, E e)              // add element e at given index
boolean addAll(int index, Collection<? extends E> c)
                                      // add contents of c at given index
E get(int index)                      // return element with given index
E remove(int index)                   // remove element with given index
E set(int index, E e)                 // replace element with given index by e
```

List<E>
+add(index : int, element) : boolean
+addAll(index : int, c : Collection<? extends E>) : boolean
+get(index) : E
+remove(index) : E
+set(index, element) : E
+indexOf(o) : int
+lastIndexOf(o) : int
+subList(fromIndex, toIndex) : List<E>
+listIterator() : ListIterator<E>
+listIterator(index) : ListIterator<E>

Figure 15.1: List

Search Methods that search for a specified object in the list and return its numerical position. These methods return -1 if the object is not present:

```
int indexOf(Object o)          // return index of first occurrence of o
int lastIndexOf(Object o)      // return index of last occurrence of o
```

Range-View A method that gets a view of a range of the list:

```
List<E> subList(int fromIndex, int toIndex)
                               // return a view of a portion of the list
```

The method subList works in a similar way to the subSet operations on SortedSet (see Section 13.2), but uses the position of elements in the list rather than their values: the returned list contains the list elements starting at fromIndex, up to but not including toIndex. The returned list has no separate existence—it is just a view of part of the list from which it was obtained, so changes in it are reflected in the original list. There is an important difference from subSet, though; changes you make to the sublist write through to the backing list, but the reverse is not always true. If elements have been inserted into or removed from the backing list by directly calling one of its "structure changing" methods (Section 12.1), any subsequent attempts to use the sublist will result in a ConcurrentModificationException.

List Iteration Methods that return a ListIterator, which is an Iterator with extended semantics to take advantage of the list's sequential nature:

```
ListIterator<E> listIterator()     // return a ListIterator for this list,
                                   // initially positioned at index 0
ListIterator<E> listIterator(int indx)
                                   // return a ListIterator for this list,
                                   // initially positioned at index indx
```

The methods added by ListIterator support traversing a list in reverse order, changing list elements or adding new ones, and getting the current position of the iterator. The current position of a ListIterator always lies between two elements, so in a list of length n, there are $n+1$ valid list iterator positions, from 0 (before the first element) to n (after the last one). The second overload of listIterator uses the supplied value to set the initial position of the listIterator to one of these positions (calling listIterator with no arguments is the same as supplying an argument of 0.)

To the Iterator methods hasNext, next, and remove, ListIterator adds the following methods:

```
public interface ListIterator<E> extends Iterator<E> {
    void add(E e);              // insert the specified element into the list
    boolean hasPrevious();     // return true if this list iterator has further
                               // elements in the reverse direction
    int nextIndex();           // return the index of the element that would be
                               // returned by a subsequent call to next
```

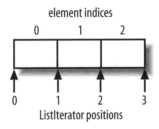

element indices

ListIterator positions

Figure 15.2: ListIterator positions

```
E previous();          // return the previous element in the list
int previousIndex();   // return the index of the element that would be
                       // returned by a subsequent call to previous
void set(E e);         // replace the last element returned by next or
                       // previous with the specified element
}
```

Figure 15.2 shows a list of three elements. Consider an iterator at position 2, either moved there from elsewhere or created there by a call to listIterator(2). The effect of most of the operations of this iterator is intuitive; add inserts an element at the current iterator position (between the elements at index 1 and 2), hasPrevious and hasNext return true, previous and next return the elements at indices 1 and 2 respectively, and previousIndex and nextIndex return those indices themselves. At the extreme positions of the list, 0 and 3 in the figure, previousIndex and nextIndex would return -1 and 3 (the size of the list) respectively, and previous or next, respectively, would throw NoSuchElementException.

The operations set and remove work differently. Their effect depends not on the current position of the iterator, but on its "current element", the one last traversed over using next or previous: set replaces the current element, and remove removes it. If there is no current element, either because the iterator has just been created, or because the current element has been removed, these methods will throw IllegalStateException.

15.1 Using the Methods of List

Let's look at examples of the use of some of these methods in the to-do manager. In the last chapter we considered representing the organization of a single day's tasks in a queue-based class with shutdown capabilities. One useful way of enlarging the scope of the application is to have a number of objects of this type, each one representing the tasks that are scheduled for a day in the future. We will store references to these objects in a List, which (to keep things simple and to avoid grappling with the distasteful details of java.util.Calendar) will be indexed on the number of days in the future that it represents. So the queue of tasks scheduled for today will be stored at element 0 of the list, the queue scheduled for tomorrow at element 1, and so on. Example 15.1 shows the scheduler.

Example 15.1. A list-based task scheduler

```java
public class TaskScheduler {
  private List<StoppableTaskQueue> schedule;
  private final int FORWARD_PLANNING_DAYS = 365;

  public TaskScheduler() {
    List<StoppableTaskQueue> temp = new ArrayList<StoppableTaskQueue>();
    for (int i = 0 ; i < FORWARD_PLANNING_DAYS ; i++) {
      temp.add(new StoppableTaskQueue());
    }
    schedule = new CopyOnWriteArrayList<StoppableTaskQueue>(temp);     //1
  }

  public PriorityTask getTask() {
    for (StoppableTaskQueue daysTaskQueue : schedule) {
      PriorityTask topTask = daysTaskQueue.getTask();
      if (topTask != null) return topTask;
    }
    return null;     // no outstanding tasks - at all!?
  }

  // at midnight, remove and shut down the queue for day 0, assign its tasks
  // to the new day 0, and create a new day's queue at the planning horizon
  public void rollOver() throws InterruptedException{
    StoppableTaskQueue oldDay = schedule.remove(0);
    Collection<PriorityTask> remainingTasks = oldDay.shutDown();
    StoppableTaskQueue firstDay = schedule.get(0);
    for (PriorityTask t : remainingTasks) {
      firstDay.addTask(t);
    }
    StoppableTaskQueue lastDay = new StoppableTaskQueue();
    schedule.add(lastDay);
  }

  public void addTask(PriorityTask task, int day) {
    if (day < 0 || day >= FORWARD_PLANNING_DAYS)
      throw new IllegalArgumentException("day out of range");
    StoppableTaskQueue daysTaskQueue = schedule.get(day);
    if (daysTaskQueue.addTask(task)) return;                          //2
    // StoppableTaskQueue.addTask returns false only when called on
    // a queue that has been shut down. In that case, it will also
    // have been removed by now, so it's safe to try again.
    if (! schedule.get(0).addTask(task)) {
      throw new IllegalStateException("failed to add task " + task);
    }
  }
}
```

Although the example aims primarily to show the use of List interface methods rather than to explore any particular implementation, we can't set it up without choosing one. Since a major factor in the choice will be the concurrency requirements of the application, we need to consider them now. They are quite straightforward: clients consuming or producing tasks only ever read the List representing the schedule, so (once it is constructed) the only occasion that it is ever written is at the end of a day. At that point the current day's queue is removed from the schedule, and a new one is added at the end (the "planning horizon", which we have set to a year in the example). We don't need to exclude clients from using the current day's queue before that happens, because the StoppableTaskQueue design of Example14.1 ensures that they will be able to complete in an orderly way once the queue is stopped. So the only exclusion required is to ensure that clients don't try to read the schedule itself while the rollover procedure is changing its values.

If you recall the discussion of CopyOnWriteArrayList in Section 11.5.3, you may see that it fills these requirements very nicely. It optimizes read access, in line with one of our requirement. In the event of a write operation, it synchronizes just long enough to create a new copy of its internal backing array, thus filling our other requirement of preventing interference between read and write operations.

With the implementation chosen, we can understand the constructor of Example15.1; writing to the list is expensive, so it is sensible to use a conversion constructor to set it up with a year's worth of task queues in one operation (line //1).

The getTask method is straightforward; we simply iterate over the task queues, starting with today's queue, looking for a scheduled task. If the method finds no outstanding tasks, it returns null—and if finding a task-free day was noteworthy, how should we celebrate a task-free year?

At midnight each day, the system will call the method rollOver, which implements the sad ritual of shutting down the old day's task queue and transferring the remaining tasks in it to the new day. The sequence of events here is important; rollOver first removes the queue from the list, at which time producers and consumers may still be about to insert or remove elements. It then calls the StoppableTaskQueue.shutDown which, as we saw in Example 14.1 returns the remaining tasks in the queue and guarantees that no more will be added. Depending on how far they have progressed, calls of addTask will either complete or will return false, indicating that they failed because the queue was shut down.

This motivates the logic of addTask: the only situation in which the addTask method of StoppableTaskQueue can return false is that in which the queue being called is already stopped. Since the only queue that is stopped is the day 0 queue, a return value of false from addTask must result from a producer thread getting a reference to this queue just before a midnight rollover. In that case, the current value of element 0 of the list is by now the new day 0, and it is safe to try again. If the second attempt fails, the thread has been suspended for 24 hours!

Notice that the rollOver method is quite expensive; it writes to the schedule twice, and since the schedule is represented by a CopyOnWriteArrayList (see Section 15.2.3), each write causes the entire backing array to be copied. The argument in favour of this implementation choice is that rollOver is very rarely invoked compared to the number of calls made on getTask, which iterates over the schedule. The alternative to CopyOnWriteArrayList would be a BlockingQueue implementation, but the improvement that would provide in the rarely-used rollOver method would come at the cost of slowing down the frequently-used getTask method, since queue iterators are not intended to be used in performance-critical situations.

Using Range-View and Iterator Methods Of the four List method groups above, Example 15.1 makes use of the methods of one group, positional access, in several places. To see how range-view and iterator methods could also be useful, consider how the TaskScheduler could export its schedule, or a part of it, for a client to modify. You would want the client to be able to view this subschedule and perhaps to insert or remove tasks, but you would definitely want to forbid the insertion or removal of elements of the list itself, since these represent the sequence of days for which tasks are being scheduled. The standard way to achieve this would be by means of an unmodifiable list, as provided by the Collections class (see Section 17.3.2). An alternative in this case would be to return a list iterator, as the snapshot iterators for copy-on-write collections do not support modification of the backing collection. So we could define a method to provide clients with a "planning window":

```
ListIterator<StoppableTaskQueue> getSubSchedule(int startDay, int endDay) {
  return schedule.subList(startDay, endDay).listIterator();
}
```

This view will be fine for today, but we have to remember to discard it at midnight, when the structural changes of removing and adding entries will invalidate it.

15.2 Implementing List

There are three concrete implementations of List in the Collections Framework (see Figure 15.3), differing in how fast they perform the various operations defined by the interface and how they behave in the face of concurrent modification; unlike Set and Queue, however, List has no subinterfaces to specify differences in functional behavior. In this and the following section we look at each implementation in turn and provide a performance comparison.

15.2.1 ArrayList

Arrays are provided as part of the Java language and have a very convenient syntax, but their key disadvantage—that, once created, they cannot be resized—makes them increasingly less popular than List implementations, which (if resizable at all) are indefinitely extensible. The most commonly used implementation of List is, in fact, ArrayList—that is, a List backed by an array.

The standard implementation of ArrayList stores the List elements in contiguous array locations, with the first element always stored at index 0 in the array. It requires an array

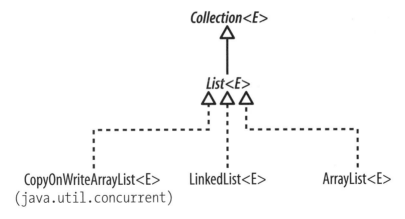

Figure 15.3: Implementations of the List interface

at least large enough (with sufficient *capacity*) to contain the elements, together with a way of keeping track of the number of "occupied" locations (the size of the List). If an ArrayList has grown to the point where its size is equal to its capacity, attempting to add another element will require it to replace the backing array with a larger one capable of holding the old contents and the new element, and with a margin for further expansion (the standard implementation actually uses a new array that is double the length of the old one). As we explained in Section 11.3, this leads to an amortized cost of $O(1)$.

The performance of ArrayList reflects array performance for "random-access" operations: set and get take constant time. The downside of an array implementation is in inserting or removing elements at arbitrary positions, because that may require adjusting the position of other elements. (We have already met this problem with the remove method of the iterators of array-based queues—for example, ArrayBlockingQueue (see Section 14.3.2). But the performance of positional add and remove methods are much more important for lists than iterator.remove is for queues.)

For example, Figure 15.4(a) shows a new ArrayList after three elements have been added by means of the following statements:

```
List<Character> charList = new ArrayList<Character>();
Collections.addAll(charList, 'a', 'b', 'c');
```

If we now want to remove the element at index 1 of an array, the implementation must preserve the order of the remaining elements and ensure that the occupied region of the array is still to start at index 0. So the element at index 2 must be moved to index 1, that at index 3 to index 2, and so on. Figure 15.4(b) shows our sample ArrayList after this operation has been carried out. Since every element must be moved in turn, the time complexity of this operation is proportional to the size of the list (even though, because this operation can usually be implemented in hardware, the constant factor is low).

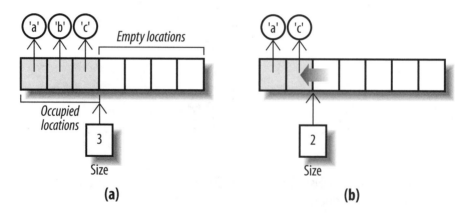

Figure 15.4: Removing an element from an ArrayList

Even so, the alert reader, recalling the discussion of the circular arrays used to implement ArrayBlockingQueue and ArrayDeque (see Section 14.4.1) may wonder why a circular array was not chosen for the implementation of ArrayList, too. It is true that the add and remove methods of a circular array show much better performance only when they are called with an index argument of 0, but this is such a common case and the overhead of using a circular array is so small, that the question remains.

Indeed, an outline implementation of a circular array list was presented by Heinz Kabutz in *The Java Specialists' Newsletter* (*http://www.javaspecialists.co.za/archive/Issue027.html*). In principle it is still possible that ArrayList may be reimplemented in this way, possibly leading to real performance gains in many existing Java applications. A possible alternative is that the circular ArrayDeque may be retrofitted to implement the methods of List. In the meantime, if your application is using a List in which the performance of element insertion and removal from the beginning of a list is more important than that of random-access operations, consider writing to the Deque interface and taking advantage of its very efficient ArrayDeque implementation.

As we mentioned in the discussion of ArrayBlockingQueue (Section 14.2), variable-size array-backed collection classes can have one configuration parameter: the initial length of the array. So besides the standard Collections Framework constructors, ArrayList has one that allows you to choose the value of the initial capacity to be large enough to accommodate the elements of the collection without frequent create-copy operations. The initial capacity of an ArrayList created by the default constructor is 10, and that of one initialized with the elements of another collection is 110% of the size of that collection.

The iterators of ArrayList are fail-fast.

15.2.2 LinkedList

We discussed LinkedList as a Deque implementation in Section 14.4.1. You will avoid it as a List implementation if your application makes much use of random access; since the list must iterate internally to reach the required position, positional add and remove have linear time complexity, on average. Where LinkedList does have a performance advantage over ArrayList is in adding and removing elements anywhere other than at the end of the list; for LinkedList this takes constant time, against the linear time required for noncircular array implementations.

15.2.3 CopyOnWriteArrayList

In Section 13.1 we met CopyOnWriteArraySet, a set implementation designed to provide thread safety together with very fast read access. CopyOnWriteArrayList is a List implementation with the same design aims. This combination of thread safety with fast read access is useful in some concurrent programs, especially when a collection of observer objects needs to receive frequent event notifications. The cost is that the array which backs the collection has to be treated as immutable, so a new copy is created whenever any changes are made to the collection. This cost may not be too high to pay if changes in the set of observers occur only rarely.

The class CopyOnWriteArraySet in fact delegates all of its operations to an instance of CopyOnWriteArrayList, taking advantage of the atomic operations addIfAbsent and addAllAbsent provided by the latter to enable the Set methods add and addAll to avoid introducing duplicates to the set. In addition to the two standard constructors (see Section 12.3), CopyOnWriteArrayList has an extra one that allows it to be created using the elements of a supplied array as its initial contents. Its iterators are snapshot iterators, reflecting the state of the list at the time of their creation.

15.3 Comparing List Implementations

Table 15.1 gives the comparative performance for some sample operations on List classes. Even though the choice here is much narrower than with lists or even sets, the same process of elimination can be used. As with queues, the first question to ask is whether your application requires thread safety. If so, you should use CopyOnWriteArrayList, if you can—that is, if writes to the list will be relatively infrequent. If not, you will have to use a synchronized wrapper (see Section17.3.1) around ArrayList or LinkedList.

For most list applications the choice is between ArrayList and LinkedList, synchronized or not. Once again, your decision will depend on how the list is used in practice. If set

Table 15.1: Comparative performance of different List implementations

	get	add	contains	next	remove(0)	iterator. remove
ArrayList	$O(1)$	$O(1)$	$O(n)$	$O(1)$	$O(n)$	$O(n)$
LinkedList	$O(n)$	$O(1)$	$O(n)$	$O(1)$	$O(1)$	$O(1)$
CopyOnWrite-ArrayList	$O(1)$	$O(n)$	$O(n)$	$O(1)$	$O(n)$	$O(n)$

and get predominate, or element insertion and removal is mainly at the end of the list, then ArrayList will be the best choice. If, instead, your application needs to frequently insert and remove elements near the start of the list as part of a process that uses iteration, LinkedList may be better. If you are in doubt, test the performance with each implementation. A Java 6 alternative for single-threaded code that may be worth considering in the last case—if the insertions and removals are actually *at* the start of the list—is to write to the Deque interface, taking advantage of its very efficient ArrayDeque implementation. For relatively infrequent random access, use an iterator, or copy the ArrayDeque elements into an array using toArray.

It is possible that, in a future release, ArrayDeque will be retrofitted to implement the List interface; if that happens, it will become the implementation of choice for both Queue and List in single-threaded environments.

Maps

The Map interface is the last of the major Collections Framework interfaces, and the only one that does not inherit from Collection. It defines the operations that are supported by a set of key-to-value associations in which the keys are unique. These operations are shown in Figure 16.1 and fall into the following four groups, broadly parallel to the four operation groups of Collection—adding elements, removing elements, querying collection contents, and providing different views of the contents of a collection.

Adding Associations

```
V put(K key, V value)          // add or replace a key-value association
                               // return the old value (may be null) if the
                               // key was present; otherwise returns null
void putAll(Map<? extends K,? extends V> m)
                               // add each of the key-value associations in
                               // the supplied map into the receiver
```

Map<K,V>
+put(key : K, value : V) : V
+putAll(t) : void
+clear() : void
+remove(key : Object) : V
+get(key : Object) : V
+containsKey(key : Object) : boolean
+containsValue(value : Object) : boolean
+size() : int
+isEmpty() : boolean
+entrySet() : Set<Map.Entry<K,V>>
+keySet() : Set<K>
+values() : Collection<V>

Figure 16.1: Map

The operations in this group are optional; calling them on an unmodifiable map will result in an `UnsupportedOperationException`.

Removing Associations

```
void clear()          // remove all associations from this map
V remove(Object key)  // remove the association, if any, with the
                      // given key; returns the value with which it
                      // was associated, or null
```

The signature of `Map.remove` is like that of the `Collection.remove` (see Section 12.1) in that it takes a parameter of type `Object` rather than the generic type. We discussed alternatives to this design in Section 2.6.

Like the addition operations of the previous group, these removal operations are optional.

Querying the Contents of a Map

```
V get(Object k)                       // return the value corresponding to k, or
                                      // null if k is not present as a key
boolean containsKey(Object k)         // return true if k is present as a key
boolean containsValue(Object v)       // return true if v is present as a value
int size()                            // return the number of associations
boolean isEmpty()                     // return true if there are no associations
```

The arguments to `containsKey` and `containsValue` may be `null` for Map implementations that allow `null` keys or values (respectively). An implementation that does not allow `null`s will throw `NullPointerException` if supplied with a `null` argument to these methods.

As with the `size` method of `Collection`, the largest element count that can be reported is `Integer.MAX_VALUE`.

Providing Collection Views of the Keys, Values, or Associations:

```
Set<Map.Entry<K, V>> entrySet() // return a Set view of the associations
Set<K> keySet()                 // return a Set view of the keys
Collection<V> values()          // return a Collection view of the values
```

The collections returned by these methods are backed by the map, so any changes to them are reflected in the map itself, and vice versa. In fact, only limited changes can be made via the view: elements can be removed, either directly or via an iterator over the view, but cannot be added; you will get an `UnsupportedOperationException` if you try. Removing a key removes the single corresponding key-value association; removing a value, on the other hand, removes only one of the associations mapping to it; the value may still be present as part of an association with a different key. An iterator over the view will become undefined if the backing map is concurrently modified.

The members of the set returned by `entrySet` implement the interface `Map.Entry`, which represents a key-value association and provides a `setValue` method which can be used to change values in the backing map. The documentation for Map.Entry is unusually specific in specifying that objects implementing the interface can only be created during iteration of the view resulting from a call of entrySet, and that such objects become invalid if the backing map is modified during this iteration. In Java 6 this restricted scenario for the creation of Map.Entry objects is insufficient, as it is the return type for a number of methods of NavigableMap (see Section 16.3).

16.1 Using the Methods of Map

One problem with basing the to-do manager on priority queues, as we have done in the last two chapters, is that priority queues are unable to preserve the order in which elements are added to them (unless that can be incorporated in the priority ordering, for example as a timestamp or sequence number). To avoid this, we could use as an alternative model a series of FIFO queues, each one assigned to a single priority. A Map would be suitable for holding the association between priorities and task queues; EnumMap in particular is a highly efficient Map implementation specialized for use with keys which are members of an enum.

This model will rely on a Queue implementation that maintains FIFO ordering. To focus on the use of the Map methods, let's assume a single-threaded client and use a series of ArrayDeques as the implementation:

```
Map<Priority,ArrayDeque<Task>> taskMap =
  new EnumMap<Priority,ArrayDeque<Task>>(Priority.class);
for (Priority p : Priority.values()) {
  taskMap.put(p, new ArrayDeque<Task>());
}
// populate the lists, for example:
taskMap.get(Priority.MEDIUM).add(mikePhone);
taskMap.get(Priority.HIGH).add(databaseCode);
```

Now, to get to one of the task queues—say, the one with the highest-priority tasks—we can write:

```
Queue<Task> highPriorityTaskList = taskMap.get(Priority.HIGH);
```

Polling this queue will now give us the high priority to-dos, in the order in which they were entered into the system.

To see the use of some of the other methods of Map, let's extend the example a little to allow for the possibility that some of these tasks might actually earn us some money by being billable. One way of representing this would be by defining a class Client:

```
class Client {...}
Client acme = new Client("Acme Corp.",...);
```

and creating a mapping from tasks to clients:

```
Map<Task,Client> billingMap = new HashMap<Task,Client>();
billingMap.put(interfaceCode, acme);
```

We need to ensure that the system can still handle nonbillable tasks. We have a choice here: we can either simply not add the name of a nonbillable task into the billingMap, or we can map it to null. In either case, as part of the code for processing a task t, we can write:

```
Task t = ...
Client client = billingMap.get(t);
if (client != null) {
  client.bill(t);
}
```

When we have finally finished all the work we were contracted to do by our client Acme Corp., the map entries that associate tasks with Acme can be removed:

```
Collection<Client> clients = billingMap.values();
for (Iterator<Client> iter = clients.iterator() ; iter.hasNext() ; ) {
  if (iter.next().equals(acme))   {
    iter.remove();
  }
}
```

A neater alternative takes advantage of the method Collections.singleton (see Section 17.2), a factory method which returns an immutable Set containing only the specified element:

```
clients.removeAll(Collections.singleton(acme));
```

Both ways cost $O(n)$, with similar constant factors in Sun's current implementation.

16.2 Implementing Map

The implementations, eight in all, that the Collections Framework provides for Map are shown in Figure 16.2. We shall discuss HashMap, LinkedHashMap, WeakHashMap, IdentityHashMap, and EnumMap here; the interfaces NavigableMap, ConcurrentMap, and ConcurrentNavigableMap are discussed, along with their implementations, in the sections following this one.

For constructors, the general rule for Map implementations is like that for Collection implementations (see Section 12.3). Every implementation excluding EnumMap has at least two constructors; taking HashMap as an example, they are:

```
public HashMap()
public HashMap(Map<? extends K,? extends V> m)
```

The first of these creates an empty map, and the second a map that will contain the key-value mappings contained in the supplied map m. The keys and values of map m must have types that are the same as (or are subtypes of) the keys and values, respectively, of the map being created. Using this second constructor has the same effect as creating an empty map with the default constructor, and then adding the contents of map m using putAll. In addition to these two, the standard implementations have other constructors for configuration purposes.

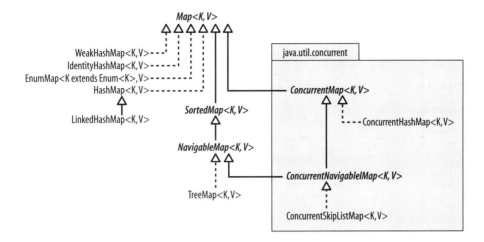

Figure 16.2: The structure of Map implementations in the Collections Framework

16.2.1 HashMap

In discussing HashSet in Section 13.1.1, we mentioned that it delegates all its operations to a private instance of HashMap. Figure 16.3(a) is similar to Figure 13.2, but without the simplification that removed the value elements from the map (all elements in a HashSet are stored as keys with the same constant value). The discussion in Section 13.1 of hash tables and their performance applies equally to HashMap. In particular, HashMap provides constant-time performance for put and get. Although in principle constant-time performance is only attainable with no collisions, it can be closely approached by the use of rehashing to control the load and thereby to minimize the number of collisions.

Iteration over a collection of keys or values requires time proportional to the capacity of the map plus the number of key-value mappings that it contains. The iterators are fail-fast.

Two constructors allow the programmer to configure a new instance of HashMap:

```
public HashMap(int initialCapacity)
public HashMap(int initialCapacity, float loadFactor)
```

These constructors are like those of HashSet, allowing specification of the initial capacity and, optionally, the load factor at which the table will be rehashed.

16.2.2 LinkedHashMap

Like LinkedHashSet (Section 13.1.2), the class LinkedHashMap refines the contract of its parent class, HashMap, by guaranteeing the order in which iterators return its elements. Unlike LinkedHashSet, however, LinkedHashMap offers a choice of iteration orders; elements can be returned either in the order in which they were inserted in the map, or in the order in which they were accessed (from least-recently to most-recently accessed). An access-

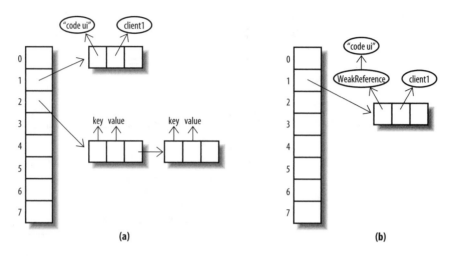

(a)   (b)

Figure 16.3: HashMap and WeakHashMap

ordered `LinkedHashMap` is created by supplying an argument of `true` for the last parameter of the constructor:

```
public LinkedHashMap(int initialCapacity,
                     float loadFactor,
                     boolean accessOrder)
```

Supplying `false` will give an insertion-ordered map. The other constructors, which are just like those of `HashMap`, also produce insertion-ordered maps. As with `LinkedHashSet`, iteration over a `LinkedHashMap` takes time proportional only to the number of elements in the map, not its capacity.

Access-ordered maps are especially useful for constructing *Least Recently Used* (*LRU*) caches. A cache is an area of memory that stores frequently accessed data for fast access. In designing a cache, the key issue is the choice of algorithm that will be used to decide what data to remove in order to conserve memory. When an item from a cached data set needs to be found, the cache will be searched first. Typically, if the item is not found in the cache, it will be retrieved from the main store and added to the cache. But the cache cannot be allowed to continue growing indefinitely, so a strategy must be chosen for removing the least useful item from the cache when a new one is added. If the strategy chosen is LRU, the entry removed will be the one least recently used. This simple strategy is suitable for situations in which an access of an element increases the probability of further access in the near future of the same element. Its simplicity and speed have made it the most popular caching strategy.

Cache construction with `LinkedHashMap` is further aided by `removeEldestEntry`, the single method that it adds to those inherited from `HashMap`:

```
protected boolean removeEldestEntry(Map.Entry<K,V> eldest)
```

The contract for removeEldestEntry states that the methods put and putAll will call removeEldestEntry whenever a new entry is added to the map, passing to it the "eldest" entry. In an insertion-ordered map, the eldest entry will be the one that was least recently added to the map, but in an access-ordered map it is the one least recently accessed (and if some entries have never been accessed, it is the one amongst these which was least recently added). In LinkedHashMap itself, removeEldestEntry does nothing and returns false, but subclasses can override it to return true under some circumstances. The contract for this method specifies that although it may itself remove the eldest entry, it must return false if it has done so, since it is expected that a return value of true will cause its calling method to do the removal. A simple example of removeEldestEntry would allow a map to grow to a given maximum size and then maintain that size by deleting the eldest entry each time a new one is added:

```
class BoundedSizeMap extends LinkedHashMap {
  private int maxEntries;
  public BoundedSizeMap(int maxEntries) {
    super(16, 0.75f, true);
    this.maxEntries = maxEntries;
  }
  protected boolean removeEldestEntry(Map.Entry eldest) {
    return size() > maxEntries;
  }
}
```

A refinement of this simple example could take into account the entry supplied as the argument to removeEldestEntry. For example, a directory cache might have a set of reserved names which should never be removed, even if the cache continues to grow as a result.

Notice that an insertion-ordered LinkedHashMap that overrides removeEldestEntry as shown above will implement a FIFO strategy. FIFO caching has often been used in preference to LRU because it is much simpler to implement in maps that do not offer access ordering. However LRU is usually more effective than FIFO, because the reduced cost of cache refreshes outweighs the overhead of maintaining access ordering.

Iteration over a collection of keys or values returned by a LinkedHashMap is linear in the number of elements. The iterators over such collections are fail-fast.

16.2.3 WeakHashMap

An ordinary Map keeps ordinary ("strong") references to all the objects it contains. That means that even when a key has become unreachable by any means other than through the map itself, it cannot be garbage collected. Often, that's exactly what we want; in the example at the beginning of this chapter, where we mapped tasks to clients, we wouldn't have wanted a mapping to disappear just because we weren't holding a reference to the task object that we had put into the HashMap. To look up the value associated with a supplied key, the `HashMap` will look for a key that matches (in the sense of `equals`) the supplied one—they don't have to be physically the same object.

But suppose that the objects of the key class are unique—that is, object equality is the same as object identity. For example, each object might contain a unique serial number. In this case, once we no longer have a reference—from outside the map—to an object being used as a key, we can never look it up again, because we can never re-create it. So the map might as well get rid of the key-value pair and, in fact, there may be a strong advantage in doing so if the map is large and memory is in short supply. That is the idea that `WeakHashMap` implements.

Internally `WeakHashMap` holds references to its key objects through references of the class `java.lang.ref.WeakReference` (see Figure 16.3(b)). A `WeakReference` introduces an extra level of indirection in reaching an object. For example, to make a weak reference to to the string `"code gui"` you would write:

```
WeakReference<String> wref = new WeakReference<String>("code gui");
```

And at a later time you would recover a strong reference to it using the `get` method of `WeakReference`:

```
String recoveredStringRef = wref.get();
```

If there are no strong references to the string `"code gui"` (or to any substring of it returned from its `subString` method), the existence of the weak reference will not by itself prevent the garbage collector from reclaiming the object. So the recovered reference value `recoveredStringRef` may, or may not, be `null`.

To see how `WeakHashMap` can be useful, think of a tracing garbage collector that works by determining which objects are reachable, and reclaiming all others. The starting points for a reachability search include the static variables of currently loaded classes and the local variables currently in scope. Only strong references are followed to determine reachability, so the keys of a `WeakHashMap` will be available to be reclaimed if they are not reachable by any other route. Note that a key cannot be reclaimed if it is strongly referenced from the corresponding value. (including from the values they correspond to).

Before most operations on a `WeakHashMap` are executed, the map checks which keys have been reclaimed. (It's not enough to check if a key is `null`, because `null` is a legal value for keys in a `WeakHashMap`. The `WeakReference` mechanism allows you to tell the garbage collector to leave information in a `ReferenceQueue` each time it reclaims a weakly referenced object.) The `WeakHashMap` then removes every entry of which the garbage collector has reclaimed the key.

What is a `WeakHashMap` good for? Imagine you have a program that allocates some transient system resource—a buffer, for example—on request from a client. Besides passing a reference to the resource back to the client, your program might also need to store information about it locally—for example, associating the buffer with the client that requested it. That could be implemented by means of a map from resource to client objects. But now, even after the client has disposed of the resource, the map will still hold a reference that will prevent the resource object from being garbage collected—if, that is, the reference is strong. Memory will gradually be used up by resources which are no longer in use. But if the reference is weak, held by a WeakHashMap, the garbage collector will be able to reclaim the object after the last strong reference has gone away, and the memory leak is prevented.

A more general use is in those applications—for example, caches—where you don't mind information disappearing if memory is low. Here, WeakHashMap is useful whether or not the keys are unique, because you can always re-create a key if necessary to see if the corresponding value is still in the cache. WeakHashMap isn't perfect for this purpose; one of its drawbacks is that it weakly references the map's keys rather than its values, which usually occupy much more memory. So even after the garbage collector has reclaimed a key, the real benefit in terms of available memory will not be experienced until the map has removed the stale entry. A second drawback is that weak references are *too* weak; the garbage collector is liable to reclaim a weakly reachable object at any time, and the programmer cannot influence this in any way. (A sister class of WeakReference, java.lang.ref.SoftReference, is treated differently: the garbage collector should postpone reclaiming these until it is under severe memory pressure. Heinz Kabutz has written a SoftReference-based map using generics; see *http://www.javaspecialists.co.za/archive/Issue098.html*.)

WeakHashMap performs similarly to HashMap, though more slowly because of the overheads of the extra level of indirection for keys. The cost of clearing out unwanted key-value associations before each operation is proportional to the number of associations that need to be removed. The iterators over collections of keys and values returned by WeakHashMap are fail-fast.

16.2.4 IdentityHashMap

An IdentityHashMap differs from an ordinary HashMap in that two keys are considered equal only if they are physically the same object: identity, rather than equals, is used for key comparison. That sets the contract for IdentityHashMap at odds with the contract for Map, the interface it implements, which specifies that equality should be used for key comparison. An alternative design could have avoided this problem by providing a weaker contract for Map, with two different subinterfaces strengthening the contract to specify the type of key comparison to use. This is another example of the problem we discussed in Section 11.4, of balancing the tradeoff between a framework's complexity and its precision in implementing its contracts.

IdentityHashMap is a specialized class, commonly used in operations such as serialization, in which a graph has to be traversed and information stored about each node. The algorithm used for traversing the graph must be able to check, for each node it encounters, whether that node has already been seen; otherwise, graph cycles could be followed indefinitely. For cyclic graphs, we must use identity rather than equality to check whether nodes are the same. Calculating equality between two graph node objects requires calculating the equality of their fields, which in turn means computing all their successors—and we are back to the

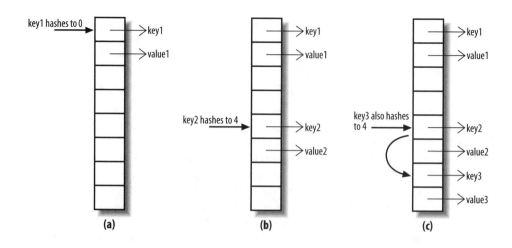

Figure 16.4: Resolving collisions by linear probing

original problem. An IdentityHashMap, by contrast, will report a node as being present only if that same node has previously been put into the map.

The standard implementation of IdentityHashMap handles collisions differently than the chaining method shown in Figure 13.2 and used by all the other variants of HashSet and HashMap. This implementation uses a technique called *linear probing*, in which the key and value references are stored directly in adjacent locations in the table itself rather than in cells referenced from it. With linear probing, collisions are handled by simply stepping along the table until the first free pair of locations is found. Figure 16.4 shows three stages in filling an IdentityHashMap with a capacity of 8. In (a) we are storing a key-value pair whose key hashes to 0, and in (b) a pair whose key hashes to 4. The third key, added in (c), also hashes to 4, so the algorithm steps along the table until it finds an unused location. In this case, the first one it tries, with index 6, is free and can be used. Deletions are trickier than with chaining; if key2 and value2 were removed from the table in Figure 13.2, key3 and value3 would have to be moved along to take their place.

Out of all the Collections Framework hash implementations, why does IdentityHashMap alone use linear probing when all the others use chaining? The motivation for using probing is that it is somewhat faster than following a linked list, but that is only true when a reference to the value can be placed directly in the array, as in Figure 16.4. That isn't practical for all other hash-based collections, because they store the hash code as well as the value. This is for reasons of efficiency: a get operation must check whether it has found the right key, and since equality is an expensive operation, it makes sense to check first whether it even has the right hash code. Of course, this reasoning doesn't apply to IdentityHashMap, which checks object identity rather than object equality.

There are three constructors for IdentityHashMap:

```
public IdentityHashMap()
public IdentityHashMap(Map<? extends K,? extends V> m)
public IdentityHashMap(int expectedMaxSize)
```

The first two are the standard constructors found in every general-purpose Map implementation. The third takes the place of the two constructors that in other HashMaps allow the user to control the initial capacity of the table and the load factor at which it will be rehashed. IdentityHashMap doesn't allow this, fixing it instead (at .67 in the standard implementation) in order to protect the user from the consequences of setting the load factor inappropriately: whereas the cost of finding a key in a table using chaining is proportional to the load factor l, in a table using linear probing it is proportional to $1/(1-l)$. So avoiding high load factors is too important to be left to the programmer! This decision is in line with the policy, mentioned earlier, of no longer providing configuration parameters when new classes are introduced into the Framework.

16.2.5 EnumMap

Implementing a mapping from an enumerated type is straightforward and very efficient, for reasons similar to those described for EnumSet (see Section 13.1.4); in an array implementation, the ordinal value of each enumerated type constant can serve as the index of the corresponding value. The basic operations of get and put can be implemented as array accesses, in constant time. An iterator over the key set takes time proportional to the number of constants in the enumerated type and returns the keys in their natural order (the order in which the enum constants are declared). Although, as with EnumSet, this class is not thread-safe, the iterators over its collection views are not fail-fast but weakly consistent.

EnumMap has three public constructors:

```
EnumMap(Class<K> keyType)           // create an empty enum map
EnumMap(EnumMap<K, ? extends V> m)  // create an enum map, with the same
                                    // key type and elements as m
EnumMap(Map<K, ? extends V> m)      // create an enum map using the elements
                                    // of the supplied Map, which (unless it
                                    // is an EnumMap) must contain at least
                                    // one association
```

An EnumMap contains a reified key type, which is used at run time for checking the validity of new entries being added to the map. This type is supplied by the three constructors in different ways. In the first, it is supplied as a class token; in the second, it is copied from the specified EnumMap. In the third, there are two possibilities: either the specified Map is actually an EnumMap, in which case it behaves like the second constructor, or the class of the first key of the specified Map is used (which is why the supplied Map may not be empty).

16.3 SortedMap and NavigableMap

Like SortedSet, the subinterface SortedMap (see Figure 16.5) adds to its contract a guarantee that its iterators will traverse the map in ascending key order. Its definition is

```
┌─────────────────────────────────────────────────────┐
│                 SortedMap<K,V>                       │
├─────────────────────────────────────────────────────┤
│ +firstKey() : K                                      │
│ +lastKey() : K                                       │
│ +comparator() : Comparator<? super K>                │
│ +subMap( fromKey : K, toKey : K ) : SortedMap<K,V>   │
│ +headMap( toKey : K ) : SortedMap<K,V>               │
│ +tailMap( fromKey : K ) : SortedMap<K,V>             │
└─────────────────────────────────────────────────────┘
```

Figure 16.5: SortedMap

similar to that of SortedSet, with methods such as firstKey and headMap corresponding to the SortedSet methods first and headSet. Also like SortedSet, the SortedMap interface has been extended in Java 6 by the subinterface NavigableMap (see Figure 16.6). This section is structured like Section13.2 for the same reasons: SortedMap has been made obsolete by NavigableMap, but it may be helpful for developers prevented for the moment from using Java 6 to have the two interfaces treated separately.

A SortedMap imposes an ordering on its keys, either that of their natural ordering or of a Comparator; but in either case the compare method must be consistent with equals, as the SortedMap will use compare to determine when a key is already in the map.

The extra methods defined by the SortedMap interface fall into three groups:

Getting the First and Last Elements

```
K firstKey()
K lastKey()
```

If the set is empty, these operations throw a NoSuchElementException.

Retrieving the Comparator

```
Comparator<? super K> comparator()
```

This method returns the map's key comparator if it has been given one, instead of relying on the natural ordering of the keys. Otherwise, it returns null.

Finding Subsequences

```
SortedMap<K,V> subMap(K fromKey, K toKey)
SortedMap<K,V> headMap(K toKey)
SortedMap<K,V> tailMap(K fromKey)
```

These operations work like the corresponding operations in SortedSet: the key arguments do not themselves have to be present in the map, and the sets returned include the fromKey—if, in fact, it is present in the map—and do not include the toKey.

NavigableMap<K,V>
+pollFirstEntry() : Map.Entry<K,V>
+pollLastEntry() : Map.Entry<K,V>
+firstEntry() : Map.Entry<K,V>
+lastEntry() : Map.Entry<K,V>
+subMap(fromKey : K, fromInclusive : boolean, toKey : K, toInclusive : boolean) : NavigableMap<K,V>
+headMap(toKey : K, toInclusive : boolean) : NavigableMap<K,V>
+tailMap(fromKey : K, fromInclusive : boolean) : NavigableMap<K,V>
+ceilingEntry(key : K) : Map.Entry<K,V>
+ceilingKey(key : K) : K
+floorEntry(key : K) : Map.Entry<K,V>
+floorKey(key : K) : K
+higherEntry(key : K) : Map.Entry<K,V>
+higherKey(key : K) : K
+lowerEntry(key : K) : Map.Entry<K,V>
+lowerKey(key : K) : K
+descendingMap() : NavigableMap<K,V>
+descendingKeySet() : NavigableSet<K>
+navigableKeySet() : NavigableSet<K>

Figure 16.6: NavigableMap

NavigableMap

NavigableMap (see Figure 16.6) extends and replaces SortedMap, in the same way as NavigableSet replaces SortedSet. Its methods correspond almost exactly to those of NavigableSet, regarding the map as a set of key-value associations represented by Map.Entry objects. So where a NavigableSet method returns an element of the set, the corresponding NavigableMap method return a result of type Map.Entry. Until now, objects of this type were only obtainable by iterating over the set returned by Map.entrySet, and were specified to become invalid in the face of concurrent modification of the map. This specification is not appropriate to Map.Entry objects returned by the new methods, and the contract for NavigableMap acknowledges this by specifying that the Map.Entry objects returned by its methods are snapshot objects reflecting the state of the map at the time they were produced, and do not support setValue.

The methods added by NavigableMap can be divided into four groups.

Getting the First and Last Elements

```
Map.Entry<K,V> pollFirstEntry()
Map.Entry<K,V> pollLastEntry()
Map.Entry<K,V> firstEntry()
Map.Entry<K,V> lastEntry()
```

The first two methods are analogous to pollFirst and pollLast in NavigableSet. The last two were introduced because the emphasis in NavigableMap on making map entries

available requires entry-returning methods corresponding to the key-returning methods
`first` and `last` inherited from `SortedMap` .

Getting Range Views

```
NavigableMap<K,V> subMap(
            K fromKey, boolean fromInclusive, K toKey, boolean toInclusive)
NavigableMap<K,V> headMap(K toKey, boolean inclusive)
NavigableMap<K,V> tailMap(K fromKey, boolean inclusive)
```

Like the `NavigableSet` methods, these provide more flexibility than the range-view methods of `SortedMap`. Instead of always returning a half-open interval, these methods accept
`boolean` parameters that are used to determine whether to include the key or keys defining
the interval.

Getting Closest Matches

```
Map.Entry<K,V> ceilingEntry(K Key)
K ceilingKey(K Key)
Map.Entry<K,V> floorEntry(K Key)
K floorKey(K Key)
Map.Entry<K,V> higherEntry(K Key)
K higherKey(K Key)
Map.Entry<K,V> lowerEntry(K Key)
K lowerKey(K Key)
```

These are similar to the corresponding closest-match methods of `NavigableSet`, but they
return `Map.Entry` objects. If you want the key belonging to one of these entries, use the
corresponding convenience key-returning method, with the performance benefit of allowing
the map to avoid the unnecessary creation of a `Map.Entry` object.

Navigating the Map

```
NavigableMap<K,V> descendingMap()    // return a reverse-order view of the map
NavigableSet<K> descendingKeySet()   // return a reverse-order key set
```

There is also a new method defined to obtain a `NavigableSet` of keys:

```
NavigableSet<K> navigableKeySet()    // return a forward-order key set
```

You might wonder why the method `keySet`, inherited from `Map`, could not simply be
overridden using a covariant return type to return a `NavigableSet`. Indeed, the platform
implementations of `NavigableMap.keySet` do return a `NavigableMap`. But there is a
compatibility concern: if `TreeMap.keySet` were to have its return type changed from `Set`
to `NavigableSet`, any existing `TreeMap` subclasses which override that method would now
fail to compile unless they too changed their return type. (This concern is similar to those
discussed in Section 8.4.)

16.3.1 TreeMap

SortedMap is implemented in the Collections Framework by TreeMap. We met trees as a data structure for storing elements in order when we discussed TreeSet (see Section 13.2.1). In fact, the internal representation of a TreeSet is just a TreeMap in which every key is associated with the same standard value, so the explanation of the mechanism and performance of red-black trees given in Section 13.2.1 applies equally here.

The constructors for TreeMap include, besides the standard ones, one that allows you to supply a Comparator and one that allows you to create one from another SortedMap, using both the same comparator and the same mappings:

```
public TreeMap(Comparator<? super K> comparator)
public TreeMap(SortedMap<K, ? extends V> m)
```

Notice that the second of these constructors suffer from a similar problem to the corresponding constructor of TreeSet (see Section 13.2.1), because the standard conversion constructor always uses the natural ordering of the keys, even when its argument is actually a SortedMap.

TreeMap has similar performance characteristics to TreeSet: the basic operations (get, put, and remove) perform in $O(\log n)$ time). The collection view iterators are fail-fast.

16.4 ConcurrentMap

Maps are often used in high-performance server applications—for example, as cache implementations—so a high-throughput thread-safe map implementation is an essential part of the Java platform. This requirement cannot be met by synchronized maps such as those provided by Collections.synchronizedMap, because with full synchronization each operation needs to obtain an exclusive lock on the entire map, effectively serializing access to it. Locking only a part of the collection at a time—*lock striping*—can achieve very large gains in throughput, as we shall see shortly with ConcurrentHashMap. But because there is no single lock for a client to hold to gain exclusive access, client-side locking no longer works, and clients need assistance from the collection itself to carry out atomic actions.

That is the purpose of the interface ConcurrentMap. It provides declarations for methods that perform compound operations atomically. There are four of these methods:

```
V putIfAbsent(K key, V value)
        // associate key with value only if key is not currently present.
        // return the old value (may be null) if the key was present,
        // otherwise return null
boolean remove(Object key, Object value)
        // remove key only if it is currently mapped to value.  Returns
        // true if the value was removed, false otherwise
```

```
V replace(K key, V value)
        // replace entry for key only if it is currently present.  Return
        // the old value (may be null) if the key was present, otherwise
        // return null
boolean replace(K key, V oldValue, V newValue)
        // replace entry for key only if it is currently mapped to oldValue.
        // return true if the value was replaced, false otherwise
```

16.4.1 ConcurrentHashMap

ConcurrentHashMap provides an implementation of ConcurrentMap and offers a highly effective solution to the problem of reconciling throughput with thread safety. It is optimized for reading, so retrievals do not block even while the table is being updated (to allow for this, the contract states that the results of retrievals will reflect the latest update operations completed before the start of the retrieval). Updates also can often proceed without blocking, because a ConcurrentHashMap consists of not one but a set of tables, called *segments*, each of which can be independently locked. If the number of segments is large enough relative to the number of threads accessing the table, there will often be no more than one update in progress per segment at any time. The constructors for ConcurrentHashMap are similar to those of HashMap, but with an extra one that provides the programmer with control over the number of segments that the map will use (its *concurrency level*):

```
ConcurrentHashMap()
ConcurrentHashMap(int initialCapacity)
ConcurrentHashMap(int initialCapacity, float loadFactor)
ConcurrentHashMap(
    int initialCapacity, float loadFactor, int concurrencyLevel)
ConcurrentHashMap(Map<? extends K,? extends V> m)
```

The class ConcurrentHashMap is a useful implementation of Map in any application where it is not necessary to lock the entire table; this is the one capability of SynchronizedMap which it does not support. That can sometimes present problems: for example, the size method attempts to count the entries in the map without using locks. If the map is being concurrently updated, however, the size method will not succeed in obtaining a consistent result. In this situation, it obtains exclusive access to the map by locking all the segments, obtaining the entry count from each, then unlocking them again. The performance cost involved in this is a justifiable tradeoff against the highly optimized performance for common operations, especially reads. Overall, ConcurrentHashMap is indispensable in highly concurrent contexts, where it performs far better than any available alternative.

Disregarding locking overheads such as those just described, the cost of the operations of ConcurrentHashMap are similar to those of HashMap. The collection views return weakly consistent iterators.

ConcurrentNavigableMap<K,V>
+subMap(fromKey : K, fromInclusive : boolean, toKey : K, toInclusive : boolean) : ConcurrentNavigableMap<K,V>
+subMap(fromKey : K, toKey : K) : ConcurrentNavigableMap<K,V>
+headMap(toKey : K, inclusive : boolean) : ConcurrentNavigableMap<K,V>
+headMap(toKey : K) : ConcurrentNavigableMap<K,V>
+tailMap(fromKey : K, inclusive : boolean) : ConcurrentNavigableMap<K,V>
+tailMap(fromKey : K) : ConcurrentNavigableMap<K,V>
+descendingMap() : ConcurrentNavigableMap<K,V>
+keySet() : NavigableSet<E>

Figure 16.7: ConcurrentNavigableMap

16.5 ConcurrentNavigableMap

ConcurrentNavigableMap (see Figure 16.7) inherits from both ConcurrentMap and
NavigableMap, and contains just the methods of these two interfaces with a few changes
to make the return types more precise. The range-view methods inherited from SortedMap
and NavigableMap now return views of type ConcurrentNavigableMap. The compatibility
concerns that prevented NavigableMap from overriding the methods of SortedMap don't
apply here to overriding the range-view methods of NavigableMap or SortedMap; because
neither of these has any implementations that have been retrofitted to the new interface, the
danger of breaking implementation subclasses does not arise. For the same reason, it is now
possible to override keySet to return NavigableSet.

16.5.1 ConcurrentSkipListMap

The relationship between ConcurrentSkipListMap and ConcurrentSkipListSet is like
that between TreeMap and TreeSet; a ConcurrentSkipListSet is implemented by a
ConcurrentSkipListMap in which every key is associated with the same standard value,
so the mechanism and performance of the skip list implementation given in Section 13.2.2
applies equally here: the basic operations (get, put, and remove) perform in $O(\log n)$ time);
iterators over the collection views execute next in constant time. These iterators are fail-fast.

16.6 Comparing Map Implementations

Table 16.1 shows the relative performance of the different platform implementations of Map
(the column headed "next" shows the cost of the next operation of iterators over the key set).
As with the implementations of queue, your choice of map class is likely to be influenced
more by the functional requirements of your application and the concurrency properties that
you need.

Some specialized situations dictate the implementation: EnumMap should always (and only)
be used for mapping from enums. Problems such as the graph traversals described in
Section 16.2.4 call for IdentityHashMap. For a sorted map, use TreeMap where thread
safety is not required, and ConcurrentSkipListMap otherwise.

Table 16.1: Comparative performance of different Map implementations

	get	containsKey	next	Notes
HashMap	$O(1)$	$O(1)$	$O(h/n)$	h is the table capacity
LinkedHashMap	$O(1)$	$O(1)$	$O(1)$	
IdentityHashMap	$O(1)$	$O(1)$	$O(h/n)$	h is the table capacity
EnumMap	$O(1)$	$O(1)$	$O(1)$	
TreeMap	$O(\log n)$	$O(\log n)$	$O(\log n)$	
ConcurrentHashMap	$O(1)$	$O(1)$	$O(h/n)$	h is the table capacity
ConcurrentSkipListMap	$O(\log n)$	$O(\log n)$	$O(1)$	

That leaves the choice of implementation for general-purpose maps. For concurrent applications, ConcurrentHashMap is the only choice. Otherwise, favor LinkedHashMap over HashMap (and accept its slightly worse performance) if you need to make use of the insertion or access order of the map—for example, to use it as a cache.

CHAPTER 17

The Collections Class

The class `java.util.Collections` consists entirely of static methods that operate on or return collections. There are three main categories: generic algorithms, methods that return empty or prepopulated collections, and methods that create wrappers. We discuss these three categories in turn, followed by a number of other methods which do not fit into a neat classification.

All the methods of `Collections` are public and static, so for readability we will omit these modifiers from the individual declarations.

17.1   Generic Algorithms

The generic algorithms fall into four major categories: changing element order in a list, changing the contents of a list, finding extreme values in a collection, and finding specific values in a list. They represent reusable functionality, in that they can be applied to `List`s (or in some cases to `Collection`s) of any type. Generifying the types of these methods has led to some fairly complicated declarations, so each section discusses the declarations briefly after presenting them.

17.1.1   Changing the Order of List Elements

There are seven methods for reordering lists in various ways. The simplest of these is `swap`, which exchanges two elements and, in the case of a `List` which implements `RandomAccess`, executes in constant time. The most complex is `sort`, which transfers the elements into an array, applies a merge sort to them in time $O(n \log n)$, and then returns them to the `List`. All of the remaining methods execute in time $O(n)$.

```
void reverse(List<?> list)
        // reverse the order of the elements
void rotate(List<?> list, int distance)
        // rotate the elements of the list; the element at index
        // i is moved to index (distance + i) % list.size()
void shuffle(List<?> list)
        // randomly permute the list elements
```

```
void shuffle(List<?> list, Random rnd)
        // randomly permute the list using the randomness source rnd
<T extends Comparable<? super T>> void sort(List<T> list)
        // sort the supplied list using natural ordering
<T> void sort(List<T> list, Comparator<? super T> c)
        // sort the supplied list using the supplied ordering
void swap(List<?> list, int i, int j)
        // swap the elements at the specified positions
```

For each of these methods, except sort and swap, there are two algorithms, one using iteration and another using random access. The method sort transfers the List elements to an array, where they are sorted using—in the current implementation—a mergesort algorithm with $n \log n$ performance. The method swap always uses random access. The standard implementations for the other methods in this section use either iteration or random access, depending on whether the list implements the RandomAccess interface (see Section 8.3). If it does, the implementation chooses the random-access algorithm; even for a list that does not implement RandomAccess, however, the random-access algorithms are used if the list size is below a given threshold, determined on a per-method basis by performance testing.

17.1.2 Changing the Contents of a List

These methods change some or all of the elements of a list. The method copy transfers elements from the source list into an initial sublist of the destination list (which has to be long enough to accommodate them), leaving any remaining elements of the destination list unchanged. The method fill replaces every element of a list with a specified object, and replaceAll replaces every occurrence of one value in a list with another—where either the old or new value can be null—returning true if any replacements were made.

```
<T> void copy(List<? super T> dest, List<? extends T> src)
        // copy all of the elements from one list into another
<T> void fill(List<? super T> list, T obj)
        // replace every element of list with obj
<T> boolean replaceAll(List<T> list, T oldVal, T newVal)
        // replace all occurrences of oldVal in list with newVal
```

The signatures of these methods can be explained using the Get and Put Principle (see Section 2.4). The signature of copy was discussed in Section 2.3. It gets elements from the source list and puts them into the destination, so the types of these lists are, respectively, ? extends T and ? super T. This fits with the intuition that the type of the source list elements should be a subtype of the destination list. Although there are simpler alternatives for the signature of copy, Section 2.3 makes the case that using wildcards where possible widens the range of permissible calls.

For fill, the Get and Put Principle dictates that you should use super if you are putting values into a parameterized collection and, for replaceAll, it states that if you are putting values into and getting values out of the same structure, you should not use wildcards at all.

17.1.3 Finding Extreme Values in a Collection

The methods min and max are supplied for this purpose, each with two overloads—one using natural ordering of the elements, and one accepting a Comparator to impose an ordering. They execute in linear time.

```
<T extends Object & Comparable<? super T>>
  T max(Collection<? extends T> coll)  // return the maximum element
                                       // using natural ordering
<T> T max(Collection<? extends T> coll, Comparator<? super T> comp)
                                  // return the maximum element
                                  // using the supplied comparator
<T extends Object & Comparable<? super T>>
  T min(Collection<? extends T> coll)  // return the minimum element
                                       // using natural ordering
<T> T min(Collection<? extends T> coll, Comparator<? super T> comp)
                                  // return the minimum element
                                  // using the supplied comparator
```

Sections 3.6 and 8.4 explain these methods and the types assigned to them.

17.1.4 Finding Specific Values in a List

Methods in this group locate elements or groups of elements in a List, again choosing between alternative algorithms on the basis of the list's size and whether it implements RandomAccess.

```
<T> int binarySearch(List<? extends Comparable<? super T>> list, T key)
        // search for key using binary search
<T> int binarySearch(List<? extends T> list, T key, Comparator<? super T> c)
        // search for key using binary search
int indexOfSubList(List<?> source, List<?> target)
        // find the first sublist of source which matches target
int lastIndexOfSubList(List<?> source, List<?> target)
        // find the last sublist of source which matches target
```

The signature of the first binarySearch overload says that you can use it to search for a key of type T in a list of objects that can have any type that can be compared with objects of type T. The second is like the Comparator overloads of min and max except that, in this case, the type parameter of the Collection must be a subtype of the type of the key, which in turn must be a subtype of the type parameter of the Comparator.

Binary search requires a sorted list for its operation. At the start of a search, the range of indices in which the search value may occur corresponds to the entire list. The binary search algorithm samples an element in the middle of this range, using the value of the sampled element to determine whether the new range should be the part of the old range above or the part below the index of the element. A third possibility is that the sampled value is equal to the search value, in which case the search is complete. Since each step halves the size of the range, m steps are required to find a search value in a list of length 2^m, and the time complexity for a list of length n is $O(\log n)$.

The methods `indexOfSubList` and `lastIndexOfSubList` do not require sorted lists for their operation. Their signatures allow the source and target lists to contain elements of any type (remember that the two wildcards may stand for two different types). The design decision behind these signatures is the same as that behind the `Collection` methods `containsAll`, `retainAll`, and `removeAll` (see Section 2.6).

17.2 Collection Factories

The `Collections` class provides convenient ways of creating some kinds of collections containing zero or more references to the same object. The simplest possible such collections are empty:

```
<T> List<T> emptyList()    // return the empty list (immutable)
<K,V> Map<K,V> emptyMap()  // return the empty map (immutable)
<T> Set<T> emptySet()      // return the empty set (immutable)
```

Empty collections can be useful in implementing methods to return collections of values, where they can be used to signify that there were no values to return. Each method returns a reference to an instance of a singleton inner class of `Collections`. Because these instances are immutable, they can safely be shared, so calling one of these factory methods does not result in object creation. The `Collections` fields `EMPTY_SET`, `EMPTY_LIST`, and `EMPTY_MAP` were commonly used for the same purpose in Java before generics, but are less useful now because their raw types generate unchecked warnings whenever they are used.

The `Collections` class also provides you with ways of creating collection objects containing only a single member:

```
<T> Set<T> singleton(T o)
        // return an immutable set containing only the specified object
<T> List<T> singletonList(T o)
        // return an immutable list containing only the specified object
<K,V> Map<K,V> singletonMap(K key, V value)
        // return an immutable map, mapping only the key K to the value V
```

Again, these can be useful in providing a single input value to a method that is written to accept a `Collection` of values.

Finally, it is possible to create a list containing a number of copies of a given object.

```
<T> List<T> nCopies(int n, T o)
        // return an immutable list containing n references to the object o
```

Because the list produced by `nCopies` is immutable, it need contain only a single physical element to provide a list view of the required length. Such lists are often used as the basis for building further collections—for example, as the argument to a constructor or an `addAll` method.

17.3 Wrappers

The `Collections` class provides wrapper objects that modify the behavior of standard collections classes in one of three ways—by synchronizing them, by making them unmodifiable, or by checking the type of elements being added to them. These wrapper objects implement the same interfaces as the wrapped objects, and they delegate their work to them. Their purpose is to restrict the circumstances under which that work will be carried out. These are examples of the use of *protection proxies* (see *Design Patterns* by Gamma, Helm, Johnson, and Vlissides, Addison-Wesley), a variant of the Proxy pattern in which the proxy controls access to the real subject.

Proxies can be created in different ways. Here, they are created by factory methods that wrap the supplied collection object in an inner class of `Collections` that implements the collection's interface. Subsequently, method calls to the proxy are (mostly) delegated to the collection object, but the proxy controls the conditions of the call: in the case of the synchronized wrappers, all method calls are delegated but the proxy uses synchronization to ensure that the collection is accessed by only one thread at a time. In the case of unmodifiable and checked collections, method calls that break the contract for the proxy fail, throwing the appropriate exception.

17.3.1 Synchronized Collections

As we explained in Section 11.5, most of the Framework classes are not thread-safe—by design—in order to avoid the overhead of unnecessary synchronization (as incurred by the legacy classes `Vector` and `Hashtable`). But there are occasions when you do need to program multiple threads to have access to the same collection, and these synchronized wrappers are provided by the `Collections` class for such situations.

There are six synchronized wrapper factory methods, corresponding to the six pre-Java 6 interfaces of the Collections Framework. (No synchronized wrappers were provided in Java 6 for `NavigableSet` or `NavigableMap`. If they had been provided, there would be very few situations in which you would choose them over the thread-safe collections `ConcurrentSkipListSet` and `ConcurrentSkipListMap`.)

```
<T> Collection<T> synchronizedCollection(Collection<T> c);
<T> Set<T> synchronizedSet(Set<T> s);
<T> List<T> synchronizedList(List<T> list);
<K, V> Map<K, V> synchronizedMap(Map<K, V> m);
<T> SortedSet<T> synchronizedSortedSet(SortedSet<T> s);
<K, V> SortedMap<K, V> synchronizedSortedMap(SortedMap<K, V> m);
```

The classes that provide these synchronized views are conditionally thread-safe (see Section 11.5); although each of their operations is guaranteed to be atomic, you may need to synchronize multiple method calls in order to obtain consistent behavior. In particular, iterators must be created and used entirely within a code block synchronized on the collection; otherwise, the result will at best be failure with `ConcurrentModificationException`. This is very coarse-grained synchronization; if your application makes heavy use of synchronized collections, its effective concurrency will be greatly reduced.

17.3.2 Unmodifiable Collections

An unmodifiable collection will throw UnsupportedOperationException in response to any attempt to change its structure or the elements that compose it. This can be useful when you want to allow clients read access to an internal data structure. Passing the structure in an unmodifiable wrapper will prevent a client from changing it. It will not prevent the client from changing the objects it contains, if they are modifiable. In some cases, you may have to protect your internal data structure by providing clients instead with a *defensive copy* made for that purpose, or by also placing these objects in unmodifiable wrappers.

There are six unmodifiable wrapper factory methods, corresponding to the six major interfaces of the Collections Framework:

```
<T> Collection<T> unmodifiableCollection(Collection<? extends T> c)
<T> Set<T> unmodifiableSet(Set<? extends T> s)
<T> List<T> unmodifiableList(List<? extends T> list)
<K, V> Map<K, V> unmodifiableMap(Map<? extends K, ? extends V> m)
<T> SortedSet<T> unmodifiableSortedSet(SortedSet<? extends T> s)
<K, V> SortedMap<K, V> unmodifiableSortedMap(SortedMap<K, ? extends V> m)
```

17.3.3 Checked Collections

Unchecked warnings from the compiler are a signal to us to take special care to avoid runtime type violations. For example, after we have passed a typed collection reference to an ungenerified library method, we can't be sure that it has added only correctly typed elements to the collection. Instead of losing confidence in the collection's type safety, we can pass in a checked wrapper, which will test every element added to the collection for membership of the type supplied when it was created. Section 8.2 shows an example of this technique.

Checked wrappers are supplied for the main interfaces:

```
static <E> Collection
    checkedCollection(Collection<E> c, Class<E> elementType)
static <E> List
    checkedList(List<E> c, Class<E> elementType)
static <E> Set
    checkedSet(Set<E> c, Class<E> elementType)
static <E> SortedSet
    checkedSortedSet(SortedSet<E> c, Class<E> elementType)
static <K, V> Map
    checkedMap(Map<K, V> c, Class<K> keyType, Class<V> valueType)
static <K, V> SortedMap
    checkedSortedMap(SortedMap<K, V> c, Class<K> keyType,Class<V> valueType)
```

17.4 Other Methods

The `Collections` class provides a number of utility methods, some of which we have already seen in use. Here we review them in alphabetical order.

addAll

```
<T> boolean addAll(Collection<? super T> c, T... elements)
        // adds all of the specified elements to the specified collection.
```

We have used this method a number of times as a convenient and efficient way of initializing a collection with individual elements, or with the contents of an array.

asLifoQueue

```
<T> Queue<T> asLifoQueue(Deque<T> deque)
        // returns a view of a Deque as a Last-in-first-out (Lifo) Queue.
```

Recall from Chapter 14 that while queues can impose various different orderings on their elements, there is no standard `Queue` implementation that provides LIFO ordering. `Dequeue` implementations, on the other hand, all support LIFO ordering if elements are removed from the same end of the dequeue as they were added. The method `asLifoQueue` allows you to use this functionality through the conveniently concise `Queue` interface.

disjoint

```
boolean disjoint(Collection<?> c1, Collection<?> c2)
        // returns true if c1 and c2 have no elements in common
```

Care is needed in using this method; implementations may iterate over either collection, testing elements of one for containment in the other. So if the two collections determine containment differently, the result of this method is undefined. This could arise if, say, one collection is a `SortedSet`, for which containment is decided by natural ordering or a comparator, and the other is a `Set`, for which containment is decided by the `equals` method of its elements.

frequency

```
int frequency(Collection<?> c, Object o)
        // returns the number of elements in c that are equal to o
```

If the supplied value o is `null`, then `frequency` returns the number of `null` elements in the collection c.

newSetFromMap

```
<E> Set<E> newSetFromMap(Map<E, Boolean> map)
        // returns a set backed by the specified map.
```

As we saw earlier, many sets (such as `TreeSet` and `NavigableSkipListSet`) are implemented by maps, and share their ordering, concurrency, and performance characteristics.

Some maps, however (such as `WeakHashMap` and `IdentityHashMap`) do not have standard `Set` equivalents. The purpose of the method `newSetFromMap` is to provide equivalent `Set` implementations for such maps. The method `newSetFromMap` wraps its argument, which must be empty when supplied and should never be subsequently accessed directly. This code shows the standard idiom for using it to create a weak `HashSet`, one whose elements are held via weak references:

```
Set<Object> weakHashSet = Collections.newSetFromMap(
    new WeakHashMap<Object, Boolean>());
```

reverseOrder

```
<T> Comparator<T> reverseOrder()
        // returns a comparator that reverses natural ordering
```

This method provides a simple way of sorting or maintaining a collection of `Comparable` objects in reverse natural order. Here is an example of its use:

```
SortedSet<Integer> s = new TreeSet<Integer>(Collections.reverseOrder());
Collections.addAll(s, 1, 2, 3);
assert s.toString().equals("[3, 2, 1]");
```

There is also a second form of this method.

```
<T> Comparator<T> reverseOrder(Comparator<T> cmp)
```

This method is like the preceding one, but instead of reversing the natural order of an object collection, it reverses the order of the `Comparator` supplied as its argument. Its behaviour when supplied with `null` is unusual for a method of the `Collections` class. The contract for `Collections` states that its methods throw a `NullPointerException` if the collections or class objects provided to them are null, but if this method is supplied with `null` it returns the same result as a call of `reverseOrder()`—that is, it returns a `Comparator` that reverses the natural order of a collection of objects.

Conclusion This completes our tour of the convenience methods provided by the `Collections` class, and our discussion of the Collections Framework. We have presented collections, sets, lists, queues, and maps, and given you the information you need to choose which interface and implementation best fits your needs.

Generics and the improved Collections Framework are possibly the most significant change to Java since its inception. We are excited about these changes, and hope we have conveyed some of this excitement to you. We hope you will see that generics and collections fit together well to make a powerful addition to your repertory of Java programming skills.

Index

About the Authors

Maurice Naftalin is Technical Director at Morningside Light Ltd., a software consultancy in the United Kingdom. He has most recently served as an architect and mentor at NSB Retail Systems plc, and as the leader of the client development team of a major U.K. government social service system. He has taught Java since 1998 at both basic and advanced levels for Learning Tree and Sun Educational Services.

Philip Wadler is professor of theoretical computer science at the University of Edinburgh, Scotland, where his research focuses on functional and logic programming. He co-authored the Generic Java standard that became the basis for generics in Sun's Java 5.0, and he also contributed to the XQuery language standard base. He received his Ph.D. in computer science from Carnegie-Mellon University and co-wrote *Introduction to Functional Programming* (Prentice-Hall).

Colophon

The animal on the cover of *Java Generics and Collections* is an alligator. Alligators are found only in southern parts of the U.S. and in China. They are rare in China, native only to the Yangtze River Basin. Alligators generally cannot tolerate salt water and therefore live in freshwater ponds, swamps, and the like.

When first born, alligators are tiny, measuring only about six inches. However, it grow extremely fast in the first years of life—a foot each year. A fully grown female is usually around 9 feet and between 150 and 200 pounds, while an adult male typically reaches 11 feet and weighs about 350 to 400 pounds. The largest known alligator on record, found in Louisiana in the early 1900s, was 19 feet, 2 inches. A key identifying characteristic of an alligator's appearance is its short, broad snout. An adult alligator's skin is a gray-black color, which turns dark black when wet, and it has a white underbelly. Young alligators have yellow and white stripes across their backs. The shape of the snout and skin color provide physical characteristics that differentiate alligators from crocodiles, which have long, thin snouts and are a tan color.

Alligators are mainly nocturnal and do most of their hunting and feeding after the sun sets. They are carnivores and eat a large variety of food, such as turtles, fish, frogs, birds, snakes, small mammals, and even smaller alligators. However, once an alligator grows into adulthood, it really faces no threats—other than humans.

The cover image is a 19th-century engraving from the *Dover Pictorial Archive*. The cover font is Adobe ITC Garamond. The text font is Linotype Birka; the heading font is Adobe Myriad Condensed; and the code font is LucasFont's TheSans Mono Condensed.

Better than e-books

Buy *Java Generics and Collections* and access
the digital edition FREE on Safari for 45 days.

Go to www.oreilly.com/go/safarienabled
and type in coupon code N1MD-8IHL-8TCI-W5MT-DW8M

Search
thousands of
top tech books

Download
whole chapters

Cut and Paste
code examples

Find
answers fast

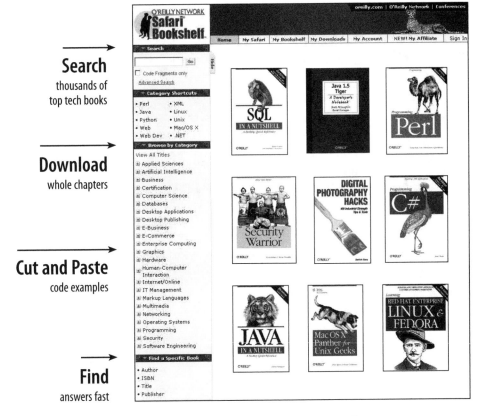

Search Safari! The premier electronic reference
library for programmers and IT professionals.

O'REILLY NETWORK
Safari Bookshelf

Addison
Wesley
AdobePress

O'REILLY
SAMS

ALPHA

New
Riders

Java
Cisco Press

Microsoft Press
que

macromedia
PRESS

Peachpit
Press

PRENTICE
HALL
PTR

Related Titles from O'Reilly

Java

Ant: The Definitive Guide,
2nd Edition

Better, Faster, Lighter Java

Beyond Java

Eclipse

Eclipse Cookbook

Eclipse IDE Pocket Guide

Enterprise JavaBeans 3.0,
5th Edition

Hardcore Java

Head First Design Patterns

Head First Design Patterns Poster

Head First Java, *2nd Edition*

Head First Servlets & JSP

Head First EJB

Hibernate: A Developer's
Notebook

J2EE Design Patterns

Java 5.0 Tiger: A Developer's
Notebook

Java & XML Data Binding

Java & XML

Java Cookbook, *2nd Edition*

Java Data Objects

Java Database Best Practices

Java Enterprise Best Practices

Java Enterprise in a Nutshell,
3nd Edition

Java Examples in a Nutshell,
3rd Edition

Java Extreme Programming
Cookbook

Java Generics and Collections

Java in a Nutshell, *5th Edition*

Java I/O, *2nd Edition*

Java Management Extensions

Java Message Service

Java Network Programming,
2nd Edition

Java NIO

Java Performance Tuning,
2nd Edition

Java RMI

Java Security, *2nd Edition*

JavaServer Faces

JavaServer Pages,
2nd Edition

Java Servlet & JSP
Cookbook

Java Servlet Programming,
2nd Edition

Java Swing, *2nd Edition*

Java Web Services
in a Nutshell

JBoss: A Developer's
Notebook

JBoss at Work: A Practical Guide

Learning Java, *2nd Edition*

Mac OS X for Java Geeks

Maven: A Developer's
Notebook

Programming Jakarta Struts,
2nd Edition

QuickTime for Java: A
Developer's Notebook

Spring: A Developer's
Notebook

Swing Hacks

Tomcat:
The Definitive Guide

WebLogic: The Definitive Guide

O'REILLY®

Our books are available at most retail and online bookstores.

To order direct: 1-800-998-9938 • *order@oreilly.com* • *www.oreilly.com*

Online editions of most O'Reilly titles are available by subscription at *safari.oreilly.com*

The O'Reilly Advantage

Stay Current and Save Money

Order books online:
www.oreilly.com/order_new

Questions about our products or your order:
order@oreilly.com

Join our email lists: Sign up to get topic specific email announcements or new books, conferences, special offers and technology news
elists@oreilly.com

For book content technical questions:
booktech@oreilly.com

To submit new book proposals to our editors:
proposals@oreilly.com

Contact us:
O'Reilly Media, Inc.
1005 Gravenstein Highway N.
Sebastopol, CA U.S.A. 95472
707-827-7000 or
800-998-9938
www.oreilly.com

Did you know that if you register your O'Reilly books, you'll get automatic notification and upgrade discounts on new editions?

And that's not all! Once you've registered your books you can:

» Win free books, T-shirts and O'Reilly Gear

» Get special offers available only to registered O'Reilly customers

» Get free catalogs announcing all our new titles (US and UK Only)

Registering is easy! Just go to www.oreilly.com/go/register

92722 - 029538

800   336 - 8896